The Sovereign Self

The Sovereign Self
Pitfalls of Identity Politics

Elisabeth Roudinesco

Translated by Catherine Porter

polity

Originally published in French as *Soi-même comme un roi. Essai sur les dérives identitaires*
© Éditions du Seuil, 2021

This English edition © Polity Press, 2022

Polity Press
65 Bridge Street
Cambridge CB2 1UR, UK

Polity Press
111 River Street
Hoboken, NJ 07030, USA

All rights reserved. Except for the quotation of short passages for the purpose of criticism and review, no part of this publication may be reproduced, stored in a retrieval system or transmitted, in any form or by any means, electronic, mechanical, photocopying, recording or otherwise, without the prior permission of the publisher.

ISBN-13: 978-1-5095-5122-4
ISBN-13: 978-1-5095-5123-1 (paperback)

A catalogue record for this book is available from the British Library.

Library of Congress Control Number: 2022935228

Typeset in 10.5 on 12 pt Sabon
by Fakenham Prepress Solutions, Fakenham, Norfolk NR21 8NL
Printed and bound in Great Britain by CPI Group (UK) Ltd, Croydon

The publisher has used its best endeavours to ensure that the URLs for external websites referred to in this book are correct and active at the time of going to press. However, the publisher has no responsibility for the websites and can make no guarantee that a site will remain live or that the content is or will remain appropriate.

Every effort has been made to trace all copyright holders, but if any have been overlooked the publisher will be pleased to include any necessary credits in any subsequent reprint or edition.

For further information on Polity, visit our website:
politybooks.com

CONTENTS

Acknowledgments	viii
Preface	ix
1. Assigning Identities	1
Beirut 2005: Who am I?	1
Secularisms	4
The politics of Narcissus	7
Berkeley 1996	8
2. The Galaxy of Gender	10
Paris 1949: One is not born a woman	10
Vienna 1912: Is anatomy destiny?	12
Highlights and disappointments of gender studies	13
Transidentities	16
Inquisitorial follies	18
Psychiatry in full retreat	21
New York: Queer Nation	24
Disseminating human gender	33
I am neither white nor woman nor man, but half Lebanese	37
3. Deconstructing Race	39
Paris 1952: Race does not exist	39
Colonialism and anticolonialism	44
"Nègre je suis"	48
Writing toward Algeria	54
Mixed-race identities	64

4. Postcolonialities 71
"Is Sartre still alive?" 71
Descartes, a white male colonialist 76
Flaubert and Kuchuk Hanem 79
Tehran 1979: Dreaming of a crusade 84
The subaltern identity 88

5. The Labyrinth of Intersectionality 104
Memories in dispute 104
"Je suis Charlie" 124
Iconoclastic rage 126

6. Great Replacements 136
Oneself against all 136
The terror of invasion 145
"Big Other": From Boulouris to *La Campagne de France* 150

Epilogue 161

Notes 163
References 199
Index 216

The brighter the light, the darker the shadows . . . One cannot fully appreciate the light without knowing the dark.

Jean-Paul Sartre

ACKNOWLEDGMENTS

Thanks to Sophie Bessis, who, from the very first steps toward the writing of this book, made available to me all her knowledge about the relations between the history of feminism and postcolonial issues.

Warm thanks to Bernard Cerquiglini for our linguistic exchanges about obscure speech and neologisms.

Thanks to Jean Khalfa, who patiently enlightened me about the life of Frantz Fanon as well as about the Anglophone interpretations of his work.

A big thank-you to Vaiju Naravane for her contribution to the recent history of sati and immolation of the body in India.

Thanks also to Dany Nobus, Chair of the Trustees of the Freud Museum of London, for our exchanges on the issue of transgendered children in Great Britain.

All my gratitude to Benjamin Stora for our discussions about colonialism and the question of shared memory.

I also thank Michel Wieviorka for our conversations about the history of the Representative Council of Black Associations in France.

Thanks to Georges Vigarello for his reflections on the issue of bodily transformations related to gender and queerness.

I thank Anthony Ballenato, who undertook considerable research in English on the Internet for this book.

Thanks to Jean-Claude Baillieul for his highly detailed corrections.

Finally, many thanks as always to Olivier Bétourné, who edited and corrected this book with talent and enthusiasm.

PREFACE

During the last 20 years or so, liberation movements have changed direction, or so it seems. Instead of seeking ways to transform the world, to make it a better place, they focus on protecting populations from what is threatening them: increasing inequalities, social invisibility, moral impoverishment.

Their goals are thus the inverse of those they had been pursuing for a century. The struggle is no longer to bring about progress; indeed, what progress has wrought is sometimes contested. Instead, suffering is put on display, offenses are denounced, free rein is given to affect: these are all markers of identity that express a desire for visibility, sometimes in order to express indignation, sometimes in order to demand recognition.[1] Art and literature are not exempt from the phenomenon, since literature has never been as preoccupied with "lived experience" as it is today. Novelists seek less to reconstruct a global reality than to tell their own stories without critical distance, through the use of autofiction[2] or even abjection; such devices allow authors to duplicate themselves ad infinitum by affirming that everything is true because it is all invented. Hence the chameleon syndrome. You put a chameleon on something green and it turns green; on something blue, and it turns blue; on something plaid, and it goes crazy, it explodes, it dies.

Gérard Noiriel, a historian of social movements, has noted that archives are less frequented by professional historians than by amateur "history lovers" who often turn to them in order to reconstitute their own family tree, to "tell the story of their village, their ancestors, their community, etc."[3] This self-affirmation – transformed into self-inflation – would thus be the distinctive sign of an epoch in which each individual seeks to be himself or herself as

PREFACE

sovereign, as king or queen rather than as someone else.[4] But, in counterpoint, there is another way of submitting to the identitarian impulse: withdrawal.

Identity can be defined in several different ways. If one says "I am myself," or "I think, therefore I am," or "Who am I if I am not what I am inhabiting," or "It thinks there where I am not," or "*I* is another,"[5] or, why not, "I depend on an alterity," or "I depend on others to know who I am," or even "I am Charlie,"[6] one is affirming the existence of a universal identity – conscious, unconscious, imbued with freedom, divided, always "other" while being oneself, independent of the contingencies of the biological body or the territory of origin. This form of self-identification rejects "belonging" in the sense of rootedness; it suggests, rather, that identity is above all multiple and that it includes the stranger in oneself.[7] But if, on the contrary, identity is conflated with belonging, the subject is thereby reduced to a single identity, or to several ranked identities; the idea that "I am myself, that's all there is to it"[8] is erased. It is this second definition of identity, largely inspired by works of post-Freudian psychoanalytic interpretation, that will be examined in the pages that follow.

In the first chapter, I consider some modern forms of identity attribution,[9] each more regrettable than the next, that translate into a determination to dismiss alterity altogether by reducing the human being to one particular experience. In the second chapter, I analyze the variations that have reshaped the notion of "gender." This notion has gradually drifted to the point where it is no longer used as a conceptual tool intended to illuminate an emancipatory approach to the history of women – as was the case until about 2000 – but is used instead to bolster, in social and political life, a normative ideology of belonging that can be stretched so far that it dissolves the boundaries between sex and gender.

In the three subsequent chapters, we shall look at the various metamorphoses of the idea of "race." After having been expunged from the discourse of science and the humanities in 1945, the notion has been put back into play by so-called "post-colonial," "subaltern," and "decolonial" studies, under the influence of a few great works by theorists of modernity, most notably Aimé Césaire, Edward Said, Franz Fanon, and Jacques Derrida. On this terrain, too, conceptual tools forged with rare finesse have been extravagantly reinterpreted, in order to shore up the ideals of a new conformity with the norm; we find traces of this as much among certain supporters of queer transgenderism as among the Indigènes de la République[10] and other

x

movements that have set out in search of an undiscoverable identity politics.

In each phase of this study, I attempt to analyze the abundant neologisms that accompany the jargonistic language of all these currents.

In the final chapter, I examine the way in which the notion of "national identity" has come back into the polemical discourse of the far right in France, haunted by the terror of a "great replacement" attributed to a demonized alterity and its manifestations: immigration, Islam, May 1968, surrogate motherhood, the French Revolution, and so on. This discourse fetishizes an imaginary past so as to promote repudiation of the present and thereby to endorse what the identitarians of the other camp condemn: identity construed as white, masculine, virile, colonialist, Western, and so forth. For these nationalist identitarians – who identify themselves moreover as Identitarians with a capital I – our villages of yesteryear, our schools, our churches, and our values are threatened by the new barbarians: Euro Disney, Indian surrogate mothers, parents who give their children unpronounceable names, polygamous communities, and so on.

In conclusion, and at the end of this immersion in the dark corners of identitarian thinking, where delirium, conspiracy theories, rejection of the other, incitement to murder, and racialized accounts of subjectivity are often part of the mix, I shall indicate several paths that may help lead us away from despair and toward a possible world in which everyone can adhere to the principle according to which "I am myself, that's all there is to it," without denying the diversity of human communities or essentializing either universality or difference. "Neither too close nor too far apart," as Claude Lévi-Strauss was wont to say in asserting that the imposition of a uniform worldview is just as deadly as the disintegration of a culture. That is the fundamental message of this study.

— 1 —

ASSIGNING IDENTITIES

Beirut 2005: Who am I?

At an evening event in Beirut, following a colloquium held in May 2005 on psychoanalysis in the Arab and Islamic world,[1] I had the opportunity to meet an important patron of the press, the erudite and elegant Ghassan Tueni. He greeted me enthusiastically: he was delighted, he said, to receive an "Orthodox" in his sumptuous residence. Astonished, I told him I was not Orthodox, and he responded at once: "But you're Romanian!" And he added that he himself belonged to the Greek Orthodox community and that his first wife was a Druze, so he was accustomed to "mixed identities." After telling him that I was neither Romanian nor Orthodox, but that my family included Jews and Protestants, I stressed that I had been brought up as a Catholic by non-believing parents who had transmitted to me so little of the traditions of the faith that I considered myself an atheist – or "a-religious" – without being necessarily anticlerical; I knew nothing about "mixed identities." Not without humor, he retorted: "So you're a Christian atheist, Orthodox in origin and Catholic by denomination." Being neither a committed atheist nor truly Christian, although I had been baptized, I ended up explaining to him that my mother, attached above all to republican *laïcité*, or secularism,[2] had come from an Alsatian family, Protestant on her father's side and "Parisian Israelite" on her mother's, and that both sides preferred the label HSP (High Protestant Society), which allowed them to bypass the word "Jew" in the name of a militant assimilationism. As for my father, who came from an ultra-Francophile and non-observant Jewish family in Bucharest, he detested synagogues and rabbis as well as popes, and he adhered to

THE SOVEREIGN SELF

the ideals of the Republic without reservation. Thus he preferred to call himself a "Voltairean," even though for strictly aesthetic reasons he was a fervent admirer of the Roman Catholic Church and especially of Renaissance painting. Italy was his second fatherland after France, and Rome was his favorite city. Alarmed by anti-Semitism and concerned with successful integration, he was inclined to lie about his origins, stressing that his father was Orthodox and that he himself had converted to Catholicism.

As for me, this way of dissimulating one's Jewishness, whether by claiming to be an "Israelite" or asserting a denominational Christian identity, struck me as a delusional practice from another era. Another guest came to join our conversation and remarked that, without being of French ancestry (*française de souche*), I had acquired "French citizenship." I was obliged to respond that that terminology did not fit my case, and moreover that I was neither a French citizen *de souche* (of French stock) – since *souches* did not exist any more than races did – nor a French citizen by acquisition, since I was born French to French parents. As for "the identity of France" he was questioning me about, I replied by citing from memory what Fernand Braudel had said on the subject. The identity of France, I said, has nothing to do with any sort of "national identity," French or otherwise. There is no such thing as a pure and perfect identity. The identity of "France" is always splintered, between its regions and its cities, for example, or between its divergent ideals, even if the French Republic is constitutionally indivisible, secular, and social.[3] France is nothing other than the France described by Jules Michelet: a plurality of Frances "stitched together," that is, the France constructed around Paris, which ended up imposing itself on the other Frances. Such is the French France, then, composed of all the migratory contributions from all over the world, with its traditions, its language, and its intellectual eminence. French civilization would not exist without the influx of strangers foreign to the "identity of France." As Braudel insisted in 1985:

> Let me start by saying once and for all that I love France with the same demanding and complicated passion as did Jules Michelet, without distinguishing between its good points and its bad, between what I like and what I find harder to accept ... I am determined to talk about France as if it were another country, another fatherland, another nation.[4]

In the course of this conversation in Beirut, which had all the elements of a certain type of Jewish joke ("You say you're going to

2

Krakow so I'll believe you're going to Łódź"), I was thus obliged for the first time in my life to explain to a highly cultured person, a reader of Paul Valéry who was well-versed in the old European humanism, that I was quite simply French, a French citizen, of French nationality, born in Paris, and that I did not speak a word of Romanian, a language that my father used only when he was mad at his sister, my elderly aunt. It was simpler for me to claim this "Frenchness" than to keep on making identitarian contortions such "I am Jewish-Romanian-Alsatian-half German," and why not a quarter Viennese by my maternal ancestor Julius Popper, conqueror of Patagonia, and also marked with the stamp of "whiteness." My interlocutor burst out laughing. "Of course! And I'm Lebanese. But let's say that you are first of all Orthodox because you have a Romanian name. So we are both attached to the canonical autocephalous Orthodox churches. Moreover, I want you to meet my second wife Chadia; she's Orthodox too, a bookseller, and passionate about psychoanalysis."

Coming from a Lebanese man accustomed to living in a country at war, affiliated with one of the 17 religions recognized by the government, there was nothing surprising about this statement. Moreover, he could only have had an exchange like this one with a foreigner: questioning a Lebanese compatriot about his identity would be seriously incongruous, because in that universe belonging to a denominational community goes without saying. And faith is a private affair, separate from any form of identity. For each subject, identity is defined on the basis of a constraint: the obligation to belong to one of the 17 communities, each of which has its own legislation and its own jurisdictions where personal status is concerned. No subjective, political, national, sexual, or social identity is possible without such a marker.[5] In this configuration, identity does not stem from any religion or faith at all, but rather from membership: in a tribe, a clan, or an ethnic group. Established under the French mandate with the best intentions in the world, this communitarian system was supposed to ensure respect for the age-old equilibriums that had been transmitted from generation to generation – the only way, it was said, to avoid erasing or reifying the various identities. And yet, during that colloquium, the Lebanese participants – and Ghassan Tueni himself – had occasion to say that they did not approve of that system and that they tended to prefer the French Enlightenment, secularism, and a conception of democracy based on citizenship that was far removed from all the denominational forms of organization of which they were at once victims, heirs, and protagonists.

3

THE SOVEREIGN SELF

The journalist and historian Samir Kassir, an editorial writer at the daily newspaper *an-Nahar* and a defender of the Palestinian cause, had helped organize the colloquium; he was convinced that psychoanalysis conveyed in itself, independently of its representatives, a form of subjectivity that was threatening to totalitarianism, nationalism, and identitarian fanaticism. He had defied censorship many times. In his talk, he demonstrated his attachment to the ideals of Arabic humanism, reiterating his preference for the universalism of the Enlightenment and his rejection of a narrow communitarianism. He was fighting against Hezbollah and the Syrian dictatorship alike. A few days after he spoke at the colloquium – an act that, as we knew, put him at great risk – he was assassinated in a car bomb attack. In December, Gebran Tueni, Ghassan's son, met the same fate.

Secularisms

For my part, I have always found the principle of secularism superior to all others for the purpose of guaranteeing freedom of conscience and the transmission of knowledge, and this was my conviction long before we were confronted with the drift toward identitarianism in France, even if the question of Islam had already arisen. Still, I feel no hostility in principle toward culturalism, relativism, or religions in general; indeed, I consider the differences among them necessary to an understanding of what is universal. But I reject the project of making secularism a new religion inhabited by a dogmatic universalism applicable to all nations. To my mind, diversity and mixing alone are sources of progress. It is nevertheless the case that, without a minimum of secularism, no nation can escape from the grip of religion, especially when religion is conflated with a project of political conquest, that is, when religious markers are on public display. This is why, even though I am well aware that numerous forms of secularism exist throughout the world, forms as respectable and effective as the French model, I would readily subscribe to the general idea according to which secularism, as such, generates more freedom than any religion invested with political power.[6]

By the same token, I contend that only secularism can guarantee freedom of conscience and, most importantly, that only secularism can keep every subject from being assigned to a particular identity. This is, moreover, the reason why I supported a law proposed in 1989 to forbid the wearing of the Islamic headscarf in schools in France, since the law affected girls who were minors. I never understood that law as leading back to some sort of "neo-colonial exclusion" aimed at the representatives of a particular community. In France, in fact, the republican school system is based on an ideal that aims to detach children to some degree from their families, their origins, and the particular features of their identity, an ideal that makes the struggle against the ascendancy of any particular religion the principle of an egalitarian education. By virtue of this principle, no pupil has the right to exhibit, on school grounds, any ostentatious sign indicating religious affiliation: a visible crucifix, kippa, or headscarf.[7] The fact remains that France is the only country in the world to proclaim such a model of republican secularism. And the model must be defended at all costs, because it embodies a tradition that grew out of the Revolution and the separation between church and state. Nevertheless, it is hard to argue that it is superior to all others and can therefore be exported. To try to impose this model on all the peoples of the world would be both imperialist and suicidal.

Very different from Ghassan Tueni, Father Sélim Abou, the rector of Saint-Joseph University and a participant in the evening event in Beirut, was a magnificent Jesuit who reminded me of Michel de Certeau. An ardent Freudian, an anticolonialist anthropologist, a keen observer of Latin America and Canada, he had studied the tragic epic of the Jesuit Republic of the Guaranis, and had reflected at great length on the "identitarian question," preferring cosmopolitanism to any form of assigned identity, even denominational.[8] He stressed, moreover, that the more economic globalization advanced, the more the equally barbaric identitarian reaction intensified, in counterpoint, as if the homogenization of lifestyles, under the impetus of the market, went hand in hand with the search for supposed "roots." In this perspective, the globalization of economic exchange was thus accompanied by a resurgence of the most reactionary identitarian anguish: fear of the abolition of sexual differences, of the erasure of sovereignties and borders, fear of the disappearance of the family, of the father, of the mother; hatred of homosexuals, Arabs, foreigners, and so on.[9]

Sélim Abou thus invoked Montesquieu's well-known judgment against that infernal spiral:

> If I knew something useful to my nation but ruinous to another, I would not offer it to my prince, because I am a man before I am a Frenchman, or because I am necessarily a man and a Frenchman only by chance. If

THE SOVEREIGN SELF

I knew something useful to me and harmful to my family, I would put it out of my mind. If I knew something useful to my family but not to my country, I would try to forget it. If I knew of something useful to my country and harmful to Europe, or useful to Europe and harmful to the human race, I would view it as a crime.[10]

Montesquieu's approach was the best antidote, Abou suggested, against extreme provocations like those of Jean-Marie Le Pen, a French far-right politician who went around reiterating ad nauseum his adherence to the principles of a hierarchy of identities based on generalized endogamy, with arguments like the following: I love my daughters more than my cousins, my cousins more than my neighbors, my neighbors more than strangers, and strangers more than my enemies. Consequently, I love the French more than the Europeans, and ultimately I love best of all, among the other countries of the world, those that are my allies and that love France.

Nothing is more regressive for civilization and socialization than to align oneself with a hierarchy of identities and memberships. To be sure, the assertion of an identity is always an attempt to counter the erasure of oppressed minorities, but it proceeds through an excess of self-centered claims, or even through a mad desire not to mix with any community but one's own. And as soon as one adopts this sort of hierarchical splintering of reality, one is condemned to invent new ostracisms with respect to those who are not included in one's immediate group. Far from being emancipatory, then, the process of identitarian reduction reconstructs what it claims to undo. How can we fail to think about the effeminate homosexual men who are rejected by those who are not effeminate? How can we fail to see that it is precisely the mechanism of identity assignment that leads Whites and Blacks to reject the mixed-race individuals derogatorily labeled "mulattos," and leads mixed-race individuals to lay claim to "the drop of blood" that would allow them to align themselves with one camp rather than another? Similarly, it leads Sephardics to discriminate against Ashkenazis, who for their part are anti-Sephardic; it leads Arabs to excoriate Blacks and vice versa; it leads Jews to become anti-Semites, sometimes owing to Jewish self-hatred and sometimes, more recently, owing to adherence to the nationalist politics of the Israeli far right. At the heart of any identitarian system, there is always the accursed place of the other, irreducible to any label, in which one is condemned to feel ashamed of being oneself.

6

ASSIGNING IDENTITIES

The politics of Narcissus

To understand the blossoming of the identitarian anxieties that have ended up reversing the ideal of struggles for freedom into its opposite, we need to go back to the emergence of what Christopher Lasch called the culture of narcissism.[11] In 1979, Lasch noted that mass culture as it had developed in American society had engendered pathologies that could not be eradicated. And he attributed to post-Freudian psychoanalysis the responsibility for having validated that culture by transforming modern subjects into victims of themselves, interested only in navel-gazing. By dint of an exclusive preoccupation with their own identitarian anxieties, subjects in the individualist American society had become slaves to a new dependency of which the tragic fate of Narcissus – much more than that of Oedipus – was the embodiment. In Greek mythology, Narcissus, fascinated by his own reflection, falls into the water and drowns because he has not managed to understand that his image is not himself. In other words, it is because he does not grasp the idea of difference between himself and otherness that he condemns himself to death. He has become dependent on a fatal identitarian anchoring that leads him to need others in order to have self-esteem, while remaining unable to conceive what authentic otherness might be.

The other is thus assimilated to an enemy, and his or her difference is denied. Since no conflictual dynamic is acknowledged, all subjects take refuge in their own little territories in order to make war on their enemies. Obsessing over one's body, acquiring a good self-image, affirming one's desires without feeling any guilt, desiring fascism or puritanism – activities such as these would determine the beliefs of a society at once depressive and narcissistic, whose new religion would declare faith in a therapy of the soul founded on the cult of an inflated ego.

In an essay published five years later, Lasch stressed that, in a troubled period such as the 1980s, daily life in America had turned into an exercise in survival: "People take one day at a time. They seldom look back, lest they succumb to a debilitating 'nostalgia'; and if they look ahead, it is to see how they can insure themselves against the disasters almost everyone now expects ... Under siege, the self contracts to a defensive core, armed against adversity. Emotional equilibrium demands a minimal self, not the imperial self of yesteryear."[12]

Lasch had the great merit of drawing attention to the emergence of a huge fantasy of identity loss. In a world recently unified and lacking

7

THE SOVEREIGN SELF

an external enemy – from the political disengagement of the 1980s to the fall of the Berlin Wall – all individuals could believe themselves personally to be victims of some ecological disaster, some nuclear accident, some network, or more simply of their neighbors: transgendered, postcolonialist, Black, Jew, Arab, sexist, rapist, zombie. The list is endless: the phenomenon has continued to grow in the early twenty-first century, as if self-preservation should be the goal of every struggle.

Berkeley 1996

In the years that followed the fall of the Wall, the culture of identity gradually took over from the culture of narcissism, and in the fluid world we currently inhabit, it has become one of the responses to the weakening of the collective ideal, to the collapse of the ideals of the French Revolution, and to the transformations of family structures. It was during those years, then, that the so-called "societal" struggles could be said to have taken the place of social struggles. The culture of identity tends to introduce its procedures of thought into the experiences of social or sexual subjective life. And from that standpoint, all behavior becomes identitarian: ways of eating, making love, sleeping, driving a car. Every neurosis, every particularity, every item of clothing refers to an attribution of identity, according to the generalized principle of conflict between oneself and the others.

I became aware of this in September 1996 during a stint in Berkeley, California – a laboratory of all the avant-garde theories. I had been invited by my friend Vincent Kaufmann, a professor of literature, who lived on campus with his family. I was astonished to discover that he was unable to bring the faculty members of his department together for a joyous, convivial banquet. They each brandished their own lifestyles like a fetish: one was a vegetarian and had to bring his own food; another suffered from horrible allergies that kept him from spending a whole evening in the company of particles deemed dangerous for his health; a third obeyed daily sleep rituals that required him to go to bed at 9 p.m. and thus to arrive for the dinner at 6; a fourth was, on the contrary, an insomniac who could not tolerate eating before 10 p.m.; yet another could not bear the idea that cheese could be served at a meal; not to mention those who were exasperated by the noise likely to be made by young children … In short, all of Kaufmann's colleagues were prepared to come at the time of their choosing and provided that they could bring

8

their own food and drink. In other respects, they were all delightful, intelligent, refined, highly cultured. All practiced the hospitality that only American intellectuals know how to offer.

That day, I could not help thinking of Michel Foucault's reflection upon arriving at the University of Vincennes in 1969:

> It was hard to say anything at all without someone asking you: "You're speaking from where?" That question always left me very dejected. It seemed to me a question befitting a police interrogation. In the guise of a theoretical and political question ("Where are you speaking from?"), in fact I was being asked about my identity: "At bottom, who are you?" "So tell us if you are a Marxist or not." "Tell us if you are an idealist or a materialist." "Tell us if you're a professor or a militant." "Show your I.D, tell us in the name of what you're going to be able to circulate so that we can tell who you are."[13]

I understand, then, why Mark Lilla, a militant on the American left and professor of humanities at Columbia University, could react with genuine outrage in 2017 when he came across yet another instance of the ravages of identity politics:

> On the [Democratic Party's] homepage, ... you find a list of links titled "People." And each link takes you to a page tailored to appeal to a distinct group and identity: women, Hispanics, "ethnic Americans," the LGBT community, Native Americans, African-Americans, Asian-Americans and Pacific Islanders ... There are seventeen such groups, and seventeen separate messages. You might well think that, by some mistake, you have landed on the website of the Lebanese government.[14]

— 2 —

THE GALAXY OF GENDER

Paris 1949: One is not born a woman

"One is not born, but rather becomes, woman."[1] When she wrote that sentence in 1949 in *Le deuxième sexe* (*The Second Sex*), Simone de Beauvoir had no idea that the book would become a major work opening the way, on the other side of the Atlantic, to all the literary, sociological, and psychoanalytical works in the 1970s that sought to distinguish between sex (or the sexed body) and gender as an identitarian construct. From Robert Stoller to Heinz Kohut to Judith Butler, from the study of transsexualism to that of the narcissistic Self and then from transgender to queer, we find everywhere, even if it is not explicit, the great Beauvoirian interrogation that made it permissible, for the first time, to cast a new gaze on the status of all the differences repressed by official history, and among those the most scandalous, that of "becoming a woman."[2]

The Second Sex provoked a scandal from the moment it was published, as if the work had come straight out of the "forbidden books" section of the French National Library (popularly known as "Hell"). And yet it resembled neither a story by the Marquis de Sade nor a pornographic text nor a treatise on eroticism. Simone de Beauvoir brought to her study of sexuality the approach of a scientist, a historian, a sociologist, an anthropologist, and a philosopher, basing her investigation on both Alfred Kinsey's survey[3] and the works of an impressive number of psychoanalysts, while taking into account not only the biological, social, and psychic reality of female sexuality but also the foundational myths about the difference between the sexes (myths conceived by men and by women) along with the domain of private life. She was speaking, then, about sexuality, and more specifically about female sexuality, in all its forms and in its smallest details.

Suddenly, the female sex erupted in a new and paradigmatic way into the field of thought: henceforth people would refer to *The Second Sex* the way they referred to Descartes's *Discourse on Method*, Rousseau's *Confessions*, or Freud's *Interpretation of Dreams*. And this magnificent book would serve as the basis for an in-depth renovation of feminist thought. Going forward, fighting for social and political equality was no longer enough. It would also be necessary to take women's sexuality into account, as an object of anthropology and as lived experience.

Simone de Beauvoir did not conceptualize the notion of gender, and she was unaware that societies had always classified sexuality variously as a function of anatomy or of identity construction. As Thomas Laqueur makes clear, in all earlier discourses about sexuality, the two notions were never conflated. Some authors asserted, as we find from Aristotle to Galen, that gender dominated sex, to the extent that men and women could be ranked according to their degree of metaphysical perfection, along an axis in which men occupied the sovereign position; other writers, as we see in the nineteenth century, asserted to the contrary that sex in the anatomical and biological sense defined gender: monism on one side (one sex was the standard), dualism on the other (there were two sexes, distinguished by anatomical differences). In both cases, masculinity was always thought to be superior to femininity: in short, phallocentrism reigned.[4]

As for the Freudian theory of sexuality, it represents a synthesis between the two models. In fact, Freud drew inspiration both from Galen and from nineteenth-century biology, taking care to establish a radical difference between the two sexes on the basis of anatomy. According to him, there was a single libido – or sex drive – that was male in essence and that defined feminine as well as masculine sexuality. This did not rule out the existence of bisexuality. In this connection, Freud revived the Platonic myth of androgyny according to which there are three genders: male, female, and androgynous. The ancestors of humans, androgynes were orb-like beings. They resembled eggs with four feet, four hands, two faces opposite each other, and two sex organs placed at the rear. Inordinately proud, they set out to besiege the heavens, which led Zeus to cut them in two. Once this punitive division – a castration – had been accomplished, each half always desired to be reunited with the other.[5]

THE SOVEREIGN SELF

Vienna 1912: Is anatomy destiny?

From this myth and from several recent studies, including those of Wilhelm Fliess, Freud retained the idea that psychic bisexuality was central in the genesis of human sexuality, especially in the cases of homosexuality and female sexuality, going so far as to assert that each sex repressed what characterized the opposite sex: penis envy on the part of the woman, desire for femininity on the part of the man. For the same reason, he maintained that the clitoris was a sort of atrophied penis and that, to reach the status of full femininity, a woman had to give up clitoral orgasms in favor of vaginal orgasms. All these theses were rightly criticized by Freud's heirs within his own movement and, of course, by Beauvoir. The fact remains that Freud produced one of the most complete theories of sexuality ever developed up to that point. He basically broke with the idea of species and races and shattered any notion of fixed identities.

In his eyes, there was no such thing as a "maternal instinct" or a female "race," except in fantasies and myths constructed by both men and women. In other words, from his perspective, all humans possessed several sexual identities, and no one was confined any longer to a single label. The social or psychic construction of sexual identity thus became, according to Freud, as important as the anatomical organization of the difference between the sexes. And this is how we must understand his famous declaration, as celebrated as Beauvoir's: "Anatomy is destiny."[6] Contrary to what has been alleged, Freud never claimed that anatomy was the only destiny possible for the human condition. As evidence, if necessary, we can turn to the fact that he borrowed the formula from Napoleon, who had sought to inscribe the history of people to come in politics rather than in a constant reference to ancient myths.[7] Even as he was revalorizing the ancient tragedies, Freud nevertheless drew on that formula to transform the great issue of sexual difference into a modern, quasi-political dramaturgy. From then on, with him and after him, and owing to the very deconstruction of the Western family that served as backdrop to the emergence of psychoanalysis, men and women alike would be condemned to idealize or debase the other, without ever reaching real fulfillment. The sexual scene described by Freud was thus inspired by the world stage and the wars between populations – as conceived by the Emperor Napoleon – even as it prefigured a new war between the sexes of which the stakes would be the reproductive organs; Freud thereby introduced into this second

12

war the language of desire and jouissance. In sum, let us say that if, for Freud, anatomy was part of human destiny, it would in no case remain, for every human being, an unsurpassable horizon. Such is indeed the theory of freedom proper to psychoanalysis: recognizing the existence of a destiny the better to free ourselves from it.

Highlights and disappointments of gender studies

Gender studies began to develop in the 1970s, from a perspective as far removed from the classic Freudian approach as from Beauvoir's: first in the Anglophone academic world, then in humanities departments more generally, and finally in various civil societies. At the outset, the goal of research in this area was to achieve a better understanding, on the one hand, of the forms of differentiation that the status of the difference between the sexes induced in a given society, and on the other, of the way the domination of patriarchal power had concealed the existence not only of women's role in history but also the role of minorities that had been oppressed owing to their sexual orientation: homosexuals, "abnormals," perverts, bisexuals, and so on. In this regard, gender studies were – and remain – of crucial importance from the standpoint of research, for historians and sociologists as well as for philosophers and specialists in literature. What would Michel Foucault's work on sexuality be, or Jacques Derrida's work on deconstruction, or Michelle Perrot's work on women's history, without the implicit reference to the question of gender? Gender studies everywhere have sought to discover the extent of sexual roles and symbolism in various societies and in different periods.[8]

However, as the world gradually ceased to be bipolar and the failure of the politics of emancipation based on the class struggle and social welfare demands became increasingly apparent, commitment to identity politics took the place of classic militancy, especially at the heart of the American left.[9] During the same period, progress in surgery made it possible to think about the question of gender in terms of direct intervention in human bodies rather than in terms of subjectivity. Two radically distinct but equally revelatory experiments attest to this shift: one a delirious approach leading to the abolition of the category of sex itself, the other a constructive reflection on the possibility of new relations between sex and gender.

The first specialist to popularize the term gender was John Money, a psychologist from New Zealand with a fundamentalist background who had specialized in hermaphroditism.[10] But he was not content to help families and the unfortunate children who were affected by that rather rare anomaly; far from it. He claimed to be pursuing, on the basis of direct observation of the phenomenon, a vast reflection on the relations between nature and culture so as to demonstrate that there was no clear-cut distinction between the two sexes; rather, there was a sort of continuum. Thus he asserted in 1955 that anatomical sex meant nothing with respect to the construction of gender, claiming that one's gender role was never established at birth but was instead constructed cumulatively through lived experience.[11] In his eyes, only the social role counted: gender without sex.[12] It would thus suffice, according to him, to raise a boy as a girl and vice versa for a child to take on an identity other than the one indicated by his or her anatomy.

In 1966, he found a guinea pig to validate his thesis in the person of David Reimer, age 18 months. The boy's penis had been burned off following a botched circumcision. On Money's advice, David's parents authorized ablation of the testicles and a name change. But in adolescence David felt that he was a man. He had surgery to regain a penis, but the surgical traumas were unbearable; he went on to commit suicide. Money's experiment was all the more scandalous in that, according to all scientific research, it is virtually impossible to bring up as a girl a child genetically programmed to be a boy. Widely attacked, Money claimed to be the victim of a far-right conspiracy.

The psychiatrist and psychoanalyst Robert Stoller approached the question of gender from a completely different standpoint in 1954 by creating the Gender Identity Research Clinic at the University of California, Los Angeles. Passionate about anthropology, literature, and history, convinced that the classic psychoanalytic theories did not suffice to account for the real relations between gender and sex, especially in the vast realm of sexual perversions, he was interested in the diversity of sexual identities and especially in transsexualism, which had been studied a year before by Harry Benjamin, an American endocrinologist.[13]

The desire to change one's sex has been observed in all societies. In Antiquity, numerous observations were made about the phenomenon, involving both transvestism and bisexuality. But what was new, in the mid-twentieth century, was that that desire could finally be translated into radical anatomical transformations by surgical and/or medicinal means. Transsexualism was now defined as very different from transvestism. The challenge was to understand the nature of a purely psychic identity problem characterized by the unshakable

14

– but not delirious – conviction of a male or female subject that he or she belonged to the opposite sex.

Through numerous studies, Stoller showed that surgical interventions – which were on the rise during this period – were beneficial only when subjects did not succeed in accepting their actual anatomy, which never corresponded to the gender to which they believed they belonged. Transsexualism provoked an immense debate in the 1970s, both among feminists and in the homosexual movement. It was finally possible to consider that the distribution of the male and female poles was not a simple matter, since both women and men could be convinced that their gender did not correspond in any way to their anatomical sex, and especially since, thanks to advances in medicine, they could finally have access to their chosen identity, or rather to the one that corresponded to an absolute certainty imposed by their subjective organization. The psyche thus had the upper hand over the biological reality, to such an extent that the former appeared capable of eliminating the latter. Surgical interventions proved to be disastrous, however, precisely because the biological reality could never be eradicated in favor of a purely psychic or social construction.

Today, before being able to benefit from a hormonal-surgical reassignment under the supervision of endocrinologists, transsexuals in France have to undergo a two-year-long evaluation; they also have to have a psychiatric assessment proving that they are neither schizophrenic nor suffering from amputomania, that is, a delirious determination to have a healthy part of the body removed (a leg, an arm, a penis). For two years, moreover, these patients must live their everyday lives as a person of the opposite sex, while the medical team oversees their meetings with their family, especially their children, who have to confront the "transition," that is, watch their mother become a man or their father become a woman. At the end of that ordeal, the patients may be authorized to follow an antihormonal treatment: anti-androgenic for men, with hair removal by electrolysis, progesterone for women. Then comes the surgical intervention: bilateral castration and creation of a neo-vagina in men, removal of the ovaries and uterus in women and then construction of a penis (phalloplasty).[14]

When we know that the hormonal treatment has to go on for the rest of the individual's life and that the transsexual provided with new organs will never again experience the slightest sexual pleasure, it is hard to keep from thinking that the pleasure felt in acquiring an entirely mutilated body is of the same nature as the pleasure experienced by the great mystics who offered to God the torment of their wounded flesh. This is at least my hypothesis.

The worldwide interest aroused by transsexualism, and more generally by the issue of transformations in sexual identity, eventually gave rise to a complete revision of the representation of the body in Western societies, and to an unprecedented expansion of theories and discourses concerning the difference between the sexes (anatomy) and gender (identity construction).

Most significantly, well after Stoller's work, and with support from the major movements aimed at the emancipation of oppressed minorities, the term "transsexualism" was rejected in favor of "transgender," a shift that allowed individuals affected by this syndrome to escape from psychiatric classifications. By adopting this label, transsexuals claimed the right to a gender identity without the obligation to undergo hormonal-surgical reassignment. And through this legitimate depsychiatrization of their fate, they formed an identity politics movement. Consequently, they demanded that their gender identity be recognized by governmental authorities, even though it did not coincide with their physical anatomy. At bottom, they reproached Robert Stoller and all the promoters of transsexualism for adopting an essentialist theory: that of the "wrong body." In order to have access to sex reassignment surgery, a transsexual had to have had a lifelong feeling of always having belonged to the "opposite" sex. In contrast, subjects who defined themselves as transgender could perfectly well avoid situating themselves in one category or the other. A trans is at once – and at will – a man or a woman, and the "transition" thus is more like an initiation, a "rite of passage," than an assignment subsequent to surgical intervention, even if the transition in one direction or the other is accompanied by hormonal treatment, plastic surgery, or crossdressing.

Transidentities

Thus several identities can cohabit depending on the way one consciously constructs a mental or corporeal universe. If evidence is needed, we have only to look at the extraordinary drag culture of the 1990s, inherited from the old tradition of drag ballrooms, where, starting in the late nineteenth century, in out-of-the-way venues, people excluded from the norm – gays, lesbians, transvestites, Blacks and Latinos – got together. Modern transgender individuals, henceforth free to exist openly, put their pride on display: on one side, transgender drag queens created a deliberately feminine identity for themselves by imitating the stereotypes of an exaggerated femininity, while transgender drag kings adopted an equally stereotypical masculine identity. Members of each group became themselves through crossdressing, with women sporting beards and penis-shaped socks, men enhancing their breasts and concealing their Adam's apples, all making outrageous use of makeup.

But for this mutation of transsexualism into transgender identity – or transidentity – to come about, an earlier event was crucial: the depsychiatrization of homosexuality. In 1973, after a stormy debate, the American Psychiatric Association finally decided to eliminate homosexuality from its list of mental illnesses. This progress toward emancipation was accompanied, moreover, by the abandonment of the very term "homosexuality" – which had been invented in 1869 along with the term "heterosexuality" – in favor of a label free of any pathological connotations: male and female homosexuals thus became gays and lesbians, forming two militant communities. This choice meant that homosexuality was no longer to be considered a "sexual orientation" – a man loves a man and a woman loves a woman – but as an identity: thus one could be gay or lesbian, it was said, without ever having had sexual relations with a person of the same sex. This thesis is clearly debatable: how can one distinguish a practitioner from a non-practitioner, when we know that abstinence is a deliberate choice that has little to do with identity and that is not necessarily a form of "asexuality"?[15] This change of paradigm nevertheless made it possible for other categories to stem not from the choice of object but from an identity. To the new community of gays and lesbians were added bisexuals, transgender persons, and hermaphrodites. In the process, the latter were rebaptized "intersexuals," a term better adapted to their new condition than the old one, which bore traces of the biological presence of two sets of organs. Members of all these groups left shame and humiliation behind in favor of pride in being themselves.

Hence the acronym LGBT, soon expanded to LGBTQIA+ (with the addition of queer, intersexual, asexual, and so on); the whole set formed a community of small communities, each demanding the end of all discrimination based on the difference between the sexes. But what forms of discrimination, exactly? The answer is simple enough. In fact, once psychiatric knowledge was set aside, members of the LGBTQIA+ communities could with good reason claim certain rights: the right to marry, to procreate, to transmit their property, to condemn their persecutors under the law. Let us note in passing that the homosexuality/heterosexuality pairing was retained, but no longer to express a difference: instead, it provided the basis for a reversal of the stigma attached to the first term. Since homosexuality had been considered an "anomaly" with respect to a "norm," it was now necessary to assert that the so-called norm was nothing but the expression of a rejection of anything that did not fit the clinical picture. Hence the creation of the word "heteronormative" to designate any oppression linked to the patriarchy, to masculine domination, to sexual relations between a man and a woman, or even to the so-called "binary" form of sexuality, as opposed to a form called "non-binary." Similarly, the invention of the word "cisgender" made it possible to characterize a sexual identity called "normative."

"Cisgender" thus became an antonym for "transgender." The latter term defined persons who did not recognize themselves in the body that had been assigned to them at birth, the underlying presupposition being that anatomy is only a construction and not a biological reality, since from this standpoint subjects have the right to recognize themselves in their own anatomy or not. In other words, the invention of this terminology functioned as a declaration of war on anatomical reality in favor of a "gendered" imperative.[16] And the terminology has now taken hold as a new norm, since the adjective "gendered" more and more often replaces the adjective "sexual" in the everyday language of journalists and politicians, and even of lawyers and judges. It could be said that the sexual, sexuality, the sexualized, in short everything that has to do with sex, is being banished in favor of a puritanism that wants to hear no more about sexuality, on the pretext that the word refers to a scandalous biology of male domination – which, however, is not the case.

Inquisitorial follies

And, from this perspective, part of the feminist movement has turned out to be hostile to fundamental freedoms in matters of behavior. It is with this branch of feminism that adherents to moral – or "politically correct"[17] – rereadings of works of art are generally associated; such rereadings ineluctably lead to acts of censure toward any expression in art or literature said to be "sexually suggestive." "Dare to be feminist!" and other such slogans have been adopted in France by this extremist tendency,[18] which aims to denounce "sexist," "macho," and similar stereotypical characterizations everywhere and in every

THE GALAXY OF GENDER

era; targets include plays and other public spectacles produced by artists deemed guilty of infringing on the dignity of women. Some of these artists have already been judged in court and have served their time; some are presumed to have committed criminal acts, while still others have been denounced publicly as ignominious on the basis of testimony that can be moving and often authentic but that can also prove very fragile when it comes to establishing proof.[19] Among the most recent campaigns waged in France, we find one called #WagonSansCouillon, women-only rail cars, protesting sexual violence in public transportation; we also find systematic and non-critical encouragements to women to denounce their "torturers," and at the same time all sorts of initiatives in favor of the headscarves worn by Muslim women, who are said to be "discriminated against" by a Republic labeled "patriarchal-heteronormative," not to mention the legally baseless denunciations and the various threats aiming to make it impossible to hold conferences and colloquia or to put on performances deemed "homophobic," "transphobic," "sexist," and so on.

To be sure, in October 2017, the #MeToo movement, a planet-wide development, finally allowed women who had been raped, tortured, or stoned under various dictatorships to exit from shame and silence, and also allowed other women to reveal to what extent, in democratic countries, rapes and various forms of harassment had not been adequately taken into account by the legal system or by public opinion. A number of murky predators such as Harvey Weinstein and Jeffrey Epstein have been brought before the courts, in a few satisfying triumphs over barbarity.[20] But these successes do not preclude criticizing the excesses of the movement. For public confession does not constitute progress in itself. An explosion of rage, however necessary, should never be a model for fighting inequalities and mistreatment. And if no one can deny the demands of a legal system based on proof and the respect for privacy, this also means that users of social networks have no business substituting themselves for judges and throwing torturers or criminals to the wolves – that is, to the court of public opinion. Similarly, this must never lead to encouraging acts of censorship or puritanism.

And yet, in November 2017, in preparation for an exhibit devoted to Balthus at the Metropolitan Museum of Art in New York, the organizers were obliged, under pressure from that sort of threat, to post a plaque at the entrance warning against the potentially disturbing nature of certain paintings. The famous *Thérèse Dreaming* was even threatened with removal after a protest, because it depicts an adolescent stretched out in a chair with her hands on her head, her skirt lifted to reveal her inner thigh and her white cotton underpants: "I was shocked to see a painting that depicts a young girl in a sexually suggestive pose," Mia Merrill stated, because it "is an evocative portrait of a prepubescent girl relaxing on a chair with her legs up and underwear exposed."[21] In the same vein, American publishers were being increasingly assailed by demands for censorship of certain books.[22]

A month after the Balthus episode, in an opinion piece published in *Libération*, the historian Laure Murat, who had been invited to Los Angeles to a film club session, recounted that she had felt duty-bound, in the name of a new theoretical approach, the "gendered gaze," to revisit a central scene of Michelangelo Antonioni's 1966 film *Blow-Up*. Tormented by the accusations of rape and harassment against Harvey Weinstein, she believed she had discerned in the film the expression of a frightful misogyny on the part of the director, a phenomenon that had been stifled for decades by servile critics:

> We see the photographer, the hero of the film, astride a mannequin that is lying on the ground, arms outstretched, in an inviting pose. A beam of luminescent rays radiates from his zoom lens, which he holds in his left hand and turns toward the face of his prey. That image, to which I would have doubtless paid little attention earlier, suddenly struck me. Was it really necessary to choose this caricatural representation of male domination in the milieu of the visual arts, at the very moment when Hollywood is still shaken by the aftermath of the Weinstein affair, which remains on the front pages?[23]

According to Laure Murat, Antonioni had made himself an accomplice to a rape scene, and his "aestheticism" served to mask a deep adherence to an "intolerable" sexism: the director was thus, by anticipation, a sort of aristocratic and highly gifted Weinstein. Reading this article, one wonders how a remarkable academic, the author of fascinating books, was able to let herself be carried away, in the name of a postmodern critique (the famous "gendered gaze"), by such reductionist fury. In fact, there is nothing in the film to justify an allegation that we are dealing with a rape scene here; similarly, nothing justifies an assertion that the director approves the violent acts of his character. Quite to the contrary, the entire staging is constructed like an account of the wanderings of a photographer on the edge of madness, locked within the labyrinth of a perpetual optical illusion.

Psychiatry in full retreat

The 1973 decision by the American Psychiatric Association to depsychiatrize homosexuality provoked a scandal. It suggested that the American psychiatric community, unable to define homosexuality "scientifically," had yielded in demagogic fashion to pressure from an identitarian group. However, if the decision to stop characterizing homosexuality as a mental illness can be attributed to the submission of medical authorities to the power of a fraction of public opinion, it was also the consequence of the negligence that prevailed at the time in psychiatric nosology. Considered a degenerate race and persecuted for centuries on the same basis as Jews, homosexuals had been regarded by psychiatrists at the end of the nineteenth century and throughout the twentieth as sexual perverts – a truly aberrant classification. As for Freud's heirs, most of them demonstrated extreme intolerance and, it must be said, profound stupidity by setting up the figure of the homosexual as a "major signifier" of all perversions; this led to the most grotesque treatments aiming to "transform" them into heterosexuals. In any case, with the appearance of the *Diagnostic and Statistical Manual of Mental Disorders (DSM)*, classic psychiatric knowledge was destroyed in favor of a ridiculous and abusive nomenclature.[24]

Between 1952 and 1968, the first two editions of the *DSM* focused on the categories of psychoanalysis and classic psychiatry, that is, on defining the psychic afflictions that corresponded to the study of human subjectivity: norms and pathologies, neuroses, psychoses, depressions, perversions. To be sure, these classifications left something to be desired, but they had a certain coherence. In contrast, starting in the 1970s, under pressure from pharmaceutical laboratories and academic departments of neuroscience concerned with instituting a vast realm of brain science that would deal with degenerative diseases as well as mild neuroses, this "dynamic" approach was contested in favor of describing behaviors on the basis of an expanding number of identitarian typologies. In other words, instead of defining the human subject according to a tripartite social, biological, and psychological approach, this new psychiatry retained just one component, behavior, or rather "behavioral difference," set up as an infinitely extendable system: the focus was no longer on subjective units but rather on identitarian variations according to each behavior.

This transformation of psychiatric knowledge has to be linked, moreover, with the epidemic of an identity disorder known as "multiple personality," a syndrome translated by the coexistence in a single subject – most often a woman – of several separate personalities, each of which could take control, in turn, of the individual's way of life.[25] Described as mystics, spirits, or visionaries capable of projecting themselves into the past or the future by adopting the identity of a historical figure or a character in a novel (in France, these could be figures such as Salammbô, Scheherazade, or Marie-Antoinette), under the influence of psychoanalysis and dynamic psychiatry, these patients had been designated as hysterics or psychotics; most had suffered childhood sexual abuse. In 1970, the notion seemed like a curiosity from another era. But in 1986, and even more in the 1990s, American psychiatrists observed a proliferation of the syndrome, to such an extent that in all major American cities, clinics sprang up specializing in the treatment of the new epidemic, which had been induced in large part by the various versions of the *DSM*. Psychiatrists thus began to see a recurrence, among their female patients, of the repressed image of a classification method that consisted in dissolving human subjectivity into multiple profiles, each having to be approached in a different way. Over the years, the epidemic faded away as these women transformed their pathology into an identitarian claim: that of victims of masculine repression.

We owe this shift in the classification of ailments of the soul to the psychiatrist Robert Leopold Spitzer. A colorful character who trusted in the virtues of the rational approach to human beings, he had been trained within the circle of classical Freudianism, which dominated psychiatric studies in the 1940s. But he later turned to the theses of Wilhelm Reich, who had been incarcerated in Lewisburg, Pennsylvania, for marketing his "orgone accumulators," devices intended to treat sexual impotence. Convinced that he was the artisan of a new scientific revolution, Spitzer surrounded himself with 14 committees, each including a large number of experts. Between 1970 and 1980, his team proceeded to an "atheoretical sweeping away" of the psychic phenomenon, substituting for the dynamic terminology of psychiatry a jargon worthy of Molière's doctors.[26] Psychiatric concepts were banished in favor of the notion of disorder and dysphoria (uneasiness, distress) that allowed the authors of the

22

DSM to add 292 imaginary maladies: timidity, fear of dying, post-traumatic stress disorder, a sense of inferiority or emptiness, and so on. In the *DSM-IV*, published in 1994, the number of such ailments went up to 410, and it has been increasing ever since.

It was in this context that Spitzer had to confront homosexual associations even as he continued to assert that, with adequate treatment methods, they could be "converted." By 2012, however, his position had changed: "I believe I owe the gay community an apology for my study making unproven claims of the efficacy of reparative therapy."[27] A sincere artisan of a dangerous universalist utopia, he had believed he was constructing a discourse on mental disorders valid for the whole planet. Instead, he had created a "monster' that became the instrument of one of the greatest errors of psychiatric history: an Orwellian system seeking to dislocate the human personality, in which all subjects could be reduced to a minuscule label, according to one or another of their behaviors.[28] Thus the American psychiatrist Allen Frances, an enthusiastic partisan of that "Big Brother" classification, ended up declaring that it was becoming harmful for society as a whole. As he said in a commentary in 2013:

> With the DSM-5, patients worried about having a medical illness will often be diagnosed with somatic symptom disorder, normal grief will be misidentified as major depressive disorder, the forgetfulness of old age will be confused with mild neurocognitive disorder, temper tantrums will be labeled disruptive mood dysregulation disorder, overeating will become binge eating disorder, and the already overused diagnosis of attention-deficit disorder will be even easier to apply to adults thanks to criteria that have been loosened further.[29]

All these processes of declassification, followed by the *DSM*'s annexation of disorders that had nothing to do with psychiatry, made it possible to transform sexual orientations formerly regarded as pathologies into multiple identities, ejecting them summarily from a body of medical knowledge that had become grotesque. From that point on, and owing to the political transformations that I signaled in the previous chapter, gender became a major concept aiming not only to abolish the difference between the sexes (in the anatomical sense) but also to redefine all sorts of sexual, social, and political disposi-tions. The extraordinary expansion of psychiatric nomenclatures was accompanied by a corresponding proliferation of identitarian studies, the second being something like the inverse of the first.

Once the term "transgender" had replaced "transsexual," the question of "vagueness" in the designation of the difference between the sexes could no longer be posed in the same way. If one can be at the same time a man and a woman because one chooses freely to be "gendered" apart from any biological reference and in an arbitrary fashion, it becomes possible to abolish the very idea of choice, even while highlighting the body in all its forms, as if the absence of reference to anatomy wiped out sexual difference even while claiming it.

New York: Queer Nation

Along similar lines, the Queer Nation movement was born in 1990, inspired by the battles of the New York branch of the Act Up group.[30] In English, the term "queer" signifies odd, weird, warped, "off": long used as a pejorative term for homosexuals, it was eventually adopted in parodic fashion by the victims themselves, in the well-known phenomenon of inverting stigmata. And it really took off as it began to allow a whole community to abolish identities based on a difference between nature and culture, sex and gender, normality and abnormality, and so on. In other words, it helped blur what had seemed self-evident, shattering by dint of performances and radicality all that had been gained in the wake of Beauvoir's work. Through the term "queer," a new identitarian – or post-feminist – politics began to emerge, based on adherence to the idea that the "abnormals" rejected from the dominant discourses could come together in a single community, a "queer nation" composed of representatives of all the "minority" sexualities – transgendered, bisexual, intersexual, and so on – but also all the victims of so-called "white oppression": people of color, Blacks, Chicanos, subalterns, migrants, colonized people, and the like.

Highly politicized, the queer movement developed an accomplished, affecting, flamboyant discourse that did not settle, as the discourse of the homosexual movement had, for demanding marriage for all and access to various modes of assisted procreation. "Performances" that were often very creative expressed a powerful desire for equality.[31] At bottom, far from seeking to become part of the traditional familial order, queer militants were claiming, in the wake of Jean Genet, pride in being "exceptional," beyond norms: "pushy femmes, radical faeries, fantasists, drags, clones, leatherfolk, ladies in tuxedos, feminist women or feminist men, masturbators, bulldaggers, divas,

Snap! queens, butch bottoms, storytellers, transsexuals, aunties, wannabes, lesbian-identified men or lesbians who sleep with men."[32]

The development of this movement went hand in hand with the valorization, in Western societies, of pornography, tattoos, plastic surgery, sexual masquerades, and deviant community practices, all of which ran counter to the self-declared puritanism of "gendered" and "antisex" feminism. Nevertheless, the movement adhered to the idea that "heteronormality" remained the enemy to be vanquished. As a result, the movement more or less unwittingly invented a new norm.

Once again, a political movement found its legitimacy in multiple texts coming from the American academic world, a thought experiment blended with life experience. While members of the LGBTQ+ movement were in the streets brandishing their six-color rainbow flag with panache,[33] scholars were publishing a large number of essays that took into account the dissolution of the sex/gender dichotomy. The birth of queer theory took place against this background.[34] Queer theorists sought not only to wipe out the idea of the anatomical determination of an individual's sex but also to make visible, through erudite performances, those on the margins of the dominant white gay or lesbian identity, those apt to elude any clear definitions. In other words, the affirmation of a blurred identity, or even an absence of identity, became a way of bringing a new identity to life.

Queer theory found an unexpected audience in the best American universities, in the very heart of gender studies departments, giving rise to myriad innovative reflections on sexual identity; at the same time, moreover, it was proving inescapable in many other disciplines: for example, in sociology, literature, psychoanalysis, psychology, history, philosophy, and biology.[35] From the standpoint of queer theory, the implication of authors in their own teaching became the condition sine qua non of an authentic theoretical experience. Talking about oneself, working on oneself, telling one's own story in the most intimate detail: such was the credo of a transmission of knowledge that inevitably incorporated a sort of self-analysis – or even autofiction – according to which one defined oneself as "gendered," "non-gendered," "binary," "non-binary," Black, white, queer, and so forth.

Just as depsychiatrization of all sexual orientations had led people formerly grouped in the large catalog of mental illnesses to express themselves in terms other than those of the nomenclature imposed by a failing body of knowledge, academics henceforth took into account their own "gender" in proclaiming their experience of identity. "Whereas subjectivity is taken into account, or even claimed by Anglo-Saxon scholars," Anne-Claire Rebreyend writes, reviewing a book by Anne Fausto-Sterling, "their French counterparts take innumerable precautions to prove that they remain completely neutral and impenetrable to anything that might make a connection between their personal lives and their objects of scholarly interest."[36] Among the various approaches to gender studies and queer theory, I propose to focus on those of Anne Fausto-Sterling and Judith Butler.

A celebrated biologist, Anne Fausto-Sterling has not hesitated to declare how fundamental her own sexual experiences have been in her work. Having spent a portion of her life as a declared heterosexual and another portion as a declared homosexual, she finally found a new identity in a situation of "transition"; she argued that "science," far from providing reliable and objective knowledge, was in reality anchored in a specific cultural context. Thus she claimed to be ridding biology of all forms of binarism; she saw anatomical sex as socially constructed, just as gender is, claiming that "sexuality is a somatic fact created by a cultural effect."[37] She proposed, then, to renew studies on hermaphroditism by replacing the two-sex system with a system encompassing five sexes: men, women, "herms" (true hermaphrodites), "merms" (male pseudo-hermaphrodites), and "ferms" (female pseudo-hermaphrodites).

From what scientific logic does the discourse of this accomplished biologist stem? If the existence of three variants of hermaphroditism can go this far in reinforcing the thesis according to which sexual difference is open to multiple forms, it means that this approach overrides any biological-genetic anomaly so as to ground a new categorization. And indeed, by dissolving binarism, Fausto-Sterling eliminates hermaphroditism in favor of a new field, "intersexuality," into which she integrates subcategories that have nothing to do with biological-genetic anomalies. And she does not hesitate to skew the figures in order to demonstrate that intersexuality is the major linchpin for understanding sexual identity in general.[38] With this hypothesis, Fausto-Sterling seeks to prove that "queerness" is not merely a social construction but a biological reality. Consequently, sexuality in her eyes is a continuum without a binary foundation. As is the case with transsexualism, progress in surgery had long since transformed the lives of hermaphrodites who had undergone surgery at birth, a procedure that was believed to spare them from having to face a dreadful fate later on.[39] With her five-sex hypothesis, Fausto-Sterling was criticizing John Money, not for the suffering he had inflicted on David Reimer but because he had made a binary choice: one must be either a man or a woman. In this way Fausto-Sterling purported to erase all borders between gender and sex by inventing a new representation of human sexuality based on the infinite variety of identitarian postures.

In so doing, she also posed a problem that transsexuals had had to confront: the obligation to make gender and anatomy coincide. But, unlike transsexuals, hermaphrodites had never had to choose, since the so-called "beneficial" operation had taken place at their birth, following a decision made by doctors with their parents' agreement. In this context, debates over gender and queerness thus brought that choice, made without the subject's consent, back into question, and led to a fierce struggle on the part of many "intersexed" individuals who, once they reached adulthood, rejected medical science in the name of a new freedom: the freedom to maintain a double anatomy with pride rather than suffer from a pathology. They too marched under the rainbow flag in order to challenge the principle of "hetero-normed" surgery.

Having become full-fledged subjects, and, what is more, self-promoting "entrepreneurs," these "declassified" people began to speak out in order to avenge themselves against the medical power of which they had been victims. Authority was no longer in the hands of scientists charged with studying "cases"; it now belonged to individuals who refused the status that medical and psychiatric science had ascribed to them. It was they – and they alone – who now had the right to tell their stories, according to the principles of emotion, "feelings," and compassion: I suffer, therefore I exist.

This is how the categories of biological science were effectively pulverized in the name of an ideal of emancipation based on an identitarian accounting that is at the very least contestable. As Vincent Guillot has written,

> Intersexuality is an identity, a culture and not a pathology or a fact of nature … We intersexuals are trying to get away from medical discourse … In reality, we represent many more people than the doctors proclaim: we constitute more than 10% of the population, for we consider that any person who does not correspond to the morpho-logical standards for males or females is de facto intersexed.[40]

Such was the new vulgate of intersexuation roughly between 1990 and 2010: it purported to annex all those who did not recognize themselves in the declared difference between the sexes – LGBTQIA+ – and whose situations generally had nothing in common beyond membership in the same identitarian movement: anti-heteronormal, anti-patriarchal, and so on.

As for the question of early intervention, it seemed to be insoluble. Some saw it as the only way for a child to acquire a stable identity, while others saw it as a mutilation, judging that the laws of bioethics should prohibit it, at least until the consent of the subject could be sought.[41] However this may be, it is essential to understand that intersexuality at birth is less an identity than a tragedy, since, treated surgically or not, these human beings will remain "of both sexes" and more importantly will be infertile; they will be all the unhappier to the extent that the truth has been kept from them.[42]

If intersexuals condemn the surgery that their parents imposed on them at birth, trans individuals demand, on the contrary, the right to "transition" at very young ages. When we know that numerous children insist that their gender does not correspond to their anatomy, boys dressing as girls and girls dressing as boys, a banal phenomenon, we can only be revolted at the idea of giving them hormone blockers and other harmful drugs, when most of the time nothing makes it possible to classify them immediately in the category of transsexuals, "gender dysphorics," or transgendered before they have at least reached the age of sexual majority, set by French law at age 15. Yet this practice is becoming more and more common, so much so that it is sometimes depicted in the press as a magnificent experience that is necessary for the full flourishing of suffering children.

In September 2020, for example, an eight-year-old French boy was classified as a transgender girl by his parents because he asserted that he was not born in the right body and that he was prepared to commit suicide if he were obliged to live according to the masculine model. Confronted with this dreadful suffering, the boy's parents decided, with the support of the Aix-Marseille school district, to enroll him in school under a new first name. After several medical examinations, the child was declared transgender, and his identity was modified in the official records. He was given the hormones required for his transition. The press then told "the moving story of Lilie, born in a boy's body,"[43] thus erasing anatomy in favor of a gendered construction that had emerged from a child's imaginary universe – a universe that we know to be populated with myths, beliefs, and fantasies in which men and women disguise themselves as animals, dragons, or chimera. Generally speaking, all the stories of children afflicted with "gender dysphoria" are presented by the progressive media as magnificent adventures in the course of which heroic parents courageously confront hostile public opinion.[44]

The fact remains that it is hard to see how anyone could affirm on the one hand, and rightly, that a child under age 15 cannot be said to consent to a sexual relation with an adult,[45] and on the other hand deem such a child sufficiently mature to make her or his own decision – that is, to consent – to undergo such a "transition." And why should surgery at a very young age be forbidden for intersexuals and then authorized when a prepubescent child asserts a desire to change his or her sex? These are the sorts of aberrant situations to which the identitarian drift can lead. And there are worse cases: many autistic, psychotic, or "borderline" children have been taken by their parents to specialized clinics and have been deemed transgender by the age of ten.

In this connection, the Gender Identity Development Service (GIDS) at the Charing Cross Hospital in London, founded in 1989 under the auspices of the prestigious Tavistock Clinic, known for harboring some of the greatest names in child psychoanalysis (from John Bowlby to Donald Woods Winnicott), has been denounced for having "accompanied," since 2011, the transition of children and preadolescents who claimed to have been born in the wrong bodies only to change their minds later on. In an internal report written in 2018, psychoanalyst David Bell noted that the number of transition requests by minors had risen vertiginously between 2010 and 2018 (by more than 200%), under the influence of social networks – most notably one called "Transgender Heaven" – that incited adolescents in distress to demand a transition that could put an end to their anguish: "Being transgender is the way you can stop thinking of yourself as shit." Bell accused doctors of accelerating transitions without taking other possible diagnoses into account. And he concluded that under such conditions no informed consent could be given; this brought him accusations of transphobia.[46] The associate director of the GIDS, Marcus Evans, who was a member of the board of the Tavistock Clinic, resigned.

> The fear of being accused of transphobia immobilizes all ability to think critically. There is nothing alarming in the fact that thousands of girls and a large number of boys are filled with disgust for their own bodies and want to change them. It is not unreasonable to wonder if there could be serious long-term consequences for mental health in permitting a young child to make decisions that modify his or her body.[47]

In December 2020, in the aftermath of that scandal, the High Court of Justice in the United Kingdom finally made a wise decision that prohibits any future transition treatment of children under the age of 16.[48]

We owe the most politically-oriented reflection on queerness to the American philosopher Judith Butler. Basing her work on that of major French thinkers from the 1970s, especially Michel Foucault, Jacques Lacan, and Jacques Derrida, in her 1990 book *Gender Trouble* she embraced the notion of borderline states, asserting that the difference between the sexes was always blurry and that, for example, the transsexualist cause could be a way of subverting the established order and rejecting the biological norm.[49] Butler had found herself early on in a borderline or beyond-the-norm state, through her identity as a Jewish woman brought up in Judaism but one who was radically critical of the politics of the Israeli state. To think through that issue, she developed an idea totally foreign to the authors from whom she drew her inspiration, according to which marginal and "disturbed" sexual behaviors – transgenderism, transvestism, transsexualism, and so on – were nothing but ways of challenging the dominant order: familialist, paternalist, heteronormal, and so on. This militant position was not rational, but it was based on a desire to reverse the norm; it was greeted with hostility by a good number of French feminists who deemed Butler a "differentialist" and reproached her for her critical attitude toward French republican secularism and toward the prohibition of religious markers in schools; Butler endorsed in particular the wearing of Islamic headscarves as a sign of identitarian revolt, denying the fact that such behavior could be *first and foremost* the stereotype of women's submission to an obscurantist, virilist, or highly paternalistic religious order.[50] Thus she was defending a universal principle of difference much more than an anti-universalist cult of difference – without the slightest concern for the thousands of women who risk their lives in refusing to wear what remains in their eyes a sign of major oppression.

From this standpoint, Butler then focused, in Foucault's wake, on the question of "precarious" or "unlivable" lives, on the "survival" of minorities of all stripes: Palestinians, the stateless, immigrants, the exploited, deviants. Hence a fine lecture title: "Can one lead a good life in a bad life?"[51] She delivered her talk in Frankfurt on September 11, 2012, when she received the prestigious Theodor W. Adorno Prize (earlier recipients had included Pierre Boulez, Jürgen Habermas, and Jean-Luc Godard). As soon as her arrival in Frankfurt was announced, Butler became the object of a grotesque cabal on the part of the Jewish community and the Israeli ambassador in Berlin. Called "depraved" for her adherence to queer theory and an "anti-Semitic enemy of Israel" for her defense of the Palestinians, she was also reproached for having claimed that Hamas and Hezbollah

THE GALAXY OF GENDER

were part of the "global left," and for her participation in actions urging boycotts, disinvestment, and sanctions (BDS) aimed at Israeli institutions.[52]

In reality, her detractors instrumentalized a statement taken out of context, in which she was replying to an interlocutor who had questioned her about the "anti-imperialist" character of Hamas and Hezbollah. As for BDS (a movement with which I myself wholly disagree), she had supported it only in relation to actions designed to implant Israeli colonies in the occupied territories. Later, Butler was unfairly dragged through the mud for a book devoted to the critique of Zionism in which she discussed at length a statement by the French philosopher Emmanuel Levinas.[53] On this occasion, insults took the place of argument, and this is what has continued to happen in a veritable war of identities that is traversing democratic societies.

It goes without saying that transgender and intersexual persons should have the right, on the same grounds as all the other minorities labeled "sexual," not to be discriminated against; this is emphasized in the 2009 appeal to the United Nations that rightly denounced the medical classification then in force that labeled such persons "mentally disordered."[54] However, where queer theory is concerned, along with the politics it deploys, it is indispensable to understand clearly the nature of a movement that aims to rid an unsettled body of psychiatric knowledge of various experiences in which the status of human sexuality is at stake: gender and sex. In this connection, queer theory and queer studies raise the problem of passing from speculative reflection to concrete political practice. For is it possible, in the name of equality of conditions, to generalize the idea that every human being can be biologically male and female, an idea that amounts to making intersexuality (hermaphroditism) something other than an anomaly of birth, something similar to transidentity – which is not an identity? Can we, in the name of that same equality, conflate psychic bisexuality, universally present in each subject, with a social identity that is simultaneously "gendered" and biologically defined, before concluding that a "neuter" or "third" sex has legal existence? Finally, can we deduce from these problematics a militant, "egalitarian" politics of identitarian differences? Must we invent new legal rules, not only to define the borders of sex and gender, but also to offer a legal framework for parentage and the reproduction of the human species based on these life experiences?

As we near the end of the first quarter of the twenty-first century, it is henceforth possible for persons in distress over identity issues

31

to take recourse to surgical procedures offered in vast clinics where the most simplistic discourse is associated with the most effective technologies: a blend of the ideology of well-being, in the style of a dating website, and delirious beliefs in the supremacy of the body over intelligence. In Montreal, at the heart of the Metropolitan Center of Surgery, the jewel of elite private hospitals founded in 1973 and endowed with the highest medical accreditation in Canada, everyone desiring to undergo a "transition" is welcomed. Breast enhancement, Adam's apple reduction, facial feminization or masculinization, vaginoplasty, phalloplasty, the sale of all sorts of objects straight out of a medical catalog that might have been revised and corrected by Krafft-Ebing[55] – fetishes, dildos, devices for compressing the genital organs, tattoos, and so on – accompanied by multiple therapies: such is the protocol of initiation, with several possible options, to which transgender persons who are looking for a satisfying or reversible identity willingly submit themselves.

"Gender dysphorics" sometimes wait several months before turning themselves over body and soul to the expert hands of surgeons specializing in body hair removal, gland reconstitution from skin taken from the scrotum, or urethra fabrication permitting urination from a standing position: "At first I did not realize [sic], I was not used to it. The first few times I saw myself in a mirror, it was as though that didn't belong to me. One often hears transgender persons say 'I'd like to wake up transitioned.' No! One must assimilate, digest, process everything."[56]

As for the question of "transgender families," it arises now in legal terms: can a transgender woman be recognized legally, through adoption, as the mother of her six-year-old daughter, given that she has been, since the girl's birth, her biological father? An example: in 2004, Raymond married Nicole, who gave birth to a baby girl. Over the years, dissatisfied with his anatomy, Raymond underwent a transition and officially became a woman named Julie, without having his genital organs modified. With Nicole's consent, he sought to become the mother of his daughter. But thanks to his male anatomy he later conceived a second child, a male named Victor. So he is at once the biological father and the social mother of this boy, the wife and husband of Nicole, and the potential adoptive mother of his daughter. "Pregnant men," Serge Hefez writes, "men or women undergoing a transition after having brought children into the world and becoming 'female fathers' or 'male mothers,' women who procreate with their own sperm ... The disorder that is disrupting our society no longer bears solely on questions of identity and gender but also cuts through the fundamental notions of procreation and parentage."[57]

This picture should make people think, especially those who oppose any transformation of the modalities of procreation and who are now convinced that the planet will eventually be populated by transgender monsters conceived on American campuses.

Disseminating human gender

In reality, there are no solutions to such contradictions. And we must be well aware that the apocalypse of transidentity will never take place. For these reasons, moreover, the queer movement is condemned to identitarian overreach, not only because it keeps on valorizing the victim experience, but also because it can act only by promoting a sort of catechism based on the avalanche of neologisms already mentioned (heteronormed, gendered, cisgendered, gay, straight, and so on). In short, it will end up reinventing the classifications of psychiatry. To grant such a prevalence of gender over sex, to the extent of dissolving anatomical difference only to return to it by a linguistic ploy (intersexuality), leads to multiplying identities ad infinitum, even as the approach to human specificity has to rest on the observation of the universal existence of the three great determining factors that shape it: the biological factor (body, anatomy, sex), the social factor (religious construction, cultural construction, family organization), and the psychic factor (subjective representation, gender, sexual orientation), it being understood that there is only one human species, whatever internal differences there may be in that species.

Among the misguided tangents that can be noted, beyond declaring prepubescent children "transgender" or wanting to be both the father and mother of one's own children, there is the will to apply the queer theory of education to children from birth onward. In this connection, nothing is more ridiculous than the idea of hiding from children their own anatomical sex, as certain parents in the LGBTQIA+ community do. Believing that they are fighting stereotypes, they explain to their offspring that when the time comes they will choose their own "gender." "Why is it important," they ask, "to know what there is between one's legs?" And they invent a new, "neuter" vocabulary, using "they" instead of "he" or "she" so as to inaugurate a "pedagogical revolution" based on the affirmation of the neuter sex. Having learned that in 2018 the state of New York rendered a judgment allowing parents to replace the mention of their children's sex on their birth certificates by four asterisks, we can only throw up our hands and wonder: by what ruse of history has it been possible to invalidate decades of fighting for progress aiming to stop treating children as imbeciles with such poppycock?[58] No doubt the next step will be to tell children that they were born in a cabbage patch, some wearing pink overalls and others wearing blue tutus ...

This is the perspective, too, from which the notion of "human species" has been surreptitiously suppressed with the appearance of disability studies, a new domain of identitarian rhetoric, born in the 1980s, dealing with handicaps. According to this well-intended new paradigm, it is urgent not only to study and care for all persons with disabilities – deafness, blindness, Down syndrome, dwarfism, schizophrenia, autism, and so on – but also to theorize the handicap as an identity, in order, it is thought, to be able to struggle against the "underrepresentation of handicapped persons in businesses and in universities," in keeping with the calls for all minorities that have suffered discrimination.[59]

Evidence for this can be found in a major study by American psychologist Andrew Solomon on the question of "human biodiversity": *Far from the Tree: Parents, Children and the Search for Identity*.[60] Solomon gathered testimony from members of more than 400 American families in search of their "vertical" (innate) and "horizontal" (acquired) identities. He says of them that they are "far from the tree," that is, from the genealogical family tree. In his improbable best-seller, he draws up a list in the manner of Georges Perec: stories of lives and suffering. Defining several categories of human beings, he observes their cohabiting just as would an animal care-taker straight out of a glass menagerie: deaf people, dwarves, people with Down syndrome, autism, or schizophrenia, prodigies, transgender people, Blacks, Latinos; people with multiple handicaps, hydrocephalics, people with cerebral palsy, blind people, and so on.

Solomon describes in minute detail the daily lives of these children and their parents. However, when one reads this study (which gave rise to a highly successful documentary film), one quickly becomes aware that the author places sexual orientation (queerness, trans-sexualism), genetic pathologies (Down syndrome, dwarfism), social situations (disturbed children), skin color, mental illness, and major handicapping conditions all on the same plane. When this objection is raised, Solomon responds by affirming that any difference is nothing but a socially constructed identity that is subjectively experienced as discrimination.

To be sure, the investigative work undertaken by Solomon is interesting, but, as the book advances, one may feel rather uneasy when the author explains how happy the parents of these children are to rear them so as to better rid themselves of the prejudices that come from the dominant society. And then one soon discovers the meaning of Solomon's battle. Where Down syndrome is concerned, affirming that the fetus is already a human being, he condemns recourse to abortion and castigates the 93% of women who make that choice after amniocentesis. In addition, in an indirect way, he advocates gender reassignment surgery for prepubescent transgender children in order to endow them with a satisfying identity. Finally, concerning Deaf people, he deplores the early use of cochlear implants, because this poses a threat to sign language, a characteristic of Deaf identity in which the Deaf are viewed as a variant of the human species. He also assigns to the "dwarfism" category (achondroplasia) all persons of small size, as if they belonged to the same community, rebaptized "identitarian" or "diversitarian."

Let us not be misled: the author is not a religious obscurantist but a progressive who explains the reasons for his militant engagement in favor of a new humanity. As does every modern identitarian researcher, in these investigations Solomon brings into play his own suffering, his weaknesses, his "borderline personality," in an approach that lies halfway between self-analysis and Christian confession. Dyslexic, born to a Jewish father and a mother haunted by Jewish self-hatred, mistreated as a child, ashamed of his homosexuality, he managed to gain access to fatherhood thanks to the wonders of surrogate motherhood. Convinced at the moment of birth that his child would be handicapped, he ended up accepting that the child was "normal" [sic]: "Sometimes, I had thought the heroic parents in this book were fools, enslaving themselves to a life's journey with their alien children, trying to breed identity out of misery. I was startled to learn that my research had built me a plank, and that I was ready to join them on their ship."[61] Thus once again a generous approach to the human condition has crumbled, under the pen of a researcher, in response to an ideal contrary to emancipation, most notably with regard to abortion or the use of medical advances to treat deafness or dwarfism. One can never repeat often enough how much the marvelous world of identitarian happiness resembles a nightmare.

Finally, and it is hardly a surprise, the manifestations of identitarian feminism attest to the fact that everywhere the most radical lesbian feminists are endlessly denouncing gay men, deeming them as guilty of masculine domination as the "dominant heterosexual males." Thus they go on to call for separatism, as a result of which men must, *as men*, be excluded from the human community.

Thus, in France, Alice Coffin, a journalist and an elected delegate to the Conseil de Paris[62] in 2020, created a sensation when she denounced another elected delegate, Christophe Girard, deputy for culture at the city hall of Paris, accusing him of complicity with certain supporters of pedophilic practices, an argument regularly used by the far right against homosexuals. Reversing the argument and defending a so-called "lesbian genius," she ended up casting men as the enemies of humanity and advocating their "elimination," white men in particular:

> All of us [women] need coats of mail, "shield-maidens," which is the name given to mythical Viking female warriors. [We need] squads and brigades for our self-defense. It is no longer enough to help each other, we must, in our turn, eliminate [men]. I no longer read books by men, I no longer watch their films, I no longer listen to their music ... Men's productions are the extension of a system of domination. They *are* the system. Art is an extension of the masculine imagination. They have already infested my mind. I am saving myself by avoiding them. ... I would enjoy taking down white men, lords, blood-letters[63] and their misdeeds, in writing. ... Which will succumb first, men, or humanity?[64]

In this incident, which was all over the news, Coffin repeated the history of a tragedy in the form of farce, in all seriousness. In a famous pamphlet of avant-garde literature, *SCUM Manifesto*,[65] self-published in the United States in 1967, Valerie Solanas – a rabid lesbian who had been raped by her father – became famous when she called for all of humanity to eliminate the money of men, the patriarchy of fathers, and the totality of male genital organs. Women, she said, no longer needed men to procreate. Since a man was but "an incomplete female," she added, a "walking abortion, aborted at the gene stage," with "a negative Midas touch – everything he touches turns to shit," he could perfectly well be eliminated.[66]

This big gesture calling for murder, lashing out against psycho-analysis, sexism, and male domination, both heterosexual and homosexual, was followed by action. After she met Andy Warhol, the pop art star, and tried to convince him to produce a piece of pornographic theater she had written, Solanas tried to assassinate him with several shots from a revolver before she turned herself in to the police. Hit in a lung, the spleen, the stomach, and the liver, Warhol barely survived; he did not file a complaint. After getting out of prison, declared to be schizophrenic, Solanas continued to persecute her hated idol even as she ensured the promotion of her manifesto and her fantasies against the penis in any form. Celebrated by several feminists, most notably in France by Virginie Despentes, Solanas was rediscovered in 1998 when her manifesto was republished with a postface by the writer Michel Houellebecq: "For my part," he said, "I have always viewed feminists as likable morons."[67] He went on to assert that the differences between men and women were genetic in nature and that Solanas's reasoning was therefore in conformity with the noblest aspirations of the Western project: to establish absolute technological control over nature.

Reading these lines, one can see that, 23 years later, the conditions were doubtless right for a re-edition of Alice Coffin's *Génie lesbien* to be published with a preface by Houellebecq, someone who, with his taste for antiphrasis, could play at pretending to support the project of this newly elected official: to replace men by women, gays by lesbians, lesbians by queers, and, ultimately, liberty by submission.

I am neither white nor woman nor man, but half Lebanese

The identitarian world is not exclusively peopled with poignant or dramatic stories. In it one often comes across comic elements worthy of great popular theater. For example, in 2016, a virtual war of succession took place in the wake of antidiscrimination measures taken under Barack Obama: transgender persons were authorized to use bathrooms and dressing rooms that corresponded to the sex they had chosen.[68] In reaction to this decision, 11 American states – for the most part southern and conservative – refused to comply. The state of North Carolina passed a law requiring transgender persons to use bathrooms corresponding to their sex at birth. The plaintiffs of all 11 states accused the federal administration of seeking to transform restrooms into gigantic sites of social experimentation.

No bathroom war has been waged in France. But in 2018, on the occasion of the PRIDE demonstration, during the television program "Arrêt sur images" (Focus on Images), Arnaud Gauthier-Fawas, administrator of the Inter-LGBT association, offended at having been presented as a *man* by the journalist Daniel Schneidermann, replied in all seriousness: "No, sir, I do not know what makes you say I am a man, for I am not a man. If we start this way, it's going to end badly." This man, claiming his "offended identity," wore a beard, and his voice and musculature did not give the impression that he

THE SOVEREIGN SELF

could be anything but male. "Gender identity and gender expression must not be confused," he added. "I am nonbinary, so neither male nor female." Instead of laughing out loud, Schneidermann apologized. At that point, another guest deplored the fact that the persons present on the set all had white skin. Whereupon the host broke out laughing, affirming that his interlocutor would doubtless claim that he was not white. "No, I'm not," he said, "for I'm Lebanese."

Unlike the Lebanese anecdote I recounted earlier, this one sent shivers down my spine: an assertion like that in effect abolishes the very idea of a subject in the sense of "I am I, that's all," as if the fact of declaring oneself "Lebanese" meant that one could be neither white nor of the male sex.

At the end of this chapter, it will have become obvious how a truly innovative conception of sexuality studies – distinguishing between gender and sex – has managed, in a few decades, to turn into its opposite and initiate a movement of normalizing regression. Everything begins with the invention of new concepts, and then the creation of an adequate vocabulary. Once solidly established, the concepts and the words are transformed into a catechism that ends up, when the time comes, by justifying acting out or intrusive interventions. Thus, without even noticing it, we pass from civilization to barbarity, from tragedy to comedy, from intelligence to stupidity, from life to a void, and from a legitimate critique of social normalcy to the reintroduction of a totalizing system.

— 3 —

DECONSTRUCTING RACE

Paris 1952: Race does not exist

In 1952, at the request of UNESCO, Claude Lévi-Strauss produced *Race and History*, a programmatic text in which he offered an astonishing reflection on the notion of race.[1] For the anthropologist, it was not enough to combat racial prejudice; in the wake of the Second World War, it was essential to denounce the monstrosities in which European nations had engaged on the basis of a purported inequality between races. Lévi-Strauss targeted Nazism, which had driven Europeans to destroy their fellow human beings, but also colonialism, which had espoused a dogmatic belief in the inferiority of non-Western peoples. At around the same time, Hannah Arendt highlighted the extent to which anti-Semitism had been the matrix for racism: having served as a theoretical backing for colonial conquests, anti-Semitism spread to the heart of colonial empires all over the world. In the colonized territories, Jews were often blamed for all sorts of plots. No sooner had the British retaken Egypt from the French, for example, than the Jews were accused of organizing all the colonial conflicts. The thesis of an international conspiracy on the part of "the Rothschilds" began to emerge outside of Europe.[2] From the late nineteenth century on, deep connections were woven between anti-Semitism, racism, and colonialism.

In this regard, it is important to be prudent in using the terms Zionism and anti-Zionism. Zionism was originally a liberation movement forged by Jews seeking to establish a state in Palestine that could encompass and integrate non-Jews. During the same period, anti-Zionism, as a movement of political and ideological opposition to Zionism, mobilized many Jews in the diaspora – including

Sigmund Freud – who opposed the conquest of a "promised land."[3] At the outset, then, anti-Zionism was entirely foreign to any sort of anti-Semitism. In its contemporary form, anti-Zionism encompasses diverse movements: some are frankly anti-Semitic, while others are hostile to Israeli policies and sometimes even to the very existence of the state of Israel. It is therefore a misuse of language to charge every anti-Zionist with anti-Semitism, all the more so since the term is often used retrospectively: it is by such abusive labeling, for example, that Freud has been labeled "anti-Semitic" not only by the Israeli far right but also by radical anti-Freudians purporting to support Zionism. There are traces of this misuse of the term in a very odd "anthology of allegations against Jews, Judaism and Zionism," published in 2007 by Paul-Éric Blanrue, a notorious anti-Freudian and a defender of Holocaust deniers and of Iranian Islamism.[4] Blanrue claimed to be unmasking the true anti-Semites whose names had been hidden, according to him, by the "official" history: the Jews themselves and their allies. Alongside the names of Goebbels and Hitler, and without ever alluding to the Holocaust (not even in the entry "Wannsee," where the "Final Solution" is mentioned), Blanrue drew up the list of the "real" anti-Semites: Moses, Isaiah, Spinoza, Lévi-Strauss, Clemenceau, Freud, Einstein, Stefan Zweig, Zola, Proust, Pierre Assouline, and so on. Under cover of support for Zionism, the author had thus written a polemical screed that was nothing but a disguised apologia for anti-Semitism.[5] Jews are identified as having the whole world against them, but especially as being themselves the artisans of their own self-hatred. Such is the Jewish identity of a Jew, according to Blanrue: oneself as a Jew, that is, as an anti-Semite.

In his 1952 text, Lévi-Strauss began by noting that races are only skin tones and that the differences between them are only matters of pigmentation. To these virtually non-existent differences he contrasted real differences, the infinite and invaluable differences that distinguish cultures. Finally, in keeping with his arguments in *The Elementary Structures of Kinship*, he refuted the idea according to which humanity has evolved through "stages" from a primitive age to another that is synonymous with "civilization."[6] From this perspective, he asserted, it is impossible to associate a biological notion of evolution, Darwinian in origin, with the organization of cultures and societies that define humanity. For all societies are characterized by the passage from nature to culture. Evidence for this is found in prohibitions of incest, ways of cooking food, and the various religious and artistic expressions that characterize humanity and do not exist in the animal world. And with this Lévi-Strauss articulated what was already the credo of structuralism[7]: "Two cultures developed by men of the same race may differ as much as, or more than, two cultures associated with groups of entirely different racial origin."[8]

While races do not exist, the attribution of inferiority to one group by another was a universal practice characteristic of all social organizations, according to Lévi-Strauss. As soon as they come together in groups or communities, humans acquire the habit of rejecting others in the name of their own cultural superiority: "In the Greater Antilles," he wrote, "a few years after the discovery of America, while the Spaniards were sending out Commissions of investigation to find out whether or not the natives had a soul, the latter spent their time drowning white prisoners in order to ascertain, by long observation, whether or not their bodies would decompose."[9]

If races do not exist, and if differences are cultural and never "natural," how can one explain why certain cultures end up becoming dominant? Lévi-Strauss's response to this question seems self-evident today: societies evolve along "diagonal" lines, but some – the so-called "Western" societies – have developed technological capabilities based on scientific thought that have allowed them to dominate others and to survive more readily by moving beyond the state of nature. These societies, having become colonizers, must henceforth protect the colonized; otherwise, by dint of domination, they risk their own annihilation by destroying humanity altogether. And it is from this perspective that Lévi-Strauss advanced a thesis to which he remained faithful all his life: every form of integral Westernization of the world, owing to the vertiginous progress of science, could only end up in disaster for all humankind. So he rightly rejected the uniformization of the world in favor of respect for each culture, cultural relativism being the only way that the universalism of the human genus could be expressed.

Both near and far: such is the law of humanity itself. If everyone is alike, humanity is dissolved into blankness; if everyone stops respecting the otherness of the other while asserting her or his identitarian difference, humanity sinks into perpetual hatred of the other. Societies thus must neither dissolve into a single model (globalization) nor close themselves off within prison-like borders (nationalism): they must remain neither too close to one another nor too far apart. The uniformization of the world always produces war and communitarianism.

Such observations make it clear that Lévi-Strauss was not satisfied simply to abolish the idea of race: for him, the struggle against racism, colonialism, and nationalism was the very principle of a mode of planetary civilization based as much on respect for differences (relativism) as on the universality of the human genus. He was thereby positioning himself in the long line of French anticolonialists, from Clemenceau through André Breton and the surrealists to Sartre. Unlike his predecessors, however, he sought to provide not simply a moral or political basis for his commitment but also a structural and anthropological foundation. Exiled from France in 1940 because he belonged to the "Jewish race," he became an ethnologist through his contacts with indigenous peoples, his cherished Indians of the Brazilian continent: Nambikwara, Caduveo, Bororo, Tupi, Mundé. He recounted his great melancholic trek in a celebrated book published in 1955, *Tristes tropiques*.[10]

The publication of *Race and History* led to an intense polemic between Lévi-Strauss and Roger Caillois, a graduate of the prestigious École normale supérieure, a former member of the surrealist movement, and a member of the informal pre-war College of Sociology. Caillois reproached Lévi-Strauss for what he called a "reverse illusion," charging him with expressing rancor against his own culture. A convinced antiracist, Caillois thought nevertheless that the West possessed a culture superior to the others by virtue of its capacity to conceptualize the others and by virtue of having developed a body of knowledge about civilizations. At bottom, he challenged his contradictor with the fact that only Western thought had been capable of inventing anthropology, rationality, and, of course, science. In Caillois and Lévi-Strauss alike, the question of race is thus shelved in favor of a debate over the capacity of societies to produce knowledge about themselves and about other societies.[11] In this controversy, the opposition was not between a progressive and a reactionary but rather between an evolutionist and a structuralist, the latter calling into question the very idea of linear progress.

As early as 1952, in any case, Lévi-Strauss took it as a fact that the notion of race should be banished from anthropological, cultural, social, and philosophical studies. As he saw it, the theories about race that had flourished since the late eighteenth century lacked any foundation, once it had been demonstrated that only cultural differences mattered. "Scientific racism," which had inscribed a racial hierarchy into biology, was discredited, on the same grounds, starting in the 1950s.[12] Yet it remains obvious that racism has not vanished from human societies. In democratic countries it has been repressed by the legal system; certain discourses are condemned by law or attributed to insanity. The word "race" itself has been removed from the French Constitution, even as it is being claimed by critical race studies.

In the 1950s, another mutation came to light, giving a new form to the old opposition between "barbarians" and "civilized" peoples. This one made it possible to justify claims of inferiority by relying on the idea that cultural differences counted less than the differences connected with the degree of civilization: certain societies were superior to others owing to their scientific or rational capacity to conceptualize the world. The controversy between Lévi-Strauss and Caillois is emblematic of this debate. The former calls "domination" what the latter calls "superiority." For Lévi-Strauss, the imperative to get rid of any notion that a given society could be superior to another was self-evident, but this did not mean that scientific rationality should be discarded in favor of mere observation of cultural differences. The proof is that all peoples aspire to overturn the regimes of domination that oppress them, but they do not want to give up the benefits of scientific and technological progress that have been invented by the so-called "dominant" Western societies.

From this perspective, Lévi-Strauss clearly advanced an approach to understanding cultures that was much more innovative than that of his adversary Caillois. Lévi-Strauss put in the same melting pot the project of absolute respect for cultural relativism and that of conceptualizing the world in a rational manner: he thus did not give up positing the bases for a possible resolution of antagonisms, while he called upon the dominant societies, with their mastery of scientific knowledge, to protect the older cultures rather than destroying them. What was *universal* about scientific thought was thus never separable from *cultural difference.*

In earlier times, the word "race" was often used to designate a noble family lineage – the "race" of the Atrides, the Labdacides, or the descendants of Abraham; starting in the mid-eighteenth century, it was sometimes also used to define a presumed subcategory of the human species, modeled on a description of the animal world: "The Negro race," Voltaire said, "is a species of men as different from ours, as the breed of spaniels is from that of greyhounds"[13] – which did not prevent him, in the name of the same theory, from passing harsh judgment on the customs of his own country and denouncing colonization:

> It must certainly be agreed that the people of Canada, and the Caffres, whom we have been pleased to stile savages, are infinitely superior

43

THE SOVEREIGN SELF

to our own. The Huron, the Algonquin, the Illinois, the Caffre, the Hottentot, have the art of fabricating every thing that is needful for them ... The colonies of America and Africa are free, and our savages have not even the idea of freedom.[14]

Colonialism and anticolonialism

Starting in the mid-nineteenth century with the development of physical anthropology against the background of Darwinism, evolutionism, and purported scientific classifications of peoples and cultures, the word "race" took on new amplitude, facilitating the establishment of typologies based not only on morphological criteria (such as skin color) but also on hierarchies: certain "races" were deemed superior to others according to the perceived degree of advancement of their civilizations. Peoples were thus classified according to a scale of cultural and psychological as well as physiological values. These classifications led to some totally arbitrary distinctions between "Aryans" and "Semites," between Asians, Blacks, or Amerindians on the one hand and Whites from Western societies on the other, with white Northern and Southern Europeans at the pinnacle of the hierarchy. These sinister racialist theories lay behind the extermination of the Jews (called "Semites") by the Nazis, who designated themselves as members of the "superior Aryan race."[15]

Later, after slavery was abolished in Europe and in the Western hemisphere, these so-called scientific categories were widely used to justify the colonial conquests that European countries had initiated – so much so that colonialism, as a doctrine and an ideology legitimizing vast territorial appropriations, immediately became a vector for racialist theses. The phenomenon was quite paradoxical, since it was in the name of the Declaration of the Rights of Man and of the Citizen (1789) – a republican ideal – that Ernest Renan, Jules Ferry, and many others became apostles of a deadly segregation based on France's "civilizing mission": "As much as the conquests among equal races have to be blamed, the regenerescence of the inferior or debased races by the superior races is in the providential order of humanity." And again: "The superior races have a right vis-à-vis the inferior races, because there is a duty for them. They have the duty to civilize the inferior races."[16]

In the course of the fight against such principles, a movement contrary to the one that had justified conquests took shape:

anticolonialism. From Georges Clemenceau to Jean-Paul Sartre and including Claude Lévi-Strauss, Maurice Blanchot, Jacques Derrida, Pierre Bourdieu, and many others, a large number of French intellectuals and politicians were the best propagandists for the fight against anti-Semitism, racism, and colonialism. In 1885, opposing colonial conquests, Clemenceau had some very harsh words for Jules Ferry: "Conquest is purely and simply an abuse of the power that scientific civilization exerts over rudimentary civilizations, in order to appropriate men, torture them, and extract from them all the strength that is in them to the profit of the purported civilizer. This is not law, it is its negation."[17] As for Sartre, who signed the Manifesto of the 121 in favor of the right of conscientious objection to the Algerian War (1960), he produced this masterful retort in his preface to Frantz Fanon's *The Wretched of the Earth* (1961):

> Fanon speaks out loud and clear. We Europeans, we can hear him. The proof is you are holding this book. Isn't he afraid that the colonial powers will take advantage of his sincerity? No. He is not afraid of anything. Our methods are outdated; they can sometimes delay emancipation, but they can't stop it. And don't believe we can readjust our methods: neo-colonialism, that lazy dream of the metropolises, is a lot of hot air.[18]

An active proponent of abolishing slavery, Victor Schoelcher[19] did not oppose the colonial adventure on the non-European continents.[20] And neither did Victor Hugo. In a speech on May 18, 1879, in Schoelcher's honor and in his presence, Hugo justified the colonial conquests in Africa in lyric terms, convinced that they would bring the enlightenment of European civilization to black people: "The Mediterranean is the Lake of civilization. It is not without a purpose that the Mediterranean has the old universe on one of its shores and the unknown universe on the other – that is to say, on one side the condensation of civilization and on the other side the condensation of barbarism." He went on to assert that Africa had no history:

> What a land, this Africa! Asia has her history, America has her history, Australia even has her history … Africa has no history; she is shrouded in a kind of legend, vast and dark. Rome laid hands on her to suppress her … The nineteenth century made a man of the negro; in the twentieth century, Europe will have made a world of Africa. Such is the problem Europe will have to solve. She will seize upon that land and take it.[21]

THE SOVEREIGN SELF

Hugo never subscribed to the thesis that one race was superior to another. Thus nothing is more absurd than to treat him as a racist, as is being done today in blog after blog.[22] Moreover, in his first novel, *Bug-Jargal*, written when he was 16 years old and revised in 1826 when he was 24, he recounted the revolt of the slaves in the Caribbean colony of Saint Dominique (San Domingo) on August 23, 1791, when the Blacks demanded rights equal to those of white citizens.[23] On the eve of the event, a highly-placed priest, Boukman, had pronounced vodou incantations while drinking the blood of a slaughtered pig and exhorting his troops to drive away the white men.[24] In a few days, under the leadership of Georges Biassou, the rebels burned the plantations and massacred a thousand colonizers before retreating into the forests.

By choosing to privilege this first episode of the revolt of the Blacks in San Domingo, Hugo launched into a fierce indictment of slavery.[25] The novel is a strange tale, in truth, offering some parallels with his later novels, *L'homme qui rit*, *Notre-Dame de Paris*, or *Quatrevingt-treize*. In this Romantic text, Hugo featured two brothers, irreconcilable enemies, each in the grip of history: a sublime slave (Bug-Jarval) who has been freed from his chains and has become the leader of his people's revolt, and a slaveholding aristocrat (Léopold d'Auvernay), the narrator, laid low by his wounds and accompanied by a lame dog. D'Auvernay is engaged to Marie, who is loved by the former slave. Bug-Jarval, gentlemanly and attached to the ideals of the French monarchy, is presented by Hugo as the very incarnation of the nobility of the Old Regime: "This Negro – there are few Whites like him."[26] As a warrior, his "African race" enables him to rise to the highest level in the civilizational order. Thus he spends his time condemning the violence inflicted by his own troops on the slaveholding masters, who lose their standing as nobles, moreover.

At the same time, the Hugolian rebels in this story resemble *chouans* (royalist insurgents in western France during the Revolutionary period): they share the cult of the throne and a love of forests. When Marie is captured by the rebels, d'Auvernay rushes after them in hot pursuit. But he is saved by Bug, who leads him to his fiancée before turning himself in to the Whites, who will take him to the stake to be executed. In the middle of the battlefield, Hugo introduces the mulatto dwarf Habibrah, Biassou's jester, who speaks in Shakespearean tones: "Think you that in being a mulatto, a dwarf and deformed, I am not a man?"[27] It hardly needs saying that this amazing novel was greeted by some as an apologia for "Negrophilia" and by others as a "Negrophobic" screed.[28]

46

A writer of the people, the wretched and the abnormal, Hugo was neither Ferry nor Clemenceau nor Lévi-Strauss nor Sartre nor Fanon. But he was not fooled by the inadequacies of abolition, for on May 19, 1848, he said:

> The proclamation of the abolition of slavery was made in Guadeloupe with solemnity. The captain of the ship Layrle, governor of the colony, read the decree of the Assembly from a raised platform in the middle of the public square surrounded by an immense crowd, under glorious sunshine. At the moment when the governor was proclaiming the equality of the white race, the mulatto race, and the black race, there were only three men on the platform, representing the three races, as it were: a white, the governor; a mulatto, holding the governor's parasol; and a Negro, holding his hat.[29]

In the aftermath of the Second World War, decolonization of the previously occupied territories began to appear inevitable for all the imperial nations. The term "colonialism," a corollary of "racism," began to be contested not only by the colonized peoples aspiring to emancipation but also by the Western peoples opposed to colonial oppression. In the struggle, the latter in turn invoked the values of the Enlightenment and the Declaration of the Rights of Man and the Citizen. From that point on, all racialist theories were challenged, as much by the peoples rebelling against colonial domination as by the representatives of the humanities and social sciences trained in the best European and North American universities, who gradually abandoned the old classifications based on the allegedly "natural" notion of race. According to Antoine Lévêque, "[i]t was during the period when the human sciences were being denaturalized, around 1950, that anthropology and ethnology abandoned the racialist paradigm under the influence of the political will of the international community."[30] In French, the designation *sciences humaines* came to replace the singular *science humaine*, while the disciplines involved – anthropology, sociology, and so on – were converted to the idea that culture alone accounted for distinctions between societies. As a result, racialist theories had to be banned from all scientific studies.

It was in this context that Lévi-Strauss's intervention in favor of liquidating the notion of race was received as a powerful call for decolonization, all the more so since the decolonizing process was already under way more or less worldwide: on the Asian continent, in India, in the former Indochina, on the African continent, and in the Maghreb.

THE SOVEREIGN SELF

"Nègre je suis"

Together with his friend Léopold Sédar Senghor, the acclaimed poet and political militant Aimé Césaire forged the concept of Negritude. Césaire was born in the Antilles, Senghor in Senegal; both had been brilliant students at the Lycée Louis-le-Grand in Paris. As such, they embodied the best products of the French republican school system. Their destinies differed: Césaire, a militant Communist until 1956, became mayor of Fort-de-France in Martinique, while Senghor served as minister under a Gaullist government and then as the first president of an independent Senegal, from 1960 to 1980; he was elected to the fabled Académie française three years later. In 1947, they both participated in the creation of the journal *Présence africaine*, founded by the Senegalese writer Alione Diop, and then in the launching of a publishing house of the same name; in 1956 they both took part in the first Congress of Black Writers and Artists (originally called the Congress of Negro Writers and Artists), held at the Sorbonne in Paris.

In no case did the term Negritude refer to an attribution of identity. Moreover, the use of the term *nègre* (Negro) – instead of *noir* (Black) – was a way to reverse the stigma by ennobling a term that had come from racist discourse: "Since the word *nègre* sufficed to define the black being in the eyes of Whites, the Blacks took it back from the Whites to contest its meaning. Since there was shame about the word *nègre*, we chose the word *nègre*."[31]

As for the journal, it was open to all anticolonialist writers, beginning with Sartre, André Breton, and the surrealists. For Senghor, Negritude was defined in positive terms, as the set of cultural, economic, political, and artistic values of the peoples of Africa, the Black minorities of America, Asia, Europe, and Oceania, whether or not they were of "mixed blood." The very idea of the existence of a "pure race" was excluded from the notion of Negritude. Senghor valorized the idea that one must see oneself as part of a universal civilization if one wanted to avoid being assimilated by force to a dominant culture. And it was through the French language – the colonizer's language – that Negritude could become a Negro culture endowed with its own particularities and its own form of *métissage*, or "mixing." Westerners, according to Senghor, brought their own culture to share, while participating in this universalism. Whence this striking assertion: "Emotion is Negro just as reason is Hellenic."[32]

48

Césaire, for his part, saw Negritude as an act of negation rather than of affirmation: a rejection of the abject image of the Black (in the style of Aunt Jemima[33]) fabricated by colonialism; a rejection, too, of the assimilation that made the Negro a sort of valet to the Whites; and, finally, an absolute rejection of any form of antiwhite racism. In short, for him, Negritude – expressed first in the French language – sought to bring to light a culture common to all peoples who were victims of segregation owing to the color of their skin, whether they were descendants of the slave trade or Black heirs to the colonial empires. Thus Negritude, as he saw it, was defined as a cry of pain and rebellion arising from the dark holds of a slave ship. But it was in no case to be cut off from the universal culture, nor should it renounce Latin or Greek, Shakespeare or the Romantics, and so on. That is why Césaire rejected the idea of a mixed-race culture proper to the Antilles or to the Caribbean world – which does not mean that he scorned mixed-race people, but, on the contrary, that he included them in the larger cultural history of Negritude.

For, as he saw it, the mixed-race culture was of African heritage first of all, insofar as no culture can be the result of a juxtaposition of cultural traits. In this sense, the Césairean concept of Negritude is devoid of anthropological significance and proposes no new ontological perspectives. Far from designating a skin color, it refers to the need for a rebellion propelled by a fundamental language: that of "literary Negroes" – or language-wielding Negroes – claiming that share of human universality of which slavery, racism, segregation, and/or colonization had deprived them.[34] Negritude thus has a memorial dimension: it is linked to a narrative of origins.

Sartre, who had written a long preface to an anthology of new Negro and Malagasy poetry,[35] did not stop at supporting the battle in favor of Negritude; he also declared that Black poetry in the French language was the only poetry of its day that could be called revolutionary.[36] He evoked an explosive moment in which the density of words resembled a mass of stones tossed in the air by a volcano, heading toward Europe and colonization.

Far from exhibiting an attitude of compassion, Sartre compared the lived experience of colonization to the existential experience of the Occupation, recalling that it was at the core of the greatest humili-ation, confronted with the enemy's cruelty, that it was possible to grasp what freedom can be: "We were brought to the verge of the deepest knowledge that man can have of himself. For the secret of a man is not his Oedipus complex or his inferiority complex: it is the limit of his own liberty, his capacity for resisting torture and death."[37]

THE SOVEREIGN SELF

Sartre compared the Negro's destiny to that of Orpheus seeking the woman he loved in the depths of hell, and Negritude to a great Orphic poem: "Negritude is the far-away tam-tam in the streets of Dakar at night; voo-doo shouts from some Haitian cellar window, ... but it is also this poem by Césaire, this slobbery, bloody poem full of phlegm, twisting in the dust like a cut-up worm."[38] Finally, he rejected the notion of race by affirming that it was simply a skin color that the Negro could never escape, unlike the Jew, even though Jews were equally humiliated:

> since [the Negro] is oppressed within the confines of his race and because of it, he must first of all become conscious of his race. ... On this point, there is no means of evasion, or of trickery, no "crossing line" that he can consider: a Jew – a white man among white men – can deny that he is a Jew, can declare himself a man among men. The negro cannot deny that he is negro, nor can he explain that he is part of some abstract colorless humanity: he is black. Thus he has his back up against the wall of authenticity: having been insulted and formerly enslaved, he picks up the word "nigger" which was thrown at him like a stone, he draws himself erect and proudly proclaims himself a black man, face to face with white men.[39]

Finally, Sartre considered Negritude as a dialectical moment rejecting the hypothesis of the superiority of the White man and leading to a raceless society. And he added that the ultimate unity bringing together all oppressed peoples in the same fight had to be preceded, in the colonies, by "what I shall call the moment of separation or negativity: this anti-racist racism is the only road that will lead to the abolition of racial differences."[40]

In turn, in his famous *Discourse on Colonialism*, Césaire spoke out violently against colonial barbarity, supporting Lévi-Strauss against Caillois and taking up the idea according to which Nazism – the theory of the superiority of the so-called "Aryan race" – had only repeated, against the Europeans, the crime that they themselves had committed against the people they had colonized, deeming them radically inferior. "Yes," he said,

> it would be worthwhile to study clinically, in detail, the steps taken by Hitler and Hitlerism and to reveal to the very distinguished, very humanistic, very Christian bourgeois of the twentieth century that without his being aware of it, he has a Hitler inside him, that Hitler *inhabits* him, that Hitler is his *demon*, that if he rails against him, he is being inconsistent and that, at bottom, what he cannot forgive

Hitler for is not *the crime* in itself, *the crime against man*, it is not *the humiliation of man as such*, it is the crime against the white man, the humiliation of the white man, and the fact that he applied to Europe colonialist procedures which until then had been reserved exclusively for the Arabs of Algeria, the "coolies" of India, and the "niggers" of Africa.[41]

Césaire declared that no Western power had succeeded in solving the two major problems to which its existence has given rise: "the problem of the proletariat and the colonial problem."[42]

By thus inscribing the history of the extermination of the Jews within that of colonial domination, which had itself originated in the slave trade, Césaire, like Lévi-Strauss, gave a logical and historical content to the lengthy process of colonialism. And by the same token he made anticolonialism a struggle as important as the one that had been waged against anti-Semitism. Still, he did not view colonialism as a genocidal enterprise comparable to that of the Nazis: the crimes perpetrated by colonialism did not aim to exterminate the populations deemed inferior but rather to exploit them by brutally repressing any attempt at insurrection. In colonialism there was neither a concerted effort at extermination nor any genocidal project deliberately pursued to its end.

As Pierre Vidal-Naquet, an anticolonialist from the outset, emphasized, in a book review written with Gilbert Meynier: "assimilating the colonial system more or less to an anticipation of the Third Reich ... is a fraudulent intellectual exercise. ... Or rather, if the colonial massacres announced Nazism, there is no reason why the bloody repression of Spartacus's rebellion or even the Saint-Barthélémy massacre would not have announced it equally."[43] Césaire never subscribed to such a misguided viewpoint, for the good reason that the fight he was engaged in with the anticolonialists aimed first of all to shatter the idea of the supposed inferiority of the colonized people, all the while affirming that it was in the name of the same racialist theories that colonial crimes and the genocide of European Jews had been perpetrated: the victims thus had a common memorial history.

This discourse was all the more potent in that, as a young elected deputy in March 1946, Césaire had supported the law that turned the four "former colonies," Guadeloupe, French Guiana, Martinique, and Réunion, into French departments. This was a fundamental step in the process of dismantling France's colonial empire, whose death warrant Charles de Gaulle, president of the French Committee of

National Liberation, had signed in his famous speech in Brazzaville on January 30, 1944. Since Europe was in the process of freeing itself from the yoke of Nazism, it was now time to liberate Europe and France from the burden of colonialism:

> There are no populations ... in the world today that are not looking up, looking beyond the present and questioning their destiny. Among the imperial powers, none more than France can feel that call. None is more aware of the need to take profound inspiration from the lessons of the [recent] events to engage, along new paths, the sixty million people who are bound up with the fate of her forty million. No power, I say, more than France herself.[44]

The fact that de Gaulle had understood at that early date that colonialism would one day be defeated did not resolve the essential question, however: deprived of the colonial empire on which it had leaned to defeat Nazism, in the world of the future France would no longer be in a position to retain its status as a great economic, cultural, and political power.

After 1945, in any case, no colonial war would ever be won by the Western powers. While the loss of certain colonies did not necessarily lead to the loss of others, the desire to hold on to them generally led either to a transfer of power, as was the case for Great Britain (which, after granting India its independence, continued to increase its influence in the Middle East) or else to a doggedness that led nowhere. Thus after having been defeated militarily in May 1954 in Indochina, at Diên Biên Pho, France sought to hold on to Algeria, at the price of a useless war that went on for eight years. It was also compelled to give up all its African colonies, and then to recenter its politics on the construction of Europe, while the United States took up the relay of the old imperial politics only to get bogged down in Korea and then in Vietnam without ever getting the better of the Communist regimes; these collapsed on their own starting in the 1980s.[45]

Césaire knew that turning colonies into departments would not put an end to colonial domination, and that it was not enough to dissolve the colonial status in order to recognize the "cultural alterity" of the formerly colonized peoples, since there was no place for that alterity according to the principle of assimilation so dear to France's republican universalism. And he thought, rightly, that the change in status was much more advantageous to French neocolonialism[46] than to the interests of the formerly colonized. Césaire sought to enlist the latter under the banner of Negritude: "*Nègre* I am, *Nègre* I shall always be," he proclaimed; he saw himself as *Nègre* at his core.[47] But he was aware that Negritude would last only for a time, that it was linked to the fact that "the *Nègres*," a conquered and humiliated people, would henceforth enter the ranks of the so-called "civilized" nations on an equal footing. And he knew that autonomy would ultimately be the only path capable of bringing recognition of their cultural traditions to the formerly colonized. That autonomy would finally lead to the fight for independence. Césaire thought this too, but it did not keep him from supporting departmentalization. And, in 1975, critiquing the population decline in Martinique in response to the need for a labor force in metropolitan France, and thus the arrival, in exchange, of a significant number of new colonizers, he declared: "I fear the devious recolonization as much as the rampant genocide."[48] He was to be widely reproached for the purported "racism" in this statement. The critique is debatable, even if the formulation was clumsy: Césaire was seeking to draw attention to the harmful effects of a neocolonialism that threatened to depopulate Martinique of its Martinican population.

In 1948, during the celebration of the Centenary of the Abolition of Slavery, Césaire had paid resounding homage to Victor Schoelcher, emphasizing the fact that the decree of 1848 had allowed the integration of the "Negro" into the human species.[49] Up to that point, Negroes had been characterized as beasts of burden, pieces of furniture, non-subjects.[50] But Césaire also said that the decree did not go far enough; he insisted that the fight waged by the slaves themselves against their own servitude must not be forgotten – a way of reminding his audience that abolition had not simply been granted by a man of the Enlightenment but had also been won by the victims of slavery.[51]

In his *Discourse on Colonialism*, Césaire adopted a different tone in vigorously denouncing the destruction committed by all colonizers: the annihilation of the Aztec and Inca civilizations, the eradication of traditional economies, the massacre of "Black nations," the degrading of Ethiopian, Bantu, and Malagasy rites and cultures, and so on. It was time to take up the fight and support the peoples who had gathered at the big meeting in Bandung, Indonesia, in 1955. It was on that occasion that the "third world"[52] made its entry onto the international political stage, with condemnations of imperialism, apartheid, and colonialism in all their forms on its agenda, along with a severe critique of the State of Israel's colonial policy, which deprived the Palestinians of their homeland.

Writing toward Algeria

Very different from Césaire, whose student he had been at the Schoelcher school, Frantz Fanon, a Martinican psychiatrist, was another of the great artisans of anticolonialist activism. His birth in 1925 in Fort-de-France, to a mother partly of Alsatian descent and a Black father who worked for the colonial administration, made him the child of a "mixed-blood" couple, marked, he said, by the fact that he was the darkest of the eight children in his family. Hostile to the politics of Marshal Pétain, he rallied the Free French forces in the Caribbean region. He joined the French Liberation Army when he was 19, only to discover that racism was present at the heart of the French anti-Nazi resistance movement. By a curious twist of fate, he was deployed in Algeria and was awarded the Croix de Guerre by Raoul Salan, commander-in-chief of the Sixth Regiment of the Senegalese Infantry.

After taking up the study of psychiatry in 1947, he published an authoritative book, *Peau noir, masques blancs* (Black Skin, White Masks), in 1952.[53] It was to become a classic, not only in the field of anticolonialism but also as a history of the psychoanalytic approach to relations between colonizers and the colonized. Fanon mobilized Hegelian dialectics, Sartrean phenomenology, and the Lacanian theory of the mirror stage to analyze the situation of colonized individuals. He stressed the fact that Blacks had no access to the struggle for recognition, which presupposed that the subject was already white. Thus he noted that Blacks wanted to be white – hence their alienation – and that mixed-race people in the Antilles wanted to be more white than black and thus sought to be closer to the Whites, notwithstanding the latter's scorn for them. Furthermore, Blacks had trouble achieving an identity, that is, self-recognition, because for them the Other was always white.[54] And Fanon asserted that there was a specific phenomenon – or specular hallucination – that led to Blacks not knowing what color they were. If you asked a man from the Antilles what color he was, for example, he would reply: "I have no color." This referred, symmetrically, to the self-evidence of racist discourse: "Mama, see the Negro! I'm frightened!" a little girl might say, passing a Black person in the street.[55] Fanon was thus depicting colonized persons not in psychological or behavioral terms but in a way that brought into relief the history of their becoming colonized individuals inhabited by self-hatred. And he deduced from this that a Black man could only free himself from his alienation by a rebellion that would lead him to achieve self-awareness; that was the only way he could break out of an identitarian assignment based on race. Such was the new humanism advocated by Fanon: the reintegration of colonized peoples into universal humanism, a humanism that would take differences into account while humanizing the human in all its variants. As a result, Blacks would no longer need to camouflage their lack of an attainable identity by donning white masks.

Fanon's book was thus a stinging response to Octave Mannoni's *Prospero and Caliban: The Psychology of Colonization.* That book, first published in French in 1950, was presented as a psychoanalytic interpretation of the colonial situation, the first of its kind.[56] Born in Lamotte-Beuvron in 1899, Mannoni was the son of the director of a penal colony. After studies in literature, Mannoni became a pure representative of the imperial Republic by taking a government position first on the island of Réunion, later in Tananarive. An early anticolonialist, he spent 18 years in Madagascar (1931–49), leading a double life: a colonial administrator by day, an anticolonialist poet and writer by night. Back in France for a time in 1945, he developed an interest in psychoanalysis, receiving his training on Jacques Lacan's couch. Three years later, he married Maud Van der Spoel, a young Belgian psychoanalyst who had studied with Françoise Dolto. Maud Mannoni was to become one of the major figures in the French psychoanalytic school, close to the English antipsychiatrists but also an ardent militant for the anticolonialist cause; she signed the Manifesto of the 121 supporting conscientious objectors to the war in Algeria.

In his book, Octave Mannoni was inspired by three characters in Shakespeare's *The Tempest* – Prospero, the master; Ariel, the valet; and Caliban, the deformed savage – to try to differentiate the Malagasy personality from that of the colonial European. According to Mannoni, the Malagasy were characterized by a dependency complex and a submissive attitude toward a religious hierarchy in which the dead, grouped together as a moral agent – a superego – determined the behavior of the living. The Europeans stood out, in contrast, by their individualism and their emancipation with respect to customs and religion. Colonization had not only woven ties between these two incompatible systems of thought, it had also had the effect of creating unease among the Malagasy: they saw the white colonizer as the equivalent of the dead ancestor from whom they sought protection and peace of mind. "The Black man is the fear the White man has of himself."[57] And Mannoni saw this dependency complex as the consequence of a specifically Malagasy Oedipus complex: Malagasy children, unable to rebel against their fathers because power was incarnated by a dead ancestor, occupied from the outset the submissive position demanded by a colonizer concerned with imposing his own will to power.

With such arguments, this work – which owed nothing to the Malagasy insurrection against colonial oppression in 1947[58] – could only hurt the partisans of the anticolonial struggle, on the one hand because of its psychologism, which implied that the colonial situation depended on a pre-established structure, and on the other hand because it reduced the death struggle between the executioner and his victim to a perverse theatricality. Early on, Césaire had already maliciously ripped into Mannoni's book by treating the author as a minor psychologist who had used psychoanalysis to justify colonialism by dint of hackneyed arguments, and here came Fanon, at the time a better reader of Lacan's work than even the one who had spent time on the master's couch, reducing Mannoni to ashes while accusing him of an Oedipalism incompatible with the analysis of the subjectivity of colonized persons.

In fact, these attacks were both unfair and far too virulent. Despite the support offered him by Francis Jeanson, Mannoni, a collaborator on the journal *Temps modernes*, was wounded by the critiques to the point of rejecting his own work and taking himself for the colonialist that he actually never was. With the passing years and the reprintings, Mannoni's book became a classic in the Anglophone world, precisely because the impact of its psychologism eventually allowed it to be read as a contribution to identity politics – so much so that it has been embraced by the proponents of postcolonial and decolonial studies.[59]

When I began my own analysis with Octave Mannoni, in January 1972, I spoke to him spontaneously about the book, which could no longer be found; I had learned of its existence from Fanon's book. Mannoni refused to lend me a copy. He pronounced a negative judgment on the work, and he took great pleasure in subscribing to Fanon's attack. He then alluded to a self-critical text written in 1966, "The decolonization of myself," in which, having become a Lacanian, he rejected his earlier position as a "psychologist of colonization." And he told me that he owed his "decolonization of himself" not to his analysis but to the trauma that followed his reading of Fanon's book. He added at once that being a "White among Negroes is like being an analyst among Whites."[60] He never got over that experience, which had robbed him simultaneously of his paired identities as colonial administrator and anticolonialist.

And yet it was through a dialectical engagement with Fanon's text that he had been able to "decolonize himself" from psychology. As for Fanon, we now know that Mannoni's book allowed him to develop a "counter-psychology" that led him to a new psychiatric approach to the identity difficulties associated with colonization. The two texts can thus be seen in the same light.

In 1952, after the publication of *Black Skin, White Masks*, Fanon crossed paths with the adventure of institutional psychotherapy when he spent time in the Saint-Alban hospital working with Catalan psychiatrist Francesc Tosquelles. It was in this mythical place that, under the Nazi occupation, a new therapeutics of mental illness had been developed, one that aimed to transform the relations between doctors and patients by fostering greater autonomy for the patients in the life of the community. At Saint-Alban one found, pell-mell, communist or anarchist militants, resisters, madmen, and intellectuals who came and went; all dreamed of freedom regained. On the strength of this crucial experience, Fanon instituted a radical reform of the "insane asylum" as an institution in 1953, when he was appointed head doctor of the psychiatric hospital of Blida, in Algeria. He developed the principles of a social therapy that he had articulated in *Black Skin, White Masks*, based on an organic and psychical approach to the patient. This was a way of radically opposing the segregationist and racialist colonial psychiatry, which looked at "natives" as impulse-driven, primitive, and infantile beings, devoid of any humanity and incapable of achieving the slightest rationality.

Antoine Porot, an important organizer of psychiatric institutions in Algeria, recalled the characteristics of the indigenous individual labeled "North African and Muslim": "No emotional expression, extremely credulous and suggestible, tenaciously stubborn, mentally puerile without the curious mind of a Western child, readily susceptible to accidents and pithiatic reactions."[61] And he went on: "The natives form a shapeless bloc of primitives, for the most part profoundly ignorant and credulous ... Boastful, mendacious, thieving, and indolent, the Muslim North African is defined as a hysteric moron, subject moreover to unpredictable homicidal impulses."[62]

After the war began, Fanon enrolled resolutely in the ranks of the FLN (National Liberation Front). He left the hospital in Blida and, under a false name, created a nonresidential psychiatric treatment center at the Charles-Nicolle Hospital. Pursued by the French police and a victim of assassination attempts, Fanon became acquainted with Sartre, who supported all the anticolonialist movements. In September 1960, Sartre – along with Pierre Vidal-Naquet and many others – had signed the Manifesto of the 121 on the right of conscientious objection to the Algerian War. Conceived and drafted by Dionys Mascolo and Maurice Blanchot, that appeal openly advocated civil disobedience and even alliance with the FLN against the French army, while denouncing militarism and the use of torture. Every signatory understood the risk, especially the academics, who could be removed from their university positions at a moment's notice. Two communist militants, Henri Alleg and Maurice Audin, were among the victims of torture. The first, born Harry Salem in London to Jews of Russian–Polish origin, had been director of the daily paper *Alger républicain*; he was a journalist with the Communist newspaper *L'Humanité* when he was arrested and tortured by French parachutists.[63] For the rest of his life he fought alongside Gisèle Halimi, Madeleine Rebérioux, Laurent Schwartz, and Germaine Tillion to get the French government to acknowledge those practices. As for the second, the mathematician Maurice Audin was assassinated during the battle of Algiers; the French Army's responsibility for that crime was not acknowledged until 2018.

Fanon published *Les damnés de la terre* (*The Wretched of the Earth*) in 1961.[64] The war was drawing to an end and colonial violence was being unleashed in Algeria. Returning to the thesis of *Black Skin, White Masks*, he stressed the extent to which the universe of colonized peoples could no longer be reconciled with that of the colonizers. And he called on the entire African continent to engage in a relentless battle for independence. Even while bringing his support to the armed struggle, Fanon condemned the desperate terrorist acts that he deemed less effective than military action spurred by an uprising of the peasant classes. Moreover, despite his admiration for Césaire, he did not share the latter's positions on Negritude, which he viewed as a "cultural trend" that did not allow the colonized to free themselves politically.

On the contrary, he thought that, in order to support access to independence, peoples ought to constitute themselves as nations founded on ancestral traditions, or even, in Algeria's case, founded on Arabization and Islam:

> This might be an appropriate time to look at the example of the Arab world. ... Colonialism used the same tactics in these regions to inculcate the notion that the precolonial history of the indigenous population had been steeped in barbarity. The struggle for national liberation was linked to a cultural phenomenon commonly known as the awakening of Islam. The passion displayed by contemporary Arab

authors in reminding their people of the great chapters of Arab history is in response to the lies of the occupier.[65]

Fanon was clearly on the side of Ho Chi Minh and Che Guevara; at no time did he support anything like an "Islamist revolution." As evidence, we can cite a letter he wrote on the eve of his death to his friend Ali Shariati, a sociologist, Islamologist, and committed democrat:

[The world of Islam] has fought against the West and colonialism ... These two old enemies [of Islam] have inflicted serious wounds on its body and soul ... I hope that your authentic intellectuals may make good use of the immense cultural and social resources harboured in Muslim societies and minds, with the aim of emancipation and the founding of another humanity ... and breathe this spirit into the weary body of the Muslim orient ... Nevertheless, I think that reviving sectarian and religious mindsets could impede this necessary unification – already difficult enough to attain – and divert that nation yet to come, which is at best a "nation in becoming."[66]

And he added that the return to Islam "appears as a withdrawal into itself" and a "depersonalization." Such is the most caustic critique that can be made of the very notion of regressive identity.

Thirteen years after having defined Negritude in the Hegelian tradition while evoking the sumptuous aesthetic of Césairean poetry, Sartre, at Fanon's request, wrote a preface to *The Wretched of the Earth*. It proved to be one of the most violent indictments ever articulated in the entire history of anticolonialism.[67] In this text, Sartre denounced the crimes committed by European nations in the name of civilization and summoned the "wretched of the earth" to an armed uprising.

Since the others are turning themselves into men against us, apparently we are the enemy of the human race; the elite is revealing its true nature – a gang. Our beloved values are losing their feathers; if you take a closer look there is not one that isn't tainted with blood. If you need proof, remember those noble words: How generous France is. Generous? Us? And what about Sétif? And what about those eight years of fierce fighting that have cost the lives of over a million Algerians? And the torture by electricity?[68]

Finally, Sartre wrote a sentence for which he will never be forgiven. "Killing a European is killing two birds with one stone, eliminating in one go oppressor and oppressed: leaving one man dead and the other man free; for the first time, the survivor feels a *national* soil under his feet."[69] Frantz Fanon had just enough time to read this text, which went well beyond his own positions: he was addressing colonized peoples who were actively liberating themselves from the yoke of the colonizers, whereas Sartre was settling his accounts with European colonialism. Suffering from leukemia, Fanon died in Washington, DC, in December 1961 at age 36. Meanwhile, on October 17, under the leadership of Maurice Papon, the Paris police had used violence and shed blood in shutting down a peaceful demonstration by Algerians organized by the FLN.[70]

Considered one of the major works of anticolonialist historiography, this book, like most of Fanon's texts, was ignored for some 30 years, in Algeria as well as in France. The neglect lasted until the renewal of studies on colonialism and decolonization revealed the extent to which Fanon had grasped the structure of the colonial situation. I was a witness to that neglect when, in 1966, as a young professor of French in the technical secondary school at Boumerdès, Algeria, where future engineers in the fossil fuel industry were being trained, I decided to put *The Wretched of the Earth* on my syllabus: I could see that my Algerian students did not know even the name of the author of that great book. Whatever you do, stop evoking the past! The war, so weighty in the students' memory, was for them just a series of massacres, and they now wanted to devote themselves to the classics of French literature – and certainly not to Césaire's poetry or to Sartre's condemnations of colonialism. Fanon had no place in their historical memory, no more than did the work of Kateb Yacine, the most talented of the Algerian writers.[71]

In 1966, Yacine had declared that the French language constituted "the spoils of the Algerian War" – to such an extent that Yacine rejected the term "Francophonie" (the French-speaking world): "The use of the French language," he said, "does not mean that one is an agent of a foreign power. ... I write in French to tell the French that I am not French."[72] And it was in the colonizer's language – that of Césaire – that he wrote *Nedjma*, even before the outbreak of the war of independence.[73] This novel told the story of four young men in love with Nedjma, the daughter of an Algerian and a French woman. But through that feminine figure transformed into a chimera, the actor dramatized the epic story of the Algerian people in search of its own identity. Thus it was a sort of foundational autobiography of a nation to come. In the strands of a deconstructed narrative,

Yacine mixed novelistic fragments that owed as much to the French *nouveau roman* (New Novel) or to Faulkner as to the Arabic literary tradition. In any case, what united all these writers fighting for decolonization – Césaire, Senghor, Fanon, and others – were shared references to the France of 1789 and to the anti-Nazi resistance. All were careful to lean on French artisans of antiracism and anticolonialism without excluding Whites from their struggle. None of them positioned himself the way many "identitarians" did, as firmly installed within a "race" or an "ethnic group"; none thought that racism was a concern for Blacks alone, or anti-Semitism for Jews alone. In this sense, they were aware that racism is as universal a phenomenon as the aspiration to freedom. And this universality always presupposes the existence of a generalized racism and anti-Semitism: that of Blacks against Whites, Whites against Blacks, both against "mulattos," Jews against other Jews, anti-Semites against Jews or against "certain Jews," and so on.[74] Fanon never forgot a statement made by one of his professors, which he evoked frequently: "When you hear anyone abusing the Jews, pay attention, he is talking about you."[75]

In this connection, moreover, let us note that Césaire, in his account of the genesis of Antillean culture, was the first Martinican to restore Jews to a privileged place. Settled in Martinique as colonizers starting in the seventeenth century, members of the Jewish community on the island were not confined to ghettos. They traded in cocoa and indigo, and they owned slaves. The wealthiest frequented the Békés, while the poorest mingled with the mixed-race population. All were victims of the anti-Jewish sentiment and then of the anti-Semitism of the French authorities from 1940 to 1943, under the laws of the Vichy government: they were denounced, persecuted, and expelled, before being rehabilitated with the Liberation. After Algeria became independent, many Sephardic Jews emigrated to the Antilles – especially to Martinique – and found work in small businesses such as jewelry or household appliances. Later, the Israel–Palestine conflict led to a revival of anti-Semitism among the Martinicans who supported the Palestinian people persecuted by the Israelis, and it rekindled the racism of the Jewish community toward the Antilleans.[76]

Césaire never separated the struggle against racism and colonialism from the fight against anti-Semitism. In his epic poem *Notebook of a Return to the Native Land*, he paid homage to the victims of all persecutions:

the famine-man, the insult-man, the torture-man you can grab anytime, beat up, kill – no joke, kill – without having to account to anyone, without having to make excuses to anyone
a jew-man
a pogrom-man
a puppy
a beggar[77]

In 1950, celebrating the memory of the Abbé Grégoire, an abolitionist from the outset, he stressed that the Abbé had passed "from the ghetto to a slave hut."[78] Nearly 50 years later, he added: "The Negro is also the Jew, the foreigner, the Amerindian, the illiterate, the untouchable, the one who is different, the one who by his very existence is threatened, excluded, marginalized, sacrificed."[79] In the end, despite his unfailing support for the Palestinian cause and his fierce criticism of Israeli policies, Césaire, like Fanon, never yielded to the sirens of anti-Semitism.

In 1968, Fanon's widow did not seem to be concerned about the fundamental importance of the link that united the fight against racism and colonialism with the struggle against anti-Semitism. She had not appreciated Sartre's support for the State of Israel during the Six-Day War, and she disapproved especially of his refusal to identify Israel with the "imperialist camp"; she thus demanded that Maspero withdraw Sartre's preface to The Wretched of the Earth. Mortified, the editor, who was very attached to the Palestinian cause and even more to freedom of expression, found an ingenious solution by inserting, in each copy, a magnificent folded poster, presenting Sartre's text in poster form under the title "'Frantz Fanon, fils de la violence [son of violence],' by Jean-Paul Sartre." Later, in a triumph of truth over small-mindedness, the preface was restored definitely to the text.[80]

How can we fail to think in this context about André Schwarz-Bart, a member of the Resistance, a Jew and a Zionist tortured by the Nazis whose family had been exterminated in the death camps? The author of an admirable book, The Last of the Just,[81] in which he traced a long list of Just (or Righteous) individuals over a thousand years, from the Middle Ages to Auschwitz, he was nevertheless attacked by French critics, Jewish writers in particular, who found him too "Christian" and accused him of plagiarism. He received the Goncourt Prize in 1959, and the book achieved worldwide success. With his wife Simone, a Guadeloupean writer, he committed himself to the anticolonial struggle, associating himself with the fate of the Blacks as well as that of the Jews.

Together, living in Pointe-à-Pitre, they worked on a cycle concerning the memory of slavery and, in 1972, André Schwarz-Bart published a superb story, *A Woman Named Solitude*, which met with no success whatsoever.[82] And yet this was a text that could have appeared in the collection of "Parallel Lives" initiated by Foucault a few years later. As Simone Schwarz-Bart said in 2020:

> It was awful, stupid, unjust ... Antilleans dared to claim that a white man could not write about Blacks! Intellectuals close to the independentists could not stand the fact that the great book on resistance to slavery was written by a Jew, and now I feel betrayed by my own people ... The heroine of his story is claimed by all Guadeloupe. ... The little Jew André Schwarz-Bart belongs without question to the patrimony of the Antilles.[83]

Based on considerable documentation, the novel is inspired by the life of a young mixed-race girl, Solitude, and that of her mother, Bayangumay, who was born in West Africa around 1750 and torn away from her family 20 years later by slave traders who took her to Guadeloupe and sold her to colonizers. Raped at the end of the journey, Bayangumay gave birth to a daughter, Rosalie, who later took the name "Solitude." Endowed with a strange charm, the young slave, with eyes of different colors, nicknamed "Two Souls," served as a *cocotte*, a living doll, for the daughters of her white masters, while her mother abandoned her to join the *marrons*.[84] Over the years, hating her condition, she turned herself into a kind of zombie, reduced to the status of an animal.

The abolition of slavery that had been decreed in February 1794 by the Convention, France's post-revolutionary government, and extended to all the French colonies, drew Guadeloupe into a war against the English, who had reconquered the island. In May 1795, troops sent by the Convention landed and integrated free Blacks into their ranks. But after the defeat of the English, the Blacks were compelled to go back to their plantations. In the middle of this troubled period, Solitude found love and became part of the last group of rebels massacred by the French when slavery was reestablished in 1802. Pregnant, she was executed the day after she gave birth.

Oscillating between a melancholic state that led her toward her fate and a state of exaltation that pushed her toward freedom, Solitude alternated, under Schwarz-Bart's pen, between defeat and fury, in a Rousseauist décor, always in search of an unattainable identity. The author concluded his book with the torture of the runaway Negroes,

THE SOVEREIGN SELF

like "the phantoms that wander the humiliated ruins of the Warsaw ghetto."[85] Thus this book paid homage as much to the memory of the last of the Just as to that of the heroic mulatto woman whose statue would soon be erected in a Parisian garden that already bore her name – there where, earlier, there had been a statue of General Alexandre Dumas, the "black count," a mulatto who was a hero of the French Revolution, the father of the writer whose ashes lie in the Pantheon.[86] Destroyed by the Nazis in 1942, the statue has been replaced by a monument representing slaves' broken chains. Might it not be fitting to rehabilitate Solitude rather than stubbornly insisting on ousting Schoelcher or wasting time and credibility calling Victor Hugo a racist?[87]

Mixed-race identities

Césaire had strongly encouraged Schwarz-Bart to associate Jewish and Black historical memory. But he lived long enough to be confronted, from his own side, with a critique of Negritude and of the political positions he had taken. In February 1987, during the first hemispheric conference of the Black peoples of the Diaspora, organized by Florida International University in Miami, he had to explain his positions before an audience of scholars who, even as they paid him homage, were already demanding a much more identitarian postcolonial discourse. To be sure, Césaire had been an advocate for such a discourse, since he had always denounced the brutality with which colonialism had destroyed the old civilizations in the name of a "civilizing mission." However, unlike the new generation emerging from American campuses, he had never supported the idea that attribution of a racial or ethnic identity could be a response to imperialist barbarity. Nevertheless, the debate during this conference bore on the question of "ethnicity," a term that was beginning to take hold throughout postcolonial studies in relation, moreover, to gender studies. While Césaire applauded the vivacity of these approaches, he rejected the word "ethnicity," even though at the same time he welcomed the term "identity." He nevertheless affirmed the necessity of maintaining the universal meaning of that term: identity, he declared, was the very kernel of human singularity, that of humans immersed in a culture, not in a race. Here he was paying tacit homage to Claude Lévi-Strauss. We must not let the term mislead us, for Negritude, Césaire insisted, had nothing to do with a biological or ethnic order.[88]

64

The real dismantling of Césaire's work and reputation was not achieved by American scholars, however, but by his Antillean compatriots, even though they owed him everything. The most notable among them was Raphaël Confiant, who published an incendiary tract presented as praise, in 1993, *Aimé Césaire: Une traversée paradoxale du siècle*.[89] Using a rather rudimentary psychoanalytical approach, Confiant claimed to be unearthing "the Césairean unconscious." According to him, Césaire had repressed his "mulatto" identity while presenting himself as more Negro than he was. Hence the invention, Confiant emphasized, of the concept of Negritude based on the idea that "blackness" was a sign of ethnic purity superior to the mixed-blood status. By the same token, Confiant asserted that Césaire preferred the language in which his father had brought him up – French – to that of his illiterate mother, who spoke only Creole.[90] In short, Césaire was deemed guilty, through the invention of Negritude, of presenting himself as heir to the language and culture of the colonizers, heir to Hugo, Rimbaud, the surrealists, and their ilk. Thus he was accused of attributing an inferior status to his true mother tongue, Creole, the better to integrate himself into colonial society. And it was for that reason, according to Confiant, that he sought to maintain the Antilles in the bosom of the French empire, rather than militating in favor of independence.

Determined to go still further into the Oedipal analysis of the Antillean and Creole identity, Confiant himself claimed to be "the son of the father," even as he acknowledged that he was that father's symbolic murderer. On the occasion of this extravagant avowal, he specified that, even as Césaire was repressing his maternal Creole side, he was immersing himself at the same time, on the occasion of his reconnection with Black Africa, in a sort of maternal symbiosis. On this account, he freed himself from the "formal shackles" of so-called "European" poetry: "Can one use a language – French, in the case in point – that, if we hold to the psychoanalytic theories themselves, carries within it the collective unconscious of the people that created it? In a word, can Black Orpheus dialogue in French with his African Eurydice?"[91] It is impossible to overemphasize how inappropriate it is to "psychologize" the colonial question in this way: Fanon can be credited, moreover, for having challenged that principle by standing up to Mannoni.

In reality, the Freudian–Jungian jargon obscured a far more complex identity quarrel. It is to the great poet Édouard Glissant, born 15 years after Césaire and a signatory of the Manifesto of the 121, that we owe the notion of "Antilleanity." Eager to leave behind

THE SOVEREIGN SELF

the great Césairean epic of Negritude without having to kill either Césaire or Sartre, or his father or his mother, Glissant thought that Antillean culture should not be conflated with Black identity and thus that Negritude could not claim to encompass that culture. In short, he criticized the concept of Negritude for eliminating the very idea of a plural identity. And he considered that the insular world of the Caribbean, with its archipelagos, its splintered geography, and its generalized racial mixing, called for purely and simply abolishing the very notion of specifiable identity.

Drawing on the work of Gilles Deleuze in his attempt to convert the "monolithism" of Negritude into an uprooted vision of subjective identity, Glissant distanced himself from Sartrean philosophy by turning to a new generation of critical philosophers. Identity, he declared, could only be "rhizomatic" and anchored in a permanent plurality, an otherness, a blending. In contrast with Césaire's Negritude, deemed too univocal, too ontological, too paternocentric, Glissant proposed the Antillean condition as an illustration of an "all-world." The statement "We-are-Antilleans-other-than-ourselves" should thus replace the statement "I-am-Negro," which had been experienced as the cry of a revolt constraining the "not-Whites-not-Blacks" to identify with a single color:

> As long as the idea, not only as a concept but in the imaginary of the humanities, that the all-world is a rhizome in which all need all, has not been accepted, it is obvious that there are cultures that will be threatened. What I am saying is that it is neither by force nor by a concept that these cultures will be protected, but by the imaginary of the all-world, that is, by the experienced necessity of this fact: that all cultures need all cultures.[92]

According to Glissant, Antilleaneity opened the way to the constitution of a new memorial history that would no longer be written exclusively by colonizers, missionaries, slave traders, or even by anticolonialists such as Clemenceau, Lévi-Strauss, Sartre, Césaire, and the like, but by the victims themselves, newly visible: the absent figures of history. However, for such an undertaking to be possible, an adequate historiography had to be constructed. Recourse to this Antilleaneity thus led also to the invention of a new way of writing that could account for the vast Antillean mixing that blended Amerindian survivors, descendants of Africans, migrants from Syria, Japan, Lebanon, and various countries in Latin America, not to mention the Béké: a veritable identitarian patchwork. A single

66

community remained outside this project, that of the Martinican Jews.

Just as the concept of Negritude had been forged by an inversion of stigmata that allowed the colonized to appropriate the language of the colonizers for themselves, and especially the fundamental language of poetry, Antilleaneity was accompanied by an attempt to regenerate a Creole language that would not be born of Negritude or Whiteness or Indianness.

Hence the identitarian claim enacted in 1989 in *Éloge de la créolité* by Jean Bernabé, Patrick Chamoiseau, and Raphaël Confiant: "Neither Europeans nor Africans nor Asians, we declare ourselves Creoles. This will be for us an inner attitude, or, better: a vigilance; or, better still, a sort of mental envelope within which our world will be built with full awareness of the world."[93] To be sure, in this Creolizing project, published the year the Bicentenary of the French Revolution was celebrated, one can see a kind of liquidation of the old adventure of Negritude, viewed by Césaire's heirs as a sort of antiquated paternalism tied to a politics of departmentalization that prevented cutting the umbilical cord tying the islands to metropolitan France.

But one can also judge that the cult of the rhizome, of infinitely deconstructed chaos, also referred to the search for an identitarianism based on wandering, a form even more redoubtable than the one its proponents were claiming to combat: it presupposed the abolition of all identity in favor of a nameless identity – an identity of identity, analogous to "queer." For seeking too eagerly to encourage the Creolization of the world entails a risk of diminishing the necessary diversity of cultures: the famous "neither too close nor too far apart" so well conceptualized by Lévi-Strauss.

I am inclined to say here that there is no antidote to identity neuroses. The only solution to these interminably deconstructed neuroses would be to renounce both the eradication of differences and the arbitrary revalorization of a unified masculinist order already in its death throes. However, this is not what has happened.

Attesting to this is the stupefying declaration by Raphaël Confiant in 2005 in which he reconnected colonization to the Revolution of 1789: "By decapitating their king and definitively abolishing the monarchic system, by proclaiming the Universal Declaration of the Rights of Man and the Citizen, by conveying to the whole world the ideals of liberty and equality of all men, the French pulled the rug out from under all claims of breaking away from the metropole on the part of their subjects in the 'American Islands' and

Guiana." And he added that Césaire was the worthy successor of Toussaint Louverture, since he had preferred departmental status to independence. Finally, Confiant reproached the French Revolution and its universal and democratic ideals for being the source of the Antilleans' inability to conceptualize their own reality.[94]

In other words, Confiant attributed the failure of the independence movement not only to Césaire and Negritude but also to republican universalism, which, while it cut off the king's head, did not allow the Antilleans to escape their feudal dependence on the colonizers. Thus he refused to see that it was in the name of these same ideals of freedom and equality that the anticolonialists had carried out their struggles against the colonial policies that claimed fidelity to those ideals. Would it be necessary to reinstall the monarchy in France in order to put an end to such a neurosis? In reality, after spectacular progress, the independence movement did not succeed in gaining the upper hand in France's overseas departments, where poverty, racism, and inequality reigned.

It hardly needs saying that with such judgments Confiant was thumbing his nose at the debates that had developed in France over the abolition of slavery, even before the Estates General met in 1789. He deliberately neglected the role played by the white, black, and mixed-race generals who had participated, most notably Generals Alexandre Dumas and Toussaint Louverture. He left out the creation by Jacques-Pierre Brissot, in 1788, of the Society of the Friends of Blacks, which advocated the immediate prohibition of the slave trade and demanded the abolition of slavery; he also failed to mention the declarations of the duke de La Rochefoucauld-Liancourt, who envisioned extending the principle of equality before the law to all slaves. Confiant paid no attention to the debates of 1789 and the declarations of Mirabeau, who called for the constitution of a sovereign Assembly in San Domingo, announcing that one day the colonies would be independent nation-states. "Against all justice," Jean-Sylvain Bailly wrote in his *Mémoires*, "people of color have been excluded from the elections, because the Negroes are slaves and are not men in the colonies. But M. Garat does not hide the fact that this great operation of justice and humanity, the cessation of slavery, the *motion of the century*, has to be prepared long before it is accomplished."[95] In reality, Confiant rejected the French Revolution just as he had rejected Césaire: he sought to be more royalist than the slaveholding French monarchy. In other words, he was insulting the entirety of the French anticolonialist movement.

After seeking to decapitate Césaire while proclaiming the merits of the Old Regime, Confiant offered his support, in 2006, to the humorist Dieudonné M'Bala M'Bala. Dieudonné had fought racism and partnered professionally with another French comedian, actor, and writer, Élie Semoun, but he later became associated with the National Front and with Holocaust deniers. In January 2005, he had characterized the celebration of the 60th anniversary of the liberation of the Nazi extermination camps as "memorial pornography," and in June of the same year he had been attacked by four members of the Jewish Defense League.[96] Hosting him at an event recorded on video, Aimé Césaire had reminded him that "our specificities nourish the universal and not particularism and communitarianism."[97] In November 2006, Dieudonné stood alongside Jean-Marie Le Pen at the Blue-White-Red festival,[98] insisting that he himself, like Le Pen, was the victim of extreme demonization. Always obsessed by the question of mixed-race identity, Confiant justified that encounter by claiming that Dieudonné was a victim of racism who got no support from the Jews. Consequently, he could be excused for associating with Le Pen since he had to suffer twice over: "once owing to his person, his mixed-race being (African father, white mother), and again owing to those people whom it is forbidden to name ... and whom I shall designate in this paper the Unnamables." And of course, in order not to name the Jews, Confiant invoked Fanon and Césaire:

> When a Euro-American lectures me on democracy, tolerance, and the rights of man, I have two reactions: first, I admire such monstrous gall. After killing off the Amerindians, enslaving the Negroes, gassing the Unnamables, torturing the Algerians, napalming the Vietnamese, and the list goes on, here's this guy posing as a model of virtue! Hats off, folks. In contrast, when an Unnamable, after everything he's gone through in the West, comes up with the same discourse and presents himself to me as a civilized Westerner, I have just one reaction. Like Dieudonné, I get mad, plain and simple.[99]

Confiant's intervention brought an immediate retort by Jacky Dahomay[100]:

> The unpardonable mistake of Raphaël Confiant is seeking to reduce every human being to an identity substantialized by Confiant himself, a process that Sartre called *chosification* ["thingifying"] with reference to the Jewish question. Confiant does not understand that the history of the Jewish people is an integral part of the West, just like a good part of the history of the Antilles, moreover. In this sense, Confiant is no

THE SOVEREIGN SELF

less a *Westerner* than [Alain] Finkelkraut, if only through his theories of nationhood, very *German* theories developed in the West. He has trouble understanding that there is not a Jewish-being, immutable and eternal, any more than there is a *Martinican-being*. That there are Jews critical of Israeli policies, Jews who have fought colonialism and racism just as whites have done, too.[101]

It would be hard to state more clearly how identity classifications lead to an impasse, caught up as they are between racial psychology and tribal interpretations.

As for the writers of Creolity, however rich their works may be in their quest for the unfindable idiom, we have to note that they have chosen the French language in order to give themselves the breadth they deserve. Thus it is in French that the magnificent novel *Texaco* is read, and rightly so, as one of the great foundational narratives of Antillean suffering, a work of collective memory.[102] For his part, Césaire always saw Creolity as a component of Negritude, and he was probably not entirely wrong, since the Creolitarians themselves forged the neologism "mulâtritude," as if it were necessary to rival the sumptuous sonority of the Negro epic that had begun to make itself heard in the interwar period.

In sum, let us say that Glissant was also defending an archipelagic identity (Antilleaneity), when his heirs were calling for insularity; to each his own "Creole," in other words, an even more narrowly defined attribution of identity.[103]

70

— 4 —

POSTCOLONIALITIES

"Is Sartre still alive?"

Between the Césairean and Sartrean epoch of Negritude and the period during which it was challenged by a project of Antilleaneity and then of global Creolization, a new line was crossed in the struggle against colonialism. The colonial empires collapsed; the colonial wars, the battles for independence, the movements in favor of autonomy or departmentalization triumphed throughout the world: in India, Algeria, Africa, Madagascar, Vietnam, the Antilles, French Guiana, and elsewhere. This is why, in 1992, the historian Daniel Rivet called for a new approach to the history of colonization, declaring that the time of colonies and the ordeal of decolonization was over, so it was necessary to think differently about the past:

> We have finally exited from the dialectics of celebration and condemnation of the colonial phenomenon that has so long and so profoundly biased the writing of its history ... Our colonial past is far enough away that we can finally establish a relation to it that is free from the complex of arrogance and the reflex of guilt.[1]

Rivet was undoubtedly formulating both an accurate diagnosis and a devout wish. For if the period of anticolonial and independence movements had indeed come to an end, other problematics were arising at the very heart of the former empires, and other actors were coming on stage, actors who sought to track down the spirit of coloniality – conscious and unconscious[2] – everywhere it was present, that is, within democracies themselves, and everywhere apartheid was practiced, apartheid being a violently repressive policy

THE SOVEREIGN SELF

that consisted in separating Blacks, Whites, mixed-race people and "coloreds." The struggle led by Nelson Mandela in Africa embodied this great battle for freedom.

A new era was dawning, then, with studies labeled "postcolonial" called to explore a new reality: that of the Western countries confronted with immigration from their former colonies and thus the reality of an *internal colonialism* presumed to exist within their own institutions and presumed to be experienced as such by those who felt that they were its victims.[3] Naturally, these new approaches banished the word *Nègre*, which had been ennobled by Césaire after it had been wrenched away from the infamy of the slave trade. It went back to the hold, not to be used again except as a racist insult.[4] Moreover, by excluding Jews from the anticolonialist new deal, the advocates of the new approach broke the pact that had for years united the fight against anti-Semitism with the fight against racism, not only in the Antilles but also in France.[5] The separatism of identities was asserting itself in tandem with the growing demands proper to postcoloniality.

In this context, it is to Jacques Derrida that we owe the most powerful challenge to the identitarian drift of Creolity. During a colloquium organized by Édouard Glissant and David Wills in 1992 at Louisiana State University in Baton Rouge, Derrida gave a talk titled "Le monolinguisme de l'autre," in which he claimed the right to appropriate the French language for himself, inasmuch as it was his only mother tongue, precisely because it was not his own: "I have only one language; it is not mine ... I am monolingual. My monolinguism dwells, and I call it my dwelling."[6] In a lyric flight he defined himself as a Franco-Maghrebian Jew, asserting that the French language did not belong to the French state nor to the French people but rather to everyone who spoke French. And he evoked his status as an Algerian Jew exiled in France in 1949 as a student at the Lycée Louis-le-Grand, then at the École normale supérieure, and later as a professor of philosophy with a post-doctorate degree (*agrégé de philosophie*), having become French and then being obliged to return to Algeria to carry out his military service in the camp of the colonialists. His itinerary has nothing in common with Sartre's, or Césaire's.

Born in El-Biar, Algeria, in 1930, Derrida was deprived of his French citizenship under the Vichy regime, which abolished the Crémieux decree in 1940.[7] Thus he had become a French subject afflicted with an "identity disorder" and deprived of his rights. He did not know Ladino,[8] and, as a Jew privileged by the decree, he had

72

belonged to the colonizers' camp. The Jewish community of Algeria had been triply "dissociated": from the Arab-Berber culture, from the French language and culture, and finally from Jewish memory. And as a subject downgraded by Vichy, Derrida had found himself in the "other camp," that of the colonized: even worse, he actually had no camp at all, since he was no longer anything, not even a native. His only fatherland was his monolinguism, his French language, the only one through which he could exist.[9]

In proclaiming his monolinguism, Derrida was helping to deconstruct all forms of identitarianism through which a subject could properly claim a language as his own. He implicitly criticized the very idea of seeking to attach an identity to an "archipelagic" language (Creole). He also rejected "linguistic nationalism," the principle according to which a language is the property of a people. No: a language, he declared, is the signature of the person who invents it, without being the inventor's property. And he even went so far as to affirm that language, as the "language of the other," imposes its own law and stems from culture, not nature. All culture is thus "originally colonial ... Every culture institutes itself through the unilateral imposition of some 'politics' of language."[10] Consequently, cultural identity never refers to any sort of belonging.[11]

Derrida did not approach the question of colonialism the way Lévi-Strauss, Césaire, and Fanon did. He never imagined for a moment that a "Creolitary" claim could contribute to a critique of colonialism, nor did he tolerate any attributions of identity. Like Albert Camus, he imagined that Algeria could one day become both French and Muslim, Jewish and Algerian, anticolonialist. He would have wanted Algeria thus to be able to save France from its imperial epic – for this he was frequently reproached, moreover. He always dreamed of a universality founded on the reconciliation of communities. And without being philosophically or politically Sartrean, he recognized his debt to Sartre, celebrating the philosopher's thought, his presence, his persona, as indispensable in the anticolonialist struggle.[12]

In 1986, with other writers (Susan Sontag, Kateb Yacine, Maurice Blanchot), Derrida offered a stirring homage to Nelson Mandela, stressing the extent to which Mandela compelled admiration, not only for his ability never to give in to adversity, but also for his political passion and his art of not separating his commitment to law from his commitment to culture and history. It is clear that Derrida saw in Mandela the sovereign figure he had dreamed of for Algeria,

THE SOVEREIGN SELF

that country so dear to his heart: a man who knew how to turn the English democratic model against the devotees of apartheid. What Césaire had achieved with Negritude, Mandela was extending across his entire country. As Derrida put it, "in all the senses of the term, Mandela remains, then, a *man of law*. He has always appealed to right even if, in appearance, he had to oppose himself to this or that determinate legality, and even if certain judges made of him, at certain moments, an outlaw."[13]

In April 1993, a year after he had deconstructed the idea of Creolity, Derrida changed registers on the occasion of a two-part lecture he gave at the University of California, Riverside, during a colloquium on Marxism, and more specifically on the decline and fall of genuine communism. And he was clearly still thinking about apartheid, because he dedicated his talk to a Communist militant from South Africa, Chris Hani, who had just been assassinated by a far-right Polish immigrant, Janusz Waluś; the killer had been hired by Clive Derby-Lewis, a member of the Afrikaner National Party. In *Specters of Marx*, one of Derrida's finest books, he called on Freud's work, and in particular on the concept of repression, to show that Western society was all the more haunted by the "specter" of Marx since it kept on announcing Marx's death and the end of communism.[14]

That lecture took place in the wake of the worldwide success of the theses of the philosopher and economist Francis Fukuyama, who as early as 1989 had announced that the universal recognition of Western liberal democracy as the most accomplished of all forms of human government had now been achieved. In short, Fukuyama appropriated the Hegelian lessons of Alexandre Kojève on the end of history. He was immediately criticized for his use of the concept of historicity. But it was above all his own mentor, Samuel Huntington, who offered an opposing vision of the future. In the post-communist world, no "end of history" will come about, Huntington declared, but rather a clash of civilizations, that is, various civilizations will clash among themselves: Western, Slavic-Orthodox, Hindu, African, Islamic, Japanese, Confucian. Far from falling back on war, he insisted, on the contrary, that the modernization of civilizations did not necessarily entail their "Westernization" but rather their reciprocal recognition of their necessary diversity.[15] The expression "clash of civilizations" took on a life of its own, not in relation to what Huntington said about it but as a way of bringing to the fore a binary organization of the world: Westernism versus Islamism.

74

It is in this context, but from a very different perspective, that Derrida too intervened, on three interrelated questions: Is the end of history conceivable? How can we think about the unpredictable? What is Europe? In *Specters of Marx*, he also proposed to reflect on the new world order after the fall of the communist regimes, to ponder the prospect of a possible future revolution that might emerge from this new order; he invited us to contemplate what an epoch that did not succeed in conceptualizing its future might bring. Derrida associated the act of terror – the assassination of Chris Hani – with three great "scenes" in Western culture: the scene in which Hamlet is confronted by the ghost of his father, who is returning in an untimely manner to demand vengeance and to entrust the mission of saving the "world from dishonor" to his son; the scene of the publication of the *Communist Manifesto*, which includes the famous statement by Marx and Engels: "A spectre is haunting Europe: the spectre of Communism"[16]; and the scene of the new world order, an order "in a manic phase," unable to complete the process of mourning what it claims to have put to death. Of course, through his statement Derrida was paying homage to Paul Valéry, who, in 1919, had devoted himself to a vast reflection on the future of Europe in the aftermath of the First World War. According to Valéry, contemporary Europeans, like Hamlet, had realized that every civilization, even that of Europe, was mortal. Thus it was now necessary to face up to the specters that threatened to destroy Europe. The imperative facing Europeans was the same as the one confronting Shakespeare's hero: facing a crisis of values, one had to save the life of the mind, or risk seeing Europe plunge into greater barbarity: thus Hamlet wavered between two abysses, order and disorder.[17]

In 1999, Derrida, coming from a European world in crisis, met Nelson Mandela, a most perfectly Westernized non-European, when the latter was more than 80 years old. Derrida was impressed by this wise, enthusiastic man who had managed, during his years in prison, to set up a sort of permanent university designed to educate militants. Mandela asked him if Sartre were still alive.[18]

It was from the standpoint of a confrontation with apartheid and through a reflection on language that Derrida took up the torch of the anticolonialist struggle at a time when colonialism had been defeated politically but had not disappeared as an ideology. And it was at that moment that, from South Africa, the name of Sartre came back to him, a sanctified name that embodied the very history of anticolonialism. Was he still alive? Was he a specter? Who else could succeed him?

Descartes, a white male colonialist

Just as the abolition by science of the notion of race did not end racism, so the end of the colonial epic did not eradicate the spirit of colonialism. In this sense, Derrida nourished the theses of postcolonial studies, since for him it was a matter of bringing to light the existence of a new colonial subject. And to that end he undertook to move from classic structuralism to poststructuralism, by decentering the symbolic figures of structuralism: the law, the signifier, the origin, identitarian belonging.

Invented in 1967, the term "deconstruction" – very poorly understood by many commentators – referred, in its initial definition, to a work of critique and decentering: a work of unconscious thought ("it deconstructs itself") that consisted in taking a hegemonic system of thought apart without destroying it. We can understand, then, why the word became wildly successful in various "studies" in American universities. In every instance, it was a matter of critiquing, decolonizing, disalienating, challenging fixed identities and the priority of one oppression or another: that of men over women, sex over gender, dominants over subalterns, Whites over Blacks, and so on. And this mode of thought aimed to reconstruct the human and social sciences by taking what had been invisible into account: the voiceless, the minorities, the excluded, the abnormal, and so on. This movement of renovation was basically the same as the one that had seen "human science" emerge from the ruins of the so-called "science of race."

We have already seen how the new "identity politics" had been imposed in North America, by way of multiculturalism. At the outset, the project was magnificent. It emanated from a collective of Black women, heirs of Rosa Parks and of the civil rights and Black Power movements, women seeking to join, as feminists, the cluster of other movements for the liberation of oppressed minorities.[19] But the synthesis among gender, sex, race, ethnicity, and subjectivity to which the project aspired ended up privileging membership in a community rather than promoting the fight for universal civic equality: hence it underwent a gradual drift toward identitarianism.

In this new identitarian framework, a synergy emerged among poststructuralism, postcolonialism, gender studies, queer theory, and the various struggles waged by all minorities against an ancestral order called "patriarchal" or "Western-centric." Convergence, or intersectionality,[20] thus became possible, even desirable; it could bring together in the same fight those excluded from "sexual normality" and the victims of coloniality. These new "studies" emerged in the wake of all the others that had developed in the cutting-edge sectors of American universities: Latino/Hispanic/Chicano Studies, Asian American Studies, Native American Studies, and so on. It was on the basis of this reality that the term "postcolonialism"[21] began to be widely used, during the 1980s and 1990s, when students from the former empires of India and Pakistan came to enroll in the best North American, Australian, and British universities. Stigmatized on the basis of their origins, they proved eager to tangle with the vestiges of a domination by which they still felt victimized, even though they had become its best representatives. As Thomas Brisson has written:

> It is indeed remarkable that the most radical challenges do not come from the individuals most deeply rooted in their original traditions but rather from Westernized intellectuals, educated in the schools and languages of Western Europe or North America ... There is a paradox here: in a context of global decentering, intellectuals installed at the very heart of the Western world are the ones who have produced the sharpest critiques of that world.[22]

Of course, the multiculturalism that characterizes North American society, based on the principle of the melting pot, lent itself perfectly to the development of such approaches – which were full of promise, moreover, in the beginning, contrary to what certain French polemicists on the left and right alike continue to argue, convinced as they are of the superiority of their own model.[23]

We know to what extent ethnoracial logic was always of crucial importance on a continent whose history corresponds to a long process of multiple colonizations, and in a country in which the abolition of slavery was achieved only in the wake of the deadly Civil War whose memory is still present in literature, politics, and Hollywood movies.

The force of this logic is attested by the traditional division of the American population into five distinct groups: Native Americans, European Americans, African Americans, Asian Americans, and Latin Americans.[24] From this perspective, it is not surprising that the notion of membership in an ethnic group has remained present in all American demographic statistics, along with religious affiliation.

And it is of course this hyper-ethnicization – or hyper-separatism – that has led to the identitarian drift. Let us note that this phenomenon fosters racism as much as antiracism, since it provides grist for supporters of segregation and white supremacy as well as for proponents of positive discrimination (affirmative action and political correctness), who maintain that ethnic inequalities (brought to light by these classifications) must be corrected by policies of compensation, repentance, or reparation for past offenses. From this standpoint, it is hardly astonishing that the struggles waged by sexual minorities (LGBTQIA+) have allied themselves with those of ethnic minorities.[25]

Classic postcolonial studies always sought to bring to light the dynamics that have arisen *since* the colonial period. In contrast, the newer postcolonial studies have proposed overall to deconstruct the remnants of the colonialist ideology proper to the formerly colonizing nations, in order to impose on those nations a new representation of the subjectivity of those whom they consider as still and always "colonized." These studies have thus never sought to rediscover the existence of repressed identities in order to revive them, but rather to describe multiple identities, individual or collective, that are put together and taken apart to the benefit of other always hybrid identities. Such a project induces a sense of vertigo: how can one describe and analyze something that is defined as permanently fluid and that escapes ontologically from any rational analysis? Postcolonial studies rest on an antihistoricism that makes the object under study vanish just as it seems within reach.

While postcolonial studies were largely confined to the Anglophone world, a different tendency, known as "decolonial," took over in Latin America. It aimed to critique so-called Western modernity, its values and its ways of life, along with its so-called neoliberal economic system, perceived as a new colonialism.[26] Undoing the "centrality" of the West in all its forms, and thus of Europe, insofar as it is perceived as the original matrix of Occidentalism: such was the critical program proposed by the advocates of this current of thought, some of whom used the term "epistemicide" to designate the supposed elimination by the West of any form of knowledge other than its own. Others went after Descartes, who became in their writings the founder of a "mystification," since the "I" of "I think, therefore I am" was necessarily that of a colonialist "white male."[27] The two currents – postcolonial and decolonial – affirm that they take their inspiration as much from Derridean deconstruction as from Michel Foucault's theses on minorities or those of Deleuze and Guattari on rhizomatic realities, those of Frantz Fanon on racism, or those of Edward Said on Orientalist alterity, even though these thinkers had never been fans of the slightest identitarian drift.[28]

They all invoke Freudian or post-Freudian thought, either positively or negatively. This is how sophisticated theories, developed in the inner circles of the greatest universities of the Western world, end up feeding into identitarian and insurrectional (post-Marxist and post-communist) political movements.

I once asked Jacques Derrida what he thought of the deviant offshoots of his work. He answered that it was not up to him to police the texts of those who took inspiration from his thought. Unlike Lacan, he knew that no thinker could master the interpretive readings to which his work gives rise. Thus he affirmed, quite rightly, that, to be faithful to a heritage one had to be unfaithful to it.

Flaubert and Kuchuk Hanem

The work and teaching of Edward Said also influenced the postcolonials and decolonials in carrying out their identitary reconversions. Born in Palestine in 1935 under the British Mandate, Said, like Derrida, was a subject in exile, though not a monolinguistic one. He was brought up in a bourgeois family; his mother, born in Nazareth, had become Lebanese, and his father was a Palestinian American. Throughout his childhood he spoke three languages: French, English, and Arabic. He never knew where his mother's English had come from, or what her nationality was. He was not unaware, however, that he had been given his first name in homage to the Prince of Wales, known for his sartorial elegance: "I have retained this unsettled sense of many identities ... all of my life, together with an acute memory of the despairing feeling that I wish we could have been all-Arab, or all-European and American, or all-Orthodox Christian, or all-Muslim, or all Egyptian." And how was he to respond to questions like these: "'You're American?' ... 'How come you were born in Jerusalem?' ... You're an Arab after all, but what kind are you? A Protestant?"[29] He was in fact living in Cairo, even though his parents returned to Palestine regularly. At school, his friends included Armenian, Jewish, and Coptic classmates, but his closest friends were English, sons of professors and diplomats. He continued his studies at Victoria College, a British-style public secondary boarding school in Alexandria, where he was bullied by a sinister prefect who later became famous in films under the stage name of Omar Sharif.

Two years after the creation of the state of Israel, experienced by Palestinians as the disappearance of their country and their identity, Said was sent by his parents to the United States. He excelled in his

THE SOVEREIGN SELF

studies at Harvard, where he earned his doctorate in comparative literature with a thesis on Joseph Conrad.[30] The choice of topic was not anodyne. Born Polish in the Russian Empire, Conrad became a captain of long-haul ships and an adventurer in distant oceans. As someone who spoke several languages, he had long searched for an impossible identity before he became a writer. He wrote his novels in the language of his adopted country, Great Britain. Even before producing *Lord Jim*, a modern prototype of a deconstructed autobiography that announced a revolution in subjective narration, he had published a long novella, *Heart of Darkness*, whose protagonist Kurtz embodied the violence of the colonial world.[31] An ivory trader immersed in the savagery of the Congo basin, a depressive at death's door, Kurtz reigned over the natives and executed his enemies, keeping their heads planted on pikes surrounding his home. In both books, Conrad introduced a double of the protagonist, the narrator Charles Marlow.

Studying one of the most subversive authors of the late nineteenth century, Said thus invented a reading that was not deconstructive but "contrapuntal," as he would qualify it later. A serious music lover, he borrowed the term from a technique according to which melodies are superimposed on one another without any particular one being perceived as dominant. Thus he started from the principle that the greatness of a work presupposed that it could be interpreted in innumerable ways depending on the context and the epoch. Shakespeare's theater, the classic novels, the literature of modernity from Proust to Joyce – all these texts had in common a complexity that gave rise to as many polyphonic readings as there were readers of divergent identities.

Every reading thus refers back to a subjective position. In this perspective, Said presented Conrad as a brilliant wanderer who, having become a writer in a language that was not his own, never managed to shed a feeling of alienation toward his adopted country, and thus lived permanently in between two worlds. And he deduced that the character of Kurtz, haunted by his own dark visions and self-destructive impulses, proved incapable of imagining an Africa other than that of colonization. In effect, Kurtz failed to perceive the presence of a world that was nevertheless resisting him. A pure representative of an imperial system that horrified him, he was thus passing through a dream whose images were destined to disappear.[32]

In 1967, with the Six-Day War, Said – who was already teaching at Columbia University[33] and had been an American citizen for some time – came to a sudden understanding of the importance of

80

his identity as an Arab. This led him to travel to Jordan to meet with friends involved in the fight for the Palestinian cause. He later became a member of the Palestinian National Council, supporting the principle of creating a binational state and militating with his friend Daniel Barenboim to bring together young Palestinian and Israeli musicians. At bottom, like Derrida, he wanted to see all communities brought together in a single state: separation between peoples, he argued, was not a solution to any of the problems that divided them.

This turning point led to the publication of his most influential book, *Orientalism*, a study marked by the principles of reading he had developed in his approach to Conrad's work.[34] Published in English in 1978, *Orientalism* was a masterpiece of erudition; it is easy to understand why it had a powerful impact. Translated into 40 languages and reprinted numerous times, in a few short years it became the Bible for postcolonial studies, though it was often read in a sense contrary to the propositions it articulated. Still, Said himself had theorized the idea of polyphonic readings. Reviewing the entire Western adventure of Orientalism as a literary and artistic movement, Said asserted that the Orient, in the generic rather than the geographic sense of the term,[35] was a sort of fictional construction through which Western discourse sought to pin down an alterity that eluded it. Orientalism as a movement of thought attested, as he saw it, to Europe's collective daydream about the Orient, a dream that supported a relation of identitarian inequality between the Western traveler and the populations visited.

Whereas the various academic "studies" focus essentially on the "other" internal to the self (homosexual, abnormal, queer, White, Black, mixed-race, and so on), Said analyzed the discourse held by one society about another: the *external* "other" – in the case in point, the Oriental. Among the Orientals, Said focused on those of the Near and Middle East, Arab and Muslim, and among the discourses produced from the outside, he privileged those from the two colonial empires, France and Great Britain, plus the American discourse that had succeeded the other two after the dismantling of colonialism:

> A vast web of interests now links all parts of the former colonial world to the United States, just as a proliferation of academic sub-specialties divides (and yet connects) all the former philological and European-based disciplines like Orientalism. The area specialist ... lays claims to regional expertise, which is put at the service of government or business, or both.[36]

Said thus took as his object of study the Orientalism of the nineteenth and twentieth centuries; by this term, he meant a discipline and a style of thinking based on the hypothesis that there existed an *Orient* as opposed to an *Occident*, a *West*, the one dominated and the other dominant. The Orient had been "Orientalized" by Western discourse so that Occidentals and Orientals could be assured of an "identity" vis-à-vis one another, even if this identity were falsified or illusory. The danger of this approach lay of course in the risk of making the Orientalist movement a mere auxiliary of colonialism.

But the book went well beyond the initial project; it did not stop at exploding the essentialism of the Western gaze on the East. In three sections, Said analyzed all the major texts devoted to the "Orient question": from Silvestre de Sacy to Louis Massignon, along with T. E. Lawrence, Chateaubriand, Baudelaire, and Hugo, not to mention the episode of Bonaparte's Egyptian expedition (1798–1801).

In the last part of the work, devoted to the creation of the state of Israel and then to the arrival on stage of American imperialism, Said noted that in the ultimate phase of Orientalism "the Arab" had been substituted for "the Jew" in Western representations of the Orient. Said declared in effect that the Arab was thus conceived as a shadow following the Jew, noting that they were both classified as "Semites." And to show the similarity between hatred of Arabs and hatred of Jews, he cited a letter written by Chaïm Weizmann in 1918, emphasizing how readily Weizmann's statements could have been applied by anti-Semites to the Jews. Weizmann in fact drew on the classic vulgate according to which Arabs were swindlers, traitors, arrogant, or worse.[37]

Among Said's most controversial pages are those he devoted to Gustave Flaubert and his "Oriental" writings, especially the passages describing his encounter with Kuchuk Hanem, a famous woman dancer who had been relegated to Esna, on the banks of the Nile. (The Egyptian government deported prostitutes to that city, treating them as tourist attractions.) Flaubert, who at age 27 was eager for new carnal sensations, was fascinated by the bordellos. He fell in love with the sumptuous courtesan and represented her as the embodiment of Oriental femininity, the most accomplished essence of the sexual power of women in general. This was not a case of dominated alterity, but rather of conquering sovereignty:

> She is a regal-looking creature, large-breasted, fleshy, with slit nostrils, enormous eyes, and magnificent knees ... I sucked her furiously, her

body was covered with sweat ... Watching that beautiful creature asleep, ... I thought of my nights in Paris brothels ... We told each other many sweet things – toward the end there was something sad and loving in the way we embraced.[38]

Intimately acquainted with Flaubert's work, Said stressed rightly that the author had been inspired by his trip to the East, and later by his travels in Tunisia, to create the characters of Salomé and then Salammbô. However, Said did not hesitate to make the famous scene with Kuchuk Hanem not only the prototype of the power relations between East and West, but also that of male domination – on the colonizers' part – over Oriental women. That particular woman, Kuchuk Hanem,

> never spoke about herself, she never represented her emotions, presence, or history. *He* [the author], spoke for her and represented her. He was foreign, comparatively wealthy, male, and these were historical facts of domination that allowed him not only to possess Kuchuk Hanem physically, but to speak for her and tell his readers in what way she was "typically Oriental." My argument is that Flaubert's situation of strength in relation to Kuchuk Hanem was not an isolated instance. It fairly stands for the pattern of relative strength between East and West, and the discourse about the Orient that it enabled.[39]

It is clear that Said was mistaken, if not about the prototype, then at least about Flaubert. Far from being the representative of any form of colonialism, the author of *Salammbô*, unquestionably fascinated by the Orient, never saw Orientals as barbarians who needed to be subjected to the benefits of Enlightenment civilization. A rebel against bourgeois society, he never stopped denouncing its hypocrisy, its received ideas, its stupidity, its morality. He liked neither monarchy nor the democracy of the masses, which led to uniformity of thought, and he was attracted to the splendors of the ancient world – and thus those of the Orient – only because he discerned in them an aesthetic of violence in harmony with his vision of a literary art that needed to distance itself from Romanticism. He was indicted in 1857 for an "offense to public morality": he had made Emma Bovary a rebellious woman who preferred suicide to mediocrity. And he vigorously supported the cause of literature against censorship and institutional authorities.[40]

Flaubert never defended one particular nation, culture, or religion against another; he never adhered to the slightest colonial epic vision. Furthermore, throughout his travels in the Orient, he always distinguished his own way of representing the Ottoman, the Oriental, or the Arab from that of Europe in general,[41] going so far as to declare that he was no more modern than ancient, no more French than Chinese. Thus he detested any attachment to a land, whether it be marked in red, black, or blue. "I am the brother in God of everything that lives," he said, "from the giraffe and the crocodile to man, and the fellow-citizen of everyone inhabiting the great furnished mansion called the universe."[42]

Clearly, Said himself was a pure product of the Orientalist configuration that he described. He too was an Orientalist, as talented as the authors whose works he studied. And that is why his book, strongly marked by his readings of Flaubert, Conrad, Freud, Foucault, and many others, resembled the self-analysis of an "Occidentalized" man who had been "Orientalized," always torn between a discourse characterized as "colonial" and another, mute, incapable, as he saw it, of inventing another Orientalism different from the one that had been manufactured by the Occident, that is, by himself. Said never defined what an Orient reinvented by the Orientals themselves might have been.[43]

Tehran 1979: Dreaming of a crusade

The situation attributed to Flaubert, the "power relation between the one (male) who speaks and the one (female) who does not," was to be retained by Said's heirs: they made it the starting point for a new advance in postcolonial and then decolonial studies. The Flaubertian prototype of "colonial-patriarchal-masculine domination" thus became the spearhead of a highly simplified battle: the dominants on one side, masculinized; the dominated on the other, feminized or "subalternized." All this accompanied by a proliferation of neologisms characterizing subcategories of humans – gendered, nongendered, ethnic, hybrid – declined according to the difference between the sexes and the social or colonial construction: bigender, agender, cisgender, gay, bisexual, transgender, intersex, heteronormed, heteropatriarchal, Arab, lesbian, racialized, intersectionalized, subaltern, and so on. In the same perspective, the neologism "racialize" (French *raciser*) originally served to designate a discriminatory attitude based on racial criteria. But later, through a process of lexical drift, the adjective "racialized" (French *racisé*) ended up designating positively a clan anxious not to mix with a white population, the idea being that setting themselves apart would allow the mute victims to express themselves without having to fear that a Flaubert would come to speak in their place.

The use of this term opened the way to an unacceptable challenge to the idea of the indivisibility of the Republic: in France, it is in fact forbidden to classify persons on the basis of their origins or skin color. No one has the right, for example to choose to be cared for by a Black doctor rather than a White one, or by a woman rather than a man, or vice versa. Remaining "among themselves" in order to protect themselves against racist aggression: this would be the infernal spiral of all identitarian questions, a spiral that can only lead to the self-enclosure of self-identified victims. I have already noted the extent to which such labeling resembles that of the famous *DSM*, the vast manual of postmodern psychiatric classifications that is more like a George Perec-style list than a scientific work.[44]

And since "studies" were multiplying, it became necessary to expand the field of identity studies. Among these, the postcolonial Middle Ages, divided into several tendencies, called for "decolonizing" the Middle Ages, which were presumed to have been treated by Western medieval historians as an inferior alterity, on the same basis as a "black continent" subjected to European imperialism.[45] Another addition to the list was Porn Studies, or alternative feminist studies in which pornography was transformed into a liberating, even gendered practice of female sexuality, separate from any form of masculine oppression. The field of Critical Race Theory, or critical studies on race, was developed in the same perspective, taking over the notion of race and making it equivalent to the notion of class. Thus, for sociologists specializing in this identitarian field, race became a concept designating a power relation detached from any idea of races (in the plural): in other words, it was locked into a past without a present or a future.[46]

Symmetrically, Whiteness Studies, largely inspired by post-Freudian psychoanalysis, developed in American universities beginning in the 1990s. While the term "whiteness" referred to a simple chromatic property, the neologism "whititude" was introduced to invite reflection on the way a subject said to be "white" could be perceived as white and as invested with a power of domination in conformity with a racialist ideology that is still present in postcolonial societies. In other words, such studies stigmatize Whites "as whites" deemed guilty of using an alleged "white privilege" the better to repress their *necessarily* racist subjectivity. The study of whiteness thus aims to make all White people admit their unconscious racism,[47] obliging them to identify Blacks by their blackness rather than ignoring color

THE SOVEREIGN SELF

in the name of a pseudo-equality called universalist, while Critical Race Studies bring back into view, whatever one may say about it, the good old Aunt Jemima on the pancake mix box. Thus a reconceptualized notion of "race" is coming back into bodies of writing that are antiracist in inspiration. The artisans of these studies, who tend to be at the very heart of departments of social science and the humanities, have in common the fact that they are waging a ruthless war against an "intimate enemy," that is, against an unconscious frame of mind that makes the dominated parties internalize the stereotypes of the dominant ones: the dominated are portrayed as victims of an internal demon named Europe or the West. As such, in some instances they seek to combat the self-hatred resulting from that internalization; in others, the damage produced in the unconscious psyche of the dominant parties by the vestiges of the colonial epoch.[48]

To explore the various facets of this new configuration, they draw on a proteiform rhetoric that, under cover of a modernity inherited from the "masters" (Derrida, Said, Foucault, Fanon, and so on), leads them to fabricate an ingroup vocabulary of prophetic proclamation, a sort of obscure language or "prophetical jargon"[49] that allows each individual to put forward his or her subjective "positionality": race, origin, gender, experience of victimization, genealogy, sexual orientation, and so on. This "obscure language" is characterized by the expression of propositions so convoluted that they say everything and its opposite, to such an extent that no critical study can ever refute them: this practice makes debate impossible outside of the inner circle. I am tempted to say that the obscurity at issue in this obscure language is inversely proportional to the depth and pertinence of the thinking.

Let us add to the list of these Studies the attribution of religious identities, which have become so powerful that a year after the appearance of Said's book a radical political Islam burst onto the global stage, claiming to substitute a new universalism for the old imperial domination: "Its first breakthrough was the Iranian revolution of 1979, its second the war in Afghanistan against the Soviet invasion of that year."[50]

The major democratic countries had hoped that the fall of communism would result not only in the triumph of human rights in the former colonial empires but also in the victory of Enlightenment values over religious obscurantism and thus in the victory of liberal democracy, as Francis Fukuyama was prepared to prophesy. But then political Islamism, the identitarian declension of Islam,[51] came

86

in to revive an anti-Western ideal among formerly colonized peoples, a veritable messianism that – why not? – promised to become the "great decolonizer" of the whole planet.

As a special envoy of the *Corriere della Sera* to Tehran, Michel Foucault met insurgents who talked about nothing but an "Islamic government," hatred of the West, readiness to die for the Prophet. And he wondered about the meaning of that event, this twentieth-century eruption of a spiritual rebellion of unbelievable strength, comparable to that of the Crusades in the West. It is true that Foucault had witnessed a prayer meeting in favor of Ayatollah Khomeini when the latter was in exile at Neauphle-le-Château in France, threatened by the dictatorship of the Shah. But Foucault did not suppose for a moment that the Islamic rebellion would lead to the formation of a political movement; in this he was seriously mistaken.[52] Nevertheless, despite the repeated accusations (especially by Franz-Olivier Giesbert and Alain Minc), at no time was he "converted to Islam" by Khomeini.[53]

Throughout the world, so-called wars of "civilization" were breaking out, nourished by this messianic and deadly new dream that would culminate in the destruction of the twin towers of the World Trade Center in New York on September 11, 2001.

It was in this context that in February 1989, the year of his death, Khomeini, the spiritual guide of the Shiite world, pronounced a fatwa against *The Satanic Verses*, a novel published a year earlier by the British writer of Indian origin Salman Rushdie.[54] This fine book dealt with the uprooting of immigrants, torn between their culture of origin and that of their host country; it described, step by step, the metamorphoses of identity, the nightmares, hallucinations, dreams, and suffering of two protagonists confronted as much by racist prejudices as by religious obscurantism: faith and fanaticism, police brutality, death, and the theme of pardon. The title came from an episode in the life of Mohammed: surrounded by polytheist dignitaries in Mecca, the Prophet allegedly pronounced some "satanic verses" authorizing belief in other divinities besides the One God, and later retracted them. The very fact of speaking about this event called for condemnation of the book's author. The book itself was henceforth considered by its Islamist enemies as "the incarnation of the satanic plots of Worldwide Arrogance and of the Zionist colonizers who can be seen under the cover of this apostasy."[55]

For ten years, Rushdie and all his editors were threatened with death throughout the world, while the book was banned in numerous countries. Supported by a majority of intellectuals, many of whom were from the Arab-Islamic world, Rushdie, a new Voltaire, had to live under police protection, changing his residence some 60 times. The fatwa was approved by millions of Muslims, not only in Pakistan, Turkey, and the countries of North Africa and the Middle East, but also by some of the enthusiasts for postcolonialism, who wanted to see the blasphemy in question as the manifestation of a colonialist racism converted into hatred of Islam. These writers too howled about "scandal" and Islamophobia, brandishing threats worthy of the Inquisition. Among the leaders of the major democratic countries, Margaret Thatcher, Jacques Chirac, and Jimmy Carter made public declarations in which they refused to support Rushdie, asserting that his outrageous statements lacked "tact" and "compassion" toward the Muslim faith. More courageous, Queen Elizabeth conferred knighthood on Rushdie.

The rise of this identitarian Islam that unleashed its fury on a talented, progressive, and antiracist writer had clear repercussions for immigrants in the Western world, who could henceforth be identified with this obscurantist, liberticide, and criminal counter-revolution. And of course it also had repercussions in university departments that were developing programs of study focused on minorities from the former empires: the Middle East, North Africa, Pakistan, India, and so on. Would these minorities be tempted by the identitarian counter-revolution, at the risk of losing themselves in the regressive quest for an imagined past, an illusory "return to oneself," or would they choose on the contrary to adapt to a "Western" way of life that would no longer be felt as hostile to their religion but rather as a distancing from the criminal fantasy that it harbored? The fact remains that the more the world became globalized, at the rhythm of the global economy, the more the artisans of identity politics sought to take postcolonial revenge on the categories of the "Western" thought of which they were pure products; they too sometimes risked drowning in their adherence to radical Islam.

The subaltern identity

Give the floor to Kuchuk Hanem. Such was the program of the Subaltern Studies popularized in the Anglophone academic world by erudite Indian historians who had been educated in Western universities. The term "subaltern" was forged by Antonio Gramsci between 1926 and 1937, during his years in prison, to designate individuals or groups falling outside all class identities, marginalized and subjected to a subordination that was simultaneously psychological and physical.[56] He was thinking about the slaves of Antiquity, the peasants of peripheral regions, and the sub-proletariat, for whom, he argued, historians ought to constitute archives and monographs.[57] Taken up by the Bengali historian Ranajit Guha, the term was interpreted differently in the framework of a formidable historiographic operation that consists in doing "history from below," that is, giving the floor to the invisible parties, those with no status, the wretched of the earth who are the most discriminated against on the basis of their sex, their race, or their caste: in a word, to the "under-others": the subalterns.[58] For its initiators, this approach was supposed to make it possible to move beyond the classic cleavage between a history conceived by the dominant party (the colonial order) and a history recreated by the new bourgeois classes that had emerged from decolonization. Thus Subaltern Studies sought to give the floor to *the other* conceived in the most absolute nakedness: to groups totally lacking in class consciousness or ideology. After a trek that took him from Calcutta to Paris, then to Manchester and London, Guha became the leader of a vast subalternist program that over the years brought together scholars seeking to bring about a synthesis among all the approaches developed by the various Studies: Gender Studies (including queer and transgendered people), Postcolonial and Decolonial Studies, and so on.[59]

This enterprise has met with great international success, and one can see why. It was a matter of unveiling *another history*, one that had been hidden by the great national narratives taught to generation after generation, colonizers and colonized, in the Western world. It was necessary to rehabilitate a subterranean history by critiquing the narrative of origins, based on the defense of the imperial conquests, on the allegedly unequalled value of European nationalisms, on "our ancestors the Gauls," on all those stories that gloss over massacres, acts of violence and crimes perpetrated over the centuries against peoples of color, against the poor, against the victims of discrimination and exploitation. To counter the infamy of these illustrious narratives, it was necessary, according to the advocates of Subaltern Studies, to construct a memorial in honor of the victims so that they could finally "have the floor," could speak for themselves. And by the same token, the subalternists opposed the classic Marxist historians as well as the upholders of a nationalist and hagiographic history centered on the heroes of independence, for example Gandhi or Nehru in India.[60]

In short, the subalternists more or less subscribed to the celebrated African adage: "As long as lions lack their own historians, hunting stories will sing the praises of the hunters alone!"[61]

In reality, the approach called subalternist only brought to the surface a historiographical tendency that was already present in many historians who were very far from any form of identitarian commitment but who had opened the way to "microhistory," to the science of what had been lived and felt: in short, to narratives of subjective experience. This was the case with the Italian historian Carlo Ginzburg, who published a major work in 1976 inspired in part by Gramsci: *The Cheese and the Worms: The Cosmos of a Sixteenth-century Miller*.[62] The book told the story of a totally unknown miller from Friuli, Domenico Scandella, called Menocchio, whose traces Ginzburg had found while exploring some archives. The man had been summoned twice to appear in court before being burned alive for heresy on the order of the Holy Office. The files produced an astonishing picture of his feelings, his aspirations, his beliefs, his reading, and his daydreams, a whole set of indications making it possible to reconstruct his vision of the world. To his stupefied judges, he had explained that the world was chaos similar to a cheese fertilized by worms that resembled angels. And he deduced from this that one religion was as good as another. In other words, he challenged the divine foundation of the Christian religion; this was why he was judged dangerous. Ginzburg thus indeed "gave the floor" to a "subaltern."

He was not the only one at the time to advocate "history from below." In fact, during the second half of the twentieth century, the idea of giving the floor to people historiography had forgotten was common to all disciplines. It was from this perspective, for example, that in 1972 Michel Foucault examined the famous story of Pierre Rivière, a young peasant in the grip of murderous madness in the late nineteenth century who wrote a detailed confession from prison.[63] And in 1978, Foucault created a collection of "Parallel Lives," designed to make known through documents what he called "the underside" of Plutarch's lives of famous men: obscure lives, and parallel to such an extent that henceforth no one can be added to the list. Herculine Barbin's memoirs appeared in that collection. It was a matter here, as elsewhere, of studying alterity in all its forms: infamous lives, minuscule lives, subaltern lives, neglected or repressed lives, daily lives, and so on. And, from this perspective, the concept of "subalternity" was highly useful. It was moreover this idea of bringing to light a buried "alterity" that gave rise not only to the subalternatist approach but also to all the revisionary work of modern historiography; the great adventure of the history of women orchestrated by Georges Duby and Michelle Perrot is a notable example:

> Women were long relegated to the shadows of history. The development of anthropology and the new emphasis on the family, on a history of *mentalités* interested in everyday life, in what was private and individual, have helped to dispel those shadows. ... but the idea that women in themselves are an object of history must be rejected firmly. What we want to understand is the place of women, the "condition" of women, women's roles and powers. We want to investigate how women acted. We want to examine their words and their silences. We want to look at their many images: goddess, Madonna, witch. Our history is fundamentally relational; we look at society as a whole, and our history of women is just as much a history of men.[64]

Many authors, historians or novelists, have followed in the same path: Michelle Perrot by retracing the story of Lucie Martin-Baud, a silk worker from the Dauphiné region, Arlette Farge by exploring forgotten lives at the heart of the eighteenth century, Kamel Daoud by giving an identity to the Arab killed by Meursault in Albert Camus' *The Stranger*, and even Virginie Despentes by writing the following lines at the beginning of *King Kong Theory*: "I am writing *as* an ugly one *for* the ugly ones: the old hags, the dykes, the frigid, the unfucked, the unfuckables, the neurotics, the psychos, for all those girls who don't get a look in the universal market of the consumable chick."[65] None of these authors adheres to any sort of identity politics, with the possible exception of Virginie Despentes, who ended up adopting, 15 years later, a lesbian-decolonial-gendered feminist morality in the style of Alice Coffin. In other words, for the majority of authors embarked on this path, if the history of women were also that of men, this meant that it could be written by men or women, whatever their origin or skin color. Moreover, it was a characteristic of their serious research that it was internationalized from the outset; it knew neither borders nor homelands.

Thus, may it not displease identitarians on all sides, it was to the American historian Robert Paxton that we owe the first great study of Vichy France. Paxton demonstrated, with evidence, that the French state had collaborated with the Nazi policy of extermination of the Jews, thus refuting the thesis according to which Pétain was a "shield" allowing the resisters to combat the invader.[66] In this connection, let us note that the idea that a "foreigner" would not

THE SOVEREIGN SELF

have the capacity or the right to conceive of a reality external to himself is absurd.

To give the floor to subalterns – from Flaubert's courtesan to Herculine Barbin to Menocchio – there had to be mediators, that is, scholars capable of excavating their lives. In the history of subalternism, Gayatri Chakravorty Spivak was at the origin of the encounter between gender studies, postcolonialism, poststructuralism, and Edward Said's theses revised and corrected from a decidedly identitarian perspective. Born in Calcutta in 1942 into an upper-caste family, Spivak pursued studies in literature before shifting toward subalternist studies throughout her academic career in the United States, a career marked by a decisive encounter with Derrida's *Of Grammatology*.[67] She translated the book into English, thereby becoming one of the voices of deconstructionist thought in the United States.

Published in French in 1967, this book constituted, for the history of French structuralism and within a configuration created by that current of thought, the first philosophical challenge to the use of linguistics in the human sciences. Derrida used the term grammatology to define the presumed rise of a "science of letters" in which, from Plato on, the *logos* (speech and reason in Western philosophy) had repressed the truth of a primacy accorded to speech. A "logocentrism" (or a debasement of writing) thus affected philosophy and served to mask the original presence of letters. In this perspective, Derrida criticized both Lévi-Strauss's structuralism and the Lacanian reading of Freud for their adherence to a master signifier claiming to achieve full speech: "When I discussed Saussure or Lacan, my criticism was aimed less at their texts than at the role their texts played on the French intellectual scene."[68] In other words, Derrida was criticizing a dogmatic turn that resulted from the systematic reliance on linguistics in the domain of thought.

As often happens, the publication of the work in English translation ten years later guaranteed a formidable notoriety not only for its author, who became a veritable star on American campuses, but also for the translator, who had supplied a preface. Derrida's approach in a sense paralleled the preoccupations of an entire generation eager to criticize the way so-called "Western" thought claimed to rule the world by imposing the primacy of a symbolic domination over the dominated, who were the "others," subalterns, people deprived of speech and identity. Of course, Derrida himself never subscribed to such a position. But that hardly mattered, since the identitarian galaxy affirmed that every work is always the sum of the interpretations to which it gives rise.

92

In an article published in 1985 and expanded three years later in an essay, Spivak took up the terms of a debate over the decentering of the *logos* in order to focus on a very different question: can subalterns speak?[69] Like Judith Butler, Spivak was keen on performative language; "as a postcolonial intellectual," she proposed to analyze the "gendered" ritual of the immolation of widows in India. She claimed to be deriving an alternative analysis making it possible to deconstruct the Westernist discourse that opposed, according to her, any discourse coming from subalterns reputed to be "mute."

"Sutteeism" is the name for an ancestral Hindu rite in which widows self-immolated on their husbands' funeral pyre and thereby became *satis*. Renouncing the world of appearances and an illusory form of "self," the sati was thus elevated toward immortality and became a saint.[70] Cremation was practiced by widows of all ages and conditions; through this sacrificial suicide they were sanctified as heroines of the most absolute fidelity. The practice of voluntary death – called suicide – is one of the great universals of the human condition, but the rites differ significantly from society to society and from epoch to epoch. Considered heroic in ancient societies and in feudal Japan, suicide was rejected by Christianity as a sin and a crime against oneself and against God. At the end of the nineteenth century, however, it escaped moral condemnation and was regarded as a social or mental illness.

It was in this context that the great collective sacrificial rites – of women and men alike – were banished or fell into disuse,[71] even as suicide ceased to be demonized if it sprang from a subject's free will. And of course the rituals in question managed to survive in transgressive forms.[72] This was the case for the immolation of widows in India (sutteeism): it was outlawed by the English colonial administration in 1929 as an "execrable custom," and then by the independentists. Aa a result, the celebration of satis was viewed as a religious rite all the more terrifying in that it had become transgressive.

> The belief held that an authentic sati did not feel physical pain. Her only suffering was proportionate with the sins committed during earlier lives ... Rarely, I believe, has religious conditioning been pushed so far as to deny her pain and especially to interpret it in terms of guilt. But India does not have a monopoly on practices of voluntary torture of the body that require a technique of absolute domination of death pangs, however cruel this may be; it is also seen in the Japanese rite of seppuku (belly-cutting, sometimes known as hara-kiri).[73]

Indian law thus condemned all forms of celebration of the rite, and people who organized such celebrations were taken to court. But at the same time, the question arose as to how to know whether women, henceforth protected from all constraints, consented or not to their own death. Without consent, the rite was a crime perpetrated by a group; with consent, it was a suicide.

In the 1980s in India, the partisans of modernity regarded sutteeism as a barbaric ritual and approved its abolition. Feminists, for their part, saw it as the remnant of a patriarchal order that had to be eradicated. They rightly denounced rape, infanticide, arranged marriage, inequality, in short, all the injustices of which Indian women were victims (these varied, moreover, from state to state). Feminists were thus opposed to the orthodox Hindus who favored the rebirth of the sati, seeing it as an expression of the sublimated identity of women. As for the relativists, they criticized the modernist discourse that had grown out of a colonialist pathology and had proved incapable, in their eyes, of understanding cultural differences and thus of comprehending the rite of the sati.

In 1987, in the northern Indian state of Rajasthan, 18-year-old Roop Kanwar underwent a ritual cremation after eight months of marriage to a young man under treatment for depression with psychotropic drugs who had died of complications from an attack of gastro-enteritis. Accused by her parents-in-law of being responsible for their son's death, she followed him onto the funeral pyre under dubious conditions after having tried to flee. Thousands of people were present at this sinister spectacle during which she asked for help and appeared to have been drugged. In the aftermath, she was consecrated as a saint, and the site of the sacrifice drew ever-increasing numbers of pilgrims venerating the fidelity of the women attached to the ancient rituals. This false suicide aroused widespread indignation and, after years of investigations followed by arrests, a law was passed to prevent such practices. The law unequivocally condemned all the tortures inflicted on women, particularly in religious practices.

After a lengthy commentary on a well-known text by Freud on children's fantasies of being beaten,[74] and while devoting many pages to presenting Derrida's theories, Gayatri Spivak composed a "performative sentence" that was supposed to interpret the silence of the subalterns who died on the funeral pyres: "White men are saving brown women from brown men."[75] This statement completely neglected the difference between suicide and crime, between a voluntary act and an act committed under pressure. All that interested Spivak was the meaning that should be attributed to her statement in which a phantasmatic structuralist-Freudian-performative trilogy was brought to the fore: white men, women of color, men of color. In other words, Spivak was trying to pin down the "identity" of the sati rite. To this end, she relied on the story of a young female independentist who had hung herself in 1926 because she had not succeeded in carrying out a mission: the assassination of an enemy. From this tragedy, Spivak concluded that there was a structure according to which subaltern women acquired an identity by simultaneously challenging the colonial order (that of the Whites) and the nationalist religious order, that of the men of color who saw immolation as a heroic act. Finally, she declared, neither colonization nor decolonization had had any impact on the subalterns, who therefore "could not speak."

Spivak had thus "re-Indianized" herself to the extent that she claimed to be giving voice to the subalterns in the language of subalternist theory, but without ever taking a position on the question of the cremation of widows: she was neither for nor against it, since she was interested only in the question of subaltern identity in its dehistoricized essence. In her eyes, the only possible involvement from the standpoint of postcolonial critique lay in challenging the immutable structure of the Western imaginary in its relation to the other. It was with this reasoning that Spivak claimed to be concerned about the disadvantaged. Her book, written in the "obscure language" of identitarian questioning, very quickly became a classic of subalternism; it was translated – not without difficulty, moreover – into many languages. Understandably, it was widely criticized by feminists and progressives alike. In effect, it eliminated any reference to social antagonisms by putting identitarian blocs in their place. More importantly, it attested to a profound disregard for the women who were fighting in their own countries for democratic freedoms that they did not by any means deem "Western-colonized"; indeed, those freedoms were deemed essential to the women's own emancipation.

Dipesh Chakrabarty, he too born in Calcutta, six years after Spivak, was a pure product of the Western culture that he helped shatter. Between self-hatred and valorization of a decentered self, he castigated India's European modernity the better to reinvent his own identitarian positioning. After completing his doctoral work at the university of Canberra, where he was close to Ranajit Guha and his cohort, Chakrabarty was hired as a professor of history at the University of Chicago. His major book, *Provincializing Europe: Postcolonial Thought and Historical Difference*, published in 2000, was phenomenally successful; it too became a classic in

Subaltern Studies.[76] In his acknowledgments, Chakrabarty mentioned around a hundred academics, mostly from the Anglophone universe: Australian, American, Mexican, English, Indian. But he also claimed to be inspired by the works of Marx, Freud, Heidegger, Derrida, Jacques Le Goff, Jean-François Lyotard, and so on, in his articulation of something that was already known and had moreover been spelled out by Samuel Huntington: Europe was no longer the center of the world politically, nor was European history the center of an academic narrative. In reality, however, European categories of thought continued to reign over all university disciplines. Thus Chakrabarty claimed to be helping Europe free itself from its own "Europe-centered thought" so it could better apprehend the modernity of the non-Western nations and the singular histories of the subalterns:

> Provincializing Europe is not a project of rejecting or discarding European thought, nor does it mean advocating some sort of "postcolonial revenge"; European thought is at once both indispensable and inadequate in helping us to think through the experiences of political modernity in non-Western nations, and provincializing Europe becomes the task of exploring how this thought ... may be renewed from and for the margins.[77]

With regard to sutteeism, Chakrabarty, too, adopted a neutral position, refusing to concern himself with the rights of women, which would have marked in his eyes a much too "European" interest. Nor did he emphasize religious cruelty. Finally, to spell out his antihistoricist conception of history, he borrowed the famous remark that Shakespeare's Hamlet made to Horatio after the encounter with his father's ghost – the father who had charged him, let us recall, with the impossible mission of setting the world to rights: "The time is out of joint." In other words, the world confronting Hamlet was disordered, disjointed, "out of joint with itself." Magnificently analyzed by Derrida in *Specters of Marx*, Hamlet's remark to his friend foreshadows the idea that the world of the late twentieth century was disorganized henceforth under an avalanche of spectral visions: according to Derrida, we are the heirs of both Shakespeare and Marx, that is, of Paul Valéry's Europe, so difficult to keep in balance.

From this Derridean commentary, Chakrabarty concluded that, in order to understand the new non-Western world, it was necessary to write a history based on the assumption "that historical time is not integral" and by that token not bound by the historical time proper to European history.[78] He also took inspiration from Marx's thought, putting it into conversation with Heidegger's in order to criticize the historicism of the former via the antimodernism of the latter. In other words, the Marxist myth of the class struggle and its resolution through the victory of the proletariat had to be corrected by the myth of the return to the Black Forest, a symbol of the Heideggerian hatred of industrial civilization. Neither progress nor primitivism: such was the choice – or rather, the non-choice – of that strange post-Marxist Derrideanist-deconstructed Heideggerianism advanced by Chakrabarty with the aim of transforming Europe into a decentered province of the world.[79]

After Spivak had made a myth of a fantasized subaltern woman, Chakrabarty claimed for his part to be provincializing Europe with the help of concepts drawn from the "European imperialism" in which he was steeped. "We can talk of provincializing [European thought]," he said, "only in an anticolonial spirit of gratitude."[80] The problem is that all these prophetic discourses paid scant attention to the *real* situation of the "subalterns," ignoring their rebellions, their words, their democratic demands, their aspiration to freedom, their determination to escape an abominable state of servitude. Moreover, these discourses all appeared to have forgotten that Europe had produced its own anticolonialist thinking and could not be reduced to the atrocities of imperialism. Haunted by the infinite specter of their unlocatable identity, the subalternists became, by virtue of sophisticated theorizing, the worst advocates of the postcolonial critique they thought they were defending. For, as they themselves affirmed, it so happened that they were speaking on a non-European stage, but certainly not without knowing that the Europe they simultaneously hated and idolized was not the Europe whose centrality they were purporting to deconstruct after having borrowed from it the best it had to offer.

All these studies were severely criticized, by excellent specialists in structuralism, Marxism, and the study of literary texts, moreover – that is, by the academic intellectual left exasperated by such anomalies. In a superbly written article published in 1999, for example, Terry Eagleton denounced their obscurantism and their deliberately opaque style.[81] He explained in particular that that movement, at once sad and monolithic, expressed the subjective disorientation experienced by a generation that had been frightened by a consumerist West and had subscribed to a radicalized cult of marginality so as to avoid any progressivist commitment. Needless to say, Eagleton was violently attacked in turn, showing in any case how ridiculous it is to believe, as many in France do, that all the identitarian evil comes from Anglo-American campuses.

Another pure product of so-called Western thought, Homi Bhabha, born in Bombay, taught in London before moving to the United States where he now teaches English literature at Harvard. An eminent figure in postcolonial studies, he went even further in the apologia of identitarian rhetoric by relying on Fanon's work – especially *Black Skin, White Masks* – but also on Lacan's rereading of Freud, on the work of V. S. Naipaul, an English writer born in Trinidad into a family of Hindu background, and also, of course, on Joseph Conrad's *Heart of Darkness*.

In publishing *The Location of Culture* in 1994, a book that was to be greeted as a masterpiece and widely translated, Bhabha intended first of all, as a good identitarian researcher, to talk about himself and his childhood in a Parsi family from the Persian Zoroastrian minority: "'Bombay' Hindustani, 'Parsi' Gujurati, mongrel Marathi, all held in a suspension of Welsh-missionary-accented English peppered with an Anglo-Indian *patois* that was sometimes cast aside for American slang picked up from the movies or popular music."[82] And also: "I'm a ..." "Who am I? What am I?" Who are the One and the Other? This question returns obsessively in Bhabha's discourse: utterances made of neologisms, words displayed as signifiers and intended to get the Western world to understand that "there is a conspiracy of silence around the colonial truth, whatever that might be."[83]

Bhabha was undoubtedly the most radical of the authors engaged in the manipulation of obscure language. Seeking to escape the colonial stereotype, he inscribed in the English language itself a number of idioms that were intended to express the stylistic differences among formerly colonized speakers: the opposite of the Derridean idea of the monolinguism of the other. Thus he overturned denominations: "otherness" instead of alterity, "cultural difference" instead of diversity of cultures, "emplacement" instead of place, desiring to write *with the other* instead of appropriating the language of the other for oneself, and so on. The result was an infinite multiplication of new terms (interstices, third space, ambivalence), suffixes and prefixes (transculturation, transidentity); pride of place goes to the word "hybridity." It is easy to understand why his translators found themselves tearing their hair.[84]

Bhabha borrowed the notion of hybridity from Latin American writers, who come from a continent that is hybrid par excellence, a place of all possible intermixings (Whites, Blacks, Native Americans, Indians, Europeans, Asians, Caribbeans, and so on). In 1933, the renowned sociologist Gilberto Freyre had offered an excellent analysis of this phenomenon in his celebrated book *The Masters and* the *Slaves*, demonstrating that Brazil offered two antagonistic faces in the guise of a rigid organization inherited from colonization.[85] On one side, there was the humanist ideal of a positivist Church, which had inspired the great reformers throughout the twentieth century; on the other, Black culture persisted, blended with White culture owing to the racial mixing of the slaves, masters and their concubines, White men and Black women, but also Black male domestic servants and young White women.

The vindication of hybridity is also found in Oswald de Andrade's "Cannibalist Manifesto."[86] Andrade, a poet, was the founder of Brazilian modernism; his manifesto, published in 1928, echoed André Breton's 1924 *Manifesto of Surrealism*.[87] "Cannibalism alone unites us," Andrade declared, asserting that all culture came from a continuous process of incorporation of the language of the other. "Tupi or not tupi, that is the question."[88]

However, Homi Bhabha's theory of hybridity had little to do with that sumptuous conception of a baroque hybridity. His interest lay in promoting a "third space," that is, a fuzzy (queer) community in which hybridity would become the terrain of a strategy of subjective resistance, capable of driving away not only the colonial power but also its double, the anticolonialist commitment that Bhabha deemed an accomplice of that same power. He rejected wholesale the Enlightenment, secularism, democracy, and Eurocentrism, while responding in advance to an imaginary adversary who would dare to attack him on his borrowings from the detested European culture: "Before I am accused of bourgeois voluntarism, liberal pragmatism, academicist pluralism [sic], and all the other '-isms' that are freely bandied about by those who take the most severe exception to 'Eurocentric' theoreticism (Derrideanism, Lacanianism, poststructuralism, etc.), I would like to clarify the goals of my opening questions."[89] There follows an interminable litany in prophetic jargon on the new languages of criticism (deconstructionism and the like). Were they "necessarily collusive with the hegemonic role of the West as a power bloc?"[90] Yes and no: they were in collusion, but without really being so, since theory was merely a pastime for the Western elite.

Like Spivak, Bhabha maintained that the true postcolonialist revolution consisted in annihilating the very idea of a historicity of struggles and identities. Under his pen, and always in a convoluted fashion, everything became systemic, structural, immobile: bodies, identities, culture in its essentialized difference. In short, a generalized chameleon. And that is why he attacked the Western progressivists, the Marxists, the anthropologists who proclaimed the diversity of cultures, the liberal academics, whom he accused of encouraging an "endemic racism" in the guise of multiculturalism.

In other words, without ever saying so clearly, he preferred the good old Aunt Jemima colonialism to the anticolonialist left: "As a critique of the left and its enthusiastic espousal of forms of rationalism and modernity, I think that the question to ask is about the left not being able to cope with certain forms of uncertainty and unfixity in the construction of political identity and its programmatic, policy implications."[91] As for Bhabha's reading of Lacan's work, it relied in part on that of Joan Copjec, an academic specializing in cinema studies who represented Lacan as an antihistoricist opposed to Foucault and to Derrida,[92] and in part on the commentary of the Slovenian philosopher Slavoj Žižek. Famous on American campuses, Žižek had transformed Lacan – an enlightened conservative and an anticolonialist – into a sort of Marxist and Hegelian guru with Leninist tendencies.[93] An outspoken critic of Derrida, Butler, gender studies, and postcolonial approaches, Žižek thus served, alongside Copjec and many others, as a major reference for the call to order through which Bhabha, who saw himself as a Lacano-Foucaldo-Derridean, claimed to be "reframing" Fanon, without noticing that Fanon had been a much better reader of Lacan than he himself was.[94] Never before had "obscure language" been pushed to such a degree of extravagance.

Following the whims of an adroit blend of Lacanianism reviewed and corrected by Žižek, a mix of Fanonism flavored with Derridean deconstructionism and Saidean post-Orientalism, Bhabha thus pronounced an indictment against the Western anticolonial left and, of course, without daring to do so directly, against the philosopher who had been its most celebrated representative in the world, Jean-Paul Sartre.

Let us recall that, in *The Wretched of the Earth*, Sartre and Fanon were not in harmony. Sartre, in his commentary, was addressing the colonizers, while Fanon was addressing the future decolonized peoples, warning them against the neocolonialist bourgeois regimes in post-independence Africa. Hence the dichotomy between two texts that were nevertheless read together for years as an anticolonialist manifesto, so much so that it was impossible to separate them. In his preface, Bhabha played skillfully on this contradiction, emphasizing that Fanon, at the end of the book, lumped together the two empires of the Cold War period, the United States and the Soviet Union, in contrast to the emerging Third World. Consequently, he insisted that

Fanon's book should be read on its own from then on, detached from its preface, as a manifesto of postcolonial thought. In addition, he cited a famous text by Hannah Arendt, written in 1970, in which the philosopher analyzed the role of violence in history, emphasizing that violence destroyed politics. To be sure, she criticized Fanon on this point, but only the better to attack Sartre, whose arguments diverged from those of the author of *The Wretched of the Earth*.[95]

With great subtlety, Bhabha thus embarked, on the one hand, on the project of "de-Westernizing" Fanon's work, and on the other, on a muted dismissal of Sartre's preface, by invoking Arendt's critique. According to Arendt, violence is always a destruction of politics, whereas in Sartre violence is conceived as a necessity and a reinvention of the self. Playing the card of a Fanon unencumbered by Sartre, Bhabha made Fanon a non-Sartrean and quasi-Arendtian spokesman for postcolonial studies. He was obviously unable to erase the preface, which would have been an act of censure, so he took advantage of the English translation of the book to invent a new Fanon capable of serving, posthumously, the interests of the victims rather than the cause of the anticolonialists as represented by Sartre.[96] On the strength of his own representation, Bhabha revived Fanon's work in a new context. But why did Bhabha seek to erase Sartre rather than situate himself in the aftermath? This is the question raised by the often obscure "interpretations" that always prefer to suppress, set aside, or eliminate anything troublesome – the weight of history – instead of coming to grips with the principle of historicity.

In France, Homi Bhabha's work flourished quite spectacularly within the department of Psychoanalytic Studies on the Paris 7 Diderot campus, an immense Freudian bastion founded in 1971 and whose existence was already under threat by advocates of the cognitive sciences. Convinced that the introduction of gender studies would make it possible to renew the old Freudian edifice and to fight simultaneously against the reactionary positions of the French psychoanalysts – who were hostile to homosexuals – and against the proponents of behavioral therapies, Laurie Laufer, a professor of psychopathology, spent several years (2010–20) in the department developing studies in which a post-Lacanian-Foucauldian concep-tuality was blithely melded with the "obscure language" of queer decolonialism.

We find traces of this in several important colloquia, most notably in one organized by Thamy Ayouch, a deconstructive Lacanian and a subscriber to the theory of hybridity.[97] In his paper, we read:

101

THE SOVEREIGN SELF

If psychoanalysis positions itself, then, as the obverse of Cartesian reason and aims, in its practice of listening, to deconstruct its own imaginary, to what extent does it grasp the ethnocentricity of its own tools? Does it not perpetuate certain implicit tenets of Western reason in defining itself in opposition to that reason? Conversely, and as the use Homi Bhabha makes of it shows, what is psychoanalysis capable of bringing to thinking about coloniality and about the decentering of "the West"? ... What does the consideration of gender and coloniality bring to psychoanalysis, in its conception of the relations of minorization and alterization?[98]

It is not surprising that, in this context, some 80 psychoanalysts – and not the least important – rose up in the name of Enlightenment universalism against the communitarian hold over decolonial thought in French universities. They were quickly followed, in a subsequent colloquium, by another collective of about a hundred scholars on the other side who were concerned, by contrast, with developing innovative studies capable of "decolonizing the Freudian teaching" that had been ravaged by an intolerable paternalistic centralism. The problem is that no one in this quarrel was ever able to show how the revolution in the concepts of gender and queer could put an end to the conservatism of the Freudian community, nor how that new conceptuality would make it possible to decolonize Freud or, on the contrary, to make him more universal.[99]

Having followed these sometimes clownish debates, I am quite prepared to subscribe to the idea that all these theories – hybridity, subalternism, decentering, postcolonialities, and so on – finally do no more than reintroduce the old theses of colonial ethnology[100] with its immutable categories, its psychology of peoples, its binary oppositions between barbarity and civilization, with the difference that the subalterns or the "hybrids" are henceforth elevated to the status of kings of an identitarian kingdom, relegating their old torturers to the trash bins of history: a way of denying to what is called "Western" thought and its actors any participation in the anticolonial struggle. Once again, unfortunate oppressed, mute, and fetishized persons, petrified in a role that is not their own, become the guinea pigs of a theorization that robs them of their desire for emancipation. That thinkers as innovative as Césaire, Foucault, Deleuze, Derrida, Lacan, Said, Fanon, and many others could serve as alibis for such a regression remains one of the great paradoxes of this identitarian folly. But we have not yet come to the end of the spectacle.

Some time later, a veritable crusade was launched against white Western homosexuals, who were accused of having finally obtained rights – the decriminalization of homosexuality, the right to marry, and so on – in democratic countries and thus had been normalized, the better to discriminate, via their Gay Pride, against Muslims, Arabs, Blacks, they too victims of this civilizational nationalism ... It is the American academic Jasbir Puar, inspired, she has said, by the texts of Foucault, Deleuze, Said, and Guattari (yes, those names again), who can be credited with inventing the term "homonationalism" to designate, especially after September 11, the collusion between homosexuality and nationalism. As Puar sees it, this collusion was generated, by the gays, lesbians, and queers who had become de facto representatives of American nationalism and thus responsible, through the recognition of their "sexual exceptionalism," for the tortures inflicted by American soldiers on Iraqi prisoners in the jails of Abu Ghraib. If we are to believe Puar, the terrorist thus tortured was the new figure of queer alterity, a victim of the worst possible discrimination. In other words, from this perspective, the American military torturers were worse than those of Saddam Hussein, since they acted in the name of a country that had granted rights to the newly normalized sexual minorities.[101] Hence the appearance of a new neologism, "pinkwashing," a portmanteau word created on the model of "whitewashing" to describe the attempt by a nation-state or group to advocate exemplary treatment in favor of homosexuals or LGBTQIA+ persons in order to feign a progressivism designed to mask other much more serious assaults on human rights.

At this stage, the study of identitarian representations resembles a bottomless pit, since it leads those who see themselves as its adherents to reproduce discriminations that they had once fought against, and to invent categories destined to create opposing camps according to the modalities of a culture of perpetual denunciation, with each camp catalogued in terms of increasingly narrow identities.

— 5 —

THE LABYRINTH OF INTERSECTIONALITY

Memories in dispute

In late twentieth-century France, historians of colonialism and anticolonialist militants had become so active in intellectual and academic life – most notably from Sartre to Vidal-Naquet and all their heirs – that it took some time for postcolonial and then decolonial studies to emerge. As for gender studies, they were already prospering in departments of history, sociology, and philosophy. In civil society, the secular republican tradition was an additional obstacle to the flourishing of the exacerbated identity politics that were reaching the country from the Anglophone world.

Nevertheless, starting in the 2000s, which saw radical Islam increasing in strength, a dangerous fracture came to light in French civil society: the children of Islamic immigrants were encouraged to embrace an identity-based hope originating in religious obscurantism and a defense of murder. The historian Pascal Blanchard, the founder of an association focused on the study of contemporary African history (ACHAC), called this rupture the "colonial fracture." Blanchard and his group clung not to the history of colonialism and anticolonialism as such but rather to their public representations, referring for example to "human zoos," the ethnic spectacles through which the French colonial empire had ensured its military, ideological, and sexual domination over the bodies of the victims of colonization, at fairs and exhibitions or in photographs and films.[1]

In introducing the notion of colonial fracture in 2005, Blanchard and those working with him insisted that France continued to be haunted by a colonial past that it kept on repressing, but that

104

resurfaced regularly through crises in the suburbs, urban violence, and the difficulty of integrating certain immigrant communities into the French republican system.[2] So there was indeed an identitarian break of a postcolonial nature at the heart of civil society. The contemporary situation, according to the authors, was not a perfect reproduction of the colonial period but rather the fruit of a return of the colonial repressed, in the Freudian sense, a return that went well beyond ordinary class conflicts.

Such theses, popularized by numerous debates in the media, were mocked by the more classical historians for their failure to conform to a rigorous historiographical approach. And yet they announced the emergence of a fracture that was no less "identitarian" than it was "colonial," since it bore upon the specularization of the self and of alterity in the construction of Western identity. Blanchard was attacked by extremists on all sides: by those nostalgic for the colonial era, by the Indigènes de la Republique,[3] and by influential polemicists who saw him as a supporter of decolonialism.[4] Nevertheless, like his friend Benjamin Stora, he kept on insisting that the Republic ought to acknowledge the idea that history as memory could be plural. He also emphasized that, if the heirs of formerly colonized peoples did not refer to the same memory-based narratives as the children of those who had served in the French army, they still shared in the same history.[5] Let us add that the children of anticolonialist parents were in the same situation: they attended republican schools without sharing the same values as those whose parents had supported French Algeria.

In reaction to this idea of "colonial fracture," the various "studies" came together through the lens of intersectionality, within a global movement of rebellion against a dominating power. Their partisans aimed, as we have seen, to deconstruct race and sex in order to substitute a new classificational vocabulary for the old definitions. From this perspective, all forms of patriarchal oppression had to be understood de facto as the expression of a colonizing, racialist, discriminatory attitude. Thus it had become urgent to construct a "gendered postcoloniality." In the words of Malek Bouyahia, a specialist in subaltern, postcolonial, and gender studies who pursued his own studies at Université Paris-8, "[g]ender and sexuality have often been the poor relations of postcolonial criticism. However, studies led by postcolonial feminists contribute to the understanding of masculinity and whiteness as foundations of imperial formations – which does not mean, of course, that gender relations operate in the same way everywhere."[6]

Between 2000 and 2015, this vocabulary began to take hold in France in departments of gender studies and postcolonial studies. The terms were supposed to revive or even renovate or revolutionize the works of great French thinkers such as Derrida, Lacan, Deleuze, Foucault, and Fanon, as if their works – which had been translated, carefully studied, and taught for over 20 years on American university campuses – had been eclipsed.

After all the prefixes – trans-, hetero-, homo-, inter-, post-, and so on – it was the turn of suffixes to be imposed at the heart of an ever more decentered vision of a West that had to be "de-Occidentalized." Hence the systematization of phobias. Originally, the suffix "-phobe" simply indicated someone with an irrational aversion to something, as opposed to "-phile." In that pairing, we find terms that had been in use for a long time, for example Francophile vs. Francophobe, Anglophile vs. Anglophobe, Judeophile vs. Judeophobe, and so on. But the pairing in the strong sense comes from the vocabulary of psychiatry, since there the word "phobia" designates a real pathology, a classification that has grown in size in each successive version of the *DSM*: there are now some 500 varieties, from agoraphobia to zoophobia. Certain pairings do not constitute true oppositions, moreover: for example, pedophilia is a major perversion, while pedophobia is a "repulsion toward children," and falls in the category of simple phobias. It is on this muddled list straight from the *DSM*, however, that the adherents to identity politics draw in order to identify all the enemies apt to discriminate against them or offend them: homophobes, transphobes, Negrophobes, nanophobes (repelled by dwarfs), Judeophobes, lesbophobes, grossophobes (repelled by overweight people), Christianophobes, people with phobias against poor people, Siamese twins, residents of the suburbs or the inner cities, and so on.

Thus the classifications of psychiatry have re-emerged in an unexpected way as substitutes for what is more simply called anti-Semitism, racism, sexism, rejection of otherness or abnormality; these terms can easily cover the other discriminations against "everything that is not oneself," "everything that one is not"[7] – not to mention the multiple neologisms such as "blackitude," "whititude," or "whitriarchy" (in French, *blantriarcat*: the term was created by "racialized" feminist associations to denounce patriarchal white supremacy). Hence the appearance in certain unintentionally humorous videos of regal identitarian self-representations: "I am transgender, intersectional with a queer-decolonial bent, ethnically Afro-Hispanic, racialized. I am discriminated against by people who

THE LABYRINTH OF INTERSECTIONALITY

are cisgendered, transphobic, lesbophobic, grossophobic, pooro-phobic, armed with white paternalist-Westernist-heteronormism, as well as by the femonationalism and the homonationalism of whites who have become heteronormalized while becoming hostile to subalternized blacks." And so on.

While the list of new "phobias" is interminable, the neologism "Islamophobia" has to be granted a special place in this configuration. It is constantly mobilized in the rhetoric used by the left against those seen as defaming Islam, insofar as such defamation is assimilated to a form of racism, whereas no breach of "the rights of God" is actionable today in most democratic countries. In France even more than elsewhere, no law either punishes or encourages blasphemy; only insults and defamations addressed toward persons or groups on the basis of their religious affiliations are penalized. As for the republican model of secularism, it is designed as much to separate the state from religion as to guarantee freedom of worship.

As for the term *islamo-gauchisme* (Islamo-leftism), it is hardly any better. Massively brandished in France by the right against the left, it targets "enemies" grouped in a vast invasive nebula made up of anti-Semites, leftists, ecologists, Trotskyites, Communists, anti-Zionists, socialists, *insoumis* (unbowed), decolonialists or postcolonialists, sociologists (preferably anticolonialist academics). In the eyes of their adversaries, members of this group constitute a vast army installed in the land of Voltaire and capable of infiltrating the institutions of the Republic thanks to their Sartrean, deconstructivist, or Foucauldian accomplices, armed with a set of concepts forged on American campuses. Who could possibly believe that the insulting use of the expression "Islamo-leftism" – like that of "Islamophobia" – could serve to elevate the debate? Things must be called by their name: these madmen purporting to act in God's name who assassinate priests, Jews, caricaturists, writers, professors, and many others, are terrorists and criminals. And all those who support them become their accomplices.

In the last analysis, the two neologisms (Islamophobia and Islamo-leftism) used as antonyms allow those who use them to avoid the rational analysis of a complex situation and to encourage the most extreme postures.[8] Moreover, we must keep in mind the fact that they are connected with a long tradition of denunciation. We should recall that the expression "Judeo-Bolshevism" served in the early twentieth century to suggest that Communists were secretly controlled by Jewish organizations eager to impose their domination on the countries of the West. And similarly, the expression "Hitlero-Trotskyitism"

107

authorized Stalinists to insult Trotsky's supporters by treating them as allies of Nazism. To designate radical Islam as a politico-religious identitarian movement, it is preferable to speak of Salafism and jihadism, the murderous tendencies within Islam that advocate a planetary holy war and the institution of a worldwide obscurantist dictatorship aiming to use terror to eradicate civil liberties, including freedom of speech, freedom of conscience, freedom to teach reason, science, literature, and even religion.[9]

In 2005, the debate over the history of French colonialism took a new turn, in a context of crisis, just as studies in gender and postcoloniality imported from American campuses were spreading in the French university world. It is important to stress the degree to which these studies were, and remain, in the minority; this accounts for the fierce activism that has surrounded them.[10] The vast majority of studies that focused on colonialism or feminism (sex and gender), which were flourishing in France well before the beginning of the identitarian drift, as we have seen, did not subscribe to any such radicality.

But when identitarian quarrels became a political issue opposing right and left in France, all those studies, which had previously remained confined to the academic world, became targets in a media-fueled political battle set off against a background of spreading radical Islam and riots in suburbs that had become ghettos, that is, sites for recruiting adolescents from immigrant communities who could be enticed to join the jihad.

That year, the notions and problematics emerging from the various "studies" were thrust onto the public stage by a debate over the historical memory of France's colonial history. Two years later, in 2007, these notions and problematics were back on the docket in the wake of Nicolas Sarkozy's initiative to redefine, under his presidential mandate, the country's "national identity" in opposition to the communitarian threat. I hardly need recall that the national identity invoked here had little to do with Fernand Braudel's definition of the identity of France. In reality, it was a matter of defending purported "values" where different "roots" came together pell-mell: Christian civilization, Cartesian rationality, Enlightenment, secularism – the entire set of values deemed incompatible with Islam.

As for gender studies, rebaptized "gender theory," they were mocked in 2012 by all those who opposed the law on homosexual marriage initiated by François Hollande when he was elected to the presidency. An outpouring of horrors ensued. On January 13, 2013, representatives of the far right and the hard right came together in a large coalition, all tendencies converging: an antigay faction relying on Catholic integralism,[11] old warriors in the quarrel, former members of the Defense Union Group, partisans of Robert Faurisson, Alain Soral, Marc-Édouard Nabe, and other illuminati offered a thundering spectacle dominated by the expression of hatred toward elites, intellectuals, women, foreigners, immigrants, cosmopolitan Europe, homosexuals, communists, socialists, and finally Jews, all this anchored in the conviction that the traditional family was dying, that the nation was being ridiculed, that public schools were on their deathbeds, that abortion threatened to become a widespread practice with the predictable demographic consequences, and that anarchy based on a supposed generalized abolition of the difference between the sexes was triumphant. "The mamas and the papas in the street are being mowed down, marriage is being defended ... Taubira is toast, families are in the street."[12] Or even: "Everyone is born from a man and a woman!"

All the theses on gender and postcoloniality that had been developed in the inner circle of specialized university exchanges then came down into the streets in France, dividing the right and the left alike; the left split into two camps, one claiming to be more republican and identitarian, the other more democratic and multiculturalist; each, in any case, took the other as its target. This quarrel gave rise to a debate over the celebration of the centenary of the 1905 law on the separation of Church and State: in reality, it was a debate about the conditions for accommodating Islam, which had become the second religion in France and was proving resistant to the model of republican secularism. One faction held that secularism ought to stand firm and work to reinforce the Republic's power to forbid any manifestation of religious identity; the other held that the Republic ought to become "more inclusive" and more tolerant. The debate was all the more disastrous in that French-style secularism, unique in the world, presupposed both firmness and inclusion, both neutrality toward religions and a guarantee to believers that they could practice their faith in complete freedom. Either secularism is intact and does not need to be qualified by any adjective whatsoever (hard, soft, open, closed, and so on), or it is tarnished and needs to be defended. One is secular or not, without qualification. Contrary to appearances and to peremptory affirmations, it turns out, moreover, that the famous French model of republican secularism is functioning correctly. A massive survey carried out by the Observatoire de la laïcité (a commission charged with advising the government on the respect and promotion of the principle of secularism) shows in fact

THE SOVEREIGN SELF

that in 2020 the persons who had abandoned the Muslim religion were twice as numerous as those who had adopted it. This would seem to show that withdrawal into the identitarian values of radical Islam may be a symptom of self-defense against the reality of a gradual secularization of the Muslim religion.[13]

The two factions on the left will never succeed in uniting around this question; thus they are condemned to keep on despising each other. The cleavage became all the more damaging because it was amplified by Manuel Valls between 2012 and 2016. First serving as Interior Minister under François Hollande's presidency, and then as Prime Minister, Valls militated in favor of the historic separation between a "bad left," characterized as Islamo-leftist, anti-Zionist, antiracist, racialized, and a "good left," blind, by choice, to the nationalist tilt of the identitarians on the right. By brandishing the accusation of Islamo-leftism and anti-Zionism against part of its own camp, this "good left" was turning a blind eye to another tragedy: that of the nationalist and religious evolution among a portion of the Jews of the Diaspora, who were being persecuted and assassinated by Islamists and had become increasingly sensitive to the appeals of the successive Israeli administrations – and in particular that of Benjamin Netanyahu. Those Jews were constantly being urged to make their *Aliyah*, on the grounds that France would never again be their country but would belong rather to Islam. Such an approach could well produce the worst of the worst where identitarianism is concerned: anti-Semitic Arabs on one side, more and more fascinated by the drift toward "legalitarian" Islam, and racist Jews on the other, constantly invoking a Zionism that, in its initial form, was fast disappearing. As Charles Enderlin so rightly reminds us: "It is the right of any Jews to declare themselves non-Zionists, or even anti-Zionist, and to reject the idea that a Jew has the right to become Israeli by immigrating to Israel. This is a political position that has nothing to do with the anti-Zionism of the jihadists and the identitarians, an anti-Zionism that is nothing but anti-Jewish hatred."[14] It must be reiterated here: the struggle against racism, obliterated by the question of Islam, should never be separated from the battle against anti-Semitism.

On the French right, then, between 2005 and 2012, following an alleged conspiracy fomented by the supporters of "gender theory," one saw the emergence of a revalorized nationalism based on the cult of an immutable familial order that was supposedly threatened by "deconstruction," by pedophiles, homosexuals, indigenists, and degenerate Americanized thinkers (Foucault, Derrida, Deleuze, and

THE LABYRINTH OF INTERSECTIONALITY

so on); it was during this period that people were beginning to forget – on the right and on the left alike – that, if France had been a colonialist nation, it was also one of the countries in which the anticolonialist movement had been most powerful. Sartre was thus more or less relegated to the garbage heap of history, both by the right and by a certain left, along with his defense of the Negro and the memory of his fight against racism and anti-Semitism. From this point on, the question of what history was to be remembered was on the agenda.

Eleven years after the adoption of the July 1990 Gayssot law, which extended the 1997 law against racism and anti-Semitism by creating the crime of negationism (Holocaust denial), several declarations inscribing the memory of historical events had been adopted by the National Assembly. The first, dated January 29, 2001, recognized the existence of the Armenian genocide committed by the Turks (1915). The second, known as the "Taubira law," adopted on May 21, 2001, recognized the slave trade and slavery as crimes against humanity; the third, known as the "Mekachera law," dated February 23, 2005 (it had been initiated in 2003 by Philippe Douste-Blazy), "expressed the gratitude of the Nation for the work accomplished in the former French departments (Algeria, Morocco, Tunisia, Indochina)." It stipulated, moreover, that school curricula had an obligation to acknowledge the positive role of the French presence overseas, and to grant "to the history and the sacrifices of the combatants of the French army originating from these territories the eminent place to which they have a right."[15]

These declarations aroused, for good reason, the anger of a majority of French historians – from Pierre Nora and Jean-Pierre Vernant to Pierre Vidal-Naquet; these scholars published a petition emphasizing that history is neither memory nor an object of law and that, in a democracy worthy of the name, the State should not govern the profession of historians. They thus demanded the abrogation of the three laws in question.[16]

However, the three more recent declarations were not identical to the Gayssot law,[17] since they did not call for any sanctions and left historians entirely free to discuss the conditions of the Armenian genocide and the characteristics of the slave trade, which was not reducible to the trans-Atlantic trade. As for the third of these proclamations, it was quite simply ridiculous, in that it claimed to impose a national narrative straight out of "Y'a bon Banania."[18] Line 2 of its article 4 concerning school curricula was withdrawn in 2006. It was violently criticized by other historians, most notably Gérard Noiriel

111

and Gilles Manceron. The protest at least made it possible to end the spiral of memory-oriented declarations initiated by the representatives of various political parties.

The fact remains, nevertheless, that competing memories had taken shape in a lasting way in the French public arena, accentuating all the identitarian claims, and especially the detestable notion of "repentance" – a notion quite different from the need for a State worthy of its status to recognize the past crimes with which it had been associated, to open its archives, to celebrate or bring to light the victims whose histories had been concealed.

For how can the guilty parties be identified when a criminal enterprise has been spread over several centuries? Must the descendants of the colonizers be condemned? Am I responsible for crimes committed in Tierre del Fuego in the mid-nineteenth century by my remote ancestor Julius Popper, a Romanian Jew known to have massacred Selk'nam Indians? Must all traces of the past be eradicated by degrading the statues, buildings, or works of art that were created by the colonizers or belonged to them? Must one censure, ban, or reinterpret art works, books, plays, and films following the dictates of a newly constructed identitarian vulgate: gendered, non-gendered, queer, decolonial, racialized? And who is to decide about what? Who will choose to destroy what? The State, the suffering subjects, the angry mobs? Who will denounce whom?

As early as 1952, Frantz Fanon had rejected all ideas of this sort: "Am I going to ask the contemporary white man to answer for the slave-ships of the seventeenth century? ... I am not the slave of the Slavery that dehumanized my ancestors."[19] Aimé Césaire had also taken a stand:

> It is already very important that Europe has come to acknowledge the reality of the black slave trade, traffic in human beings that constitutes a crime. But I am not so much in favor of repentance or reparations. There is even, in my opinion, a danger in this idea of reparations. I would not want to see that one fine day Europe says: "All right then, here's the cash, or a check; let's say no more about it!" There is no possible reparation for something that is so irreparable and unquantifiable. The fact remains that the nations responsible for the black slave trade must become aware that they have a duty to aid those countries that they helped plunge into poverty. From there to putting a price tag on that crime against humanity.[20]

Jacques Derrida said the same thing, in 2004, in his vast reflection on the question of pardon. "Every time pardon is at the service of an aim, be it noble and spiritual (reparation or redemption, reconciliation, salvation), every time it tends to re-establish a form of normalcy (social, national, political, psychological) through a work of mourning, through some therapy or ecology of memory, then 'pardon' is not pure – nor its concept."[21] As for Benjamin Stora, the author of a large body of work on the colonial question and immigration, he has persistently reminded readers that the identity of France does not lie in the history of the dissemination of various identities but rather in the history of a reflection on shared memories.

> What seems of capital importance to me is the transmission of the memory of the anticolonial struggles. Yet, unfortunately, we are witnessing a sort of effacement of the memory of those who have not accepted the history of colonization. Some French politicians stood in opposition, from the nineteenth century until political independence [of the colonies] was achieved. But this was also true of great intellectuals such as Jean-Paul Sartre, Simone de Beauvoir, Henri Alleg, and Paul Ricoeur, and also the Communist Party militants who fought against the war in Indochina, and republican figures such as Clemenceau, Catholic intellectuals such as André Mandouze or Pierre-Henri Simon, leaders of Jewish or Muslim communities ... There is a memory that must be preserved and transmitted to the young generations. If *this memory of refusal* of what that period was like is not transmitted, we are left with the feeling of a homogeneous France that has accepted the principles of colonization from time immemorial.[22]

This was obviously not the position of the founders of a new identitarian movement who, under the leadership of Houria Bouteldja and Sadri Khiari, launched an appeal in January 2005, designating themselves as the "Indigenous of the Republic."[23] They called for a memorial march to take place on May 8 of that year, the 60th anniversary of the Sétif uprising, which had been crushed in a bloodbath. This was not an anodyne choice, since it implied that the republican regime of the 2000s was beholden to a colonial statism comparable to that of the Third Republic. It was in 1881, under the administration of Jules Ferry, that the famous Code de l'Indigénat had been instituted; this regime of governmental sanctions applying to colonial subjects was abrogated on December 12, 1945. Designating oneself as "indigenous," for a French citizen in 2005, amounted to affirming that one was subject to a civil statute authorizing the seizure of property, arbitrary imprisonment, and disciplinary measures with no possible legal recourse.

In short, the founders of the movement felt themselves to be, according to the credo of postcolonialism, the victims of an imaginary "colonial continuum" that had nothing to do with their actual situation, nor with the real racial discriminations of which they were indeed victims in France. Insofar as this collective had all the reasons in the world to create a new antiracist movement, to that same extent it placed itself in a senseless situation by claiming that France remained a colonial state, based on a so-called "systemic" – that is, immutable – racism.

"We are the Indigenous of the Republic": this "we" signified that it was indeed a matter of communitarian separation, and thus of affirming the definition of an "indigenist identity" reconstructed according to a hierarchy of "ethnicities" and thus "racialized." The petition brought together militants from all sides who, categorically refusing any theorization whatsoever of the class struggle, were tacitly reintroducing a politics of race. To be sure, it was no longer a question of claiming old-style biological racialism, but rather of affirming that race did indeed exist. For the Indigenists, race became an identity marker at the heart of which one could define oneself as belonging to the community: "As capital produces classes, as patriarchy produces genders, so European-worldwide colonialism produces races." Consequently, it was necessary to set the "racialized" community in opposition to the civic racialization instituted by the Republic.

By the same token, all the principles of secularism were ridiculed as signs of colonial barbarity. The indigenous militants thus rejected the law of March 15, 2004, that banned religious symbols in schools, deeming this law the perpetuation of a colonialist undertaking. In addition, they vaunted the merits of a neofeminism based on the loyalty of Arab women toward their men – fathers, spouses, and brothers, men who were themselves victims of the colonial phenomenon and under pressure to bring the neofeminists back to religious obscurantism. Without ever concerning themselves with the fate of the women of the Arab world who, throughout the world, were rejecting the mandatory wearing of headscarves, or *enfoulardisation*,[24] they denounced white, Western, oppressive or "civilizational" feminism, "civilizational" being the term used by Françoise Vergès, a political scientist henceforth converted to the new wave of decolonialism. Carried away by her decolonial faith, Vergès accused Gisèle Halimi and Simone de Beauvoir of representing an unconscious colonialism. She reproached the former for having been the attorney for Djamila Boupacha, a militant of the

THE LABYRINTH OF INTERSECTIONALITY

FLN arrested and viciously tortured by the French army in 1960, and she reproached the latter for having created a support committee for the young woman by mobilizing the entire French anticolonialist intelligentsia, in particular Louis Aragon, Geneviève de Gaulle, Aimé Césaire, and Germaine Tillion.[25]

This was how Françoise Vergès undertook to rewrite the history of French anticolonialism as a partisan of French Algeria might have done. Worse still, she maintained that Beauvoir and Halimi had manipulated Boupacha, a poor Algerian militant, to serve the interests of a white anticolonialism that was, as Vergès saw it, nothing but a grotesque figure of colonialism.[26] She denounced French feminist culture as a whole, renouncing her own history in the process. She had in fact been an influential feminist herself; she had been a long-time member of the group "Psychanalyse et politique" founded by Antoinette Fouque. As Vergès wrote in 2019:

> Racialized women are accepted in the ranks of civilizational feminists provided that they adhere to the Western interpretation of the rights of women. From the perspective of their ideology, the feminists of the global South remain unassimilable, for they demonstrate the impossibility of resolving, in terms of integration, parity, and diversity, the contradictions produced by imperialism and capitalism. Counterrevolutionary feminism then takes the form of femonationalism, femoimperialism, femofascism or marketplace feminism.[27]

When I met Françoise Vergès in Berkeley in 1996, she was a respected historian, a friend of Aimé Césaire, a daughter of the brilliant bourgeois communist intellectuals Paul Vergès and Laurence Deroin, open to any innovative work and raised in the purest tradition of critical thinking.[28] There was no apparent reason to suppose that one day she would let herself be won over by such fanaticism, to the point of seeing herself as a victim of "white ferocity" and of the "whitriarchy."

So after "homonationalism" (homosexuals normalized), here is "femonationalism," a term invented by the English sociologist Sara R. Farris to define the European feminists, heirs of Simone de Beauvoir (Élisabeth Badinter, Alice Schwarzer, and many others) whom the author deems neoliberal, civilizational, universalist, Islamophobic, reactionary, guilty not only of neglecting the unfortunate subalterns of color overexploited by savage capitalism (female employees, street sweepers, house cleaners, cash register operators, and so on), but also guilty of mistreating Muslim men, of stigmatizing them as potential rapists. These femonationals would in the last analysis simply be accomplices of an anti-Arab racism seeking to promote the idea that the migrants faced with drowning in the Mediterranean would be, ontologically, less rapist than their Western counterparts from the "whitriarchy." These women can thus be seen as degrading migrant communities while claiming to emancipate them from their backward cultures.[29]

In addition, the Indigenes of the Republic tried to connect their grievances as "victims of the Republic" with the grievances of Palestinians, who had been robbed of their territory. This authorized the Indigenes to characterize anyone who dared criticize the Muslim religion as "Islamophobic." From this perspective, it became imperative to enlist in a "non-Islamophobic" – that is, Islamist – movement, the better to support the Palestinians' claims.

This radicality only grew more pronounced over the years.[30] The indigenists and their allies did not rely on the obscure language used by the subalternist academics; instead, they adopted a more or less classic militant style generously sprinkled with neologisms. But their texts, often written in inclusive language, were studded with stereotypical depictions of immigrants, the young people of the suburbs, the undocumented, and the abuses committed by the white enemy that was constantly seeking to hide the truth. The term "as," or "in the capacity of," appears constantly in their texts, to emphasize the extent to which the Republic stigmatized Arabs, Blacks, Muslims, the formerly colonized, in the name of an alleged universalism grounded in integration, the source of all the indignities. As for the two founders of the movement, Sadri Khiari and Houra Bouteldja, they asserted that their principal adversaries were not only the antiracist movements on the left but also the LGBTQIA+ movements, whose adherents had acquired rights and had thus been normalized. In this way the indigenous identitarians rejected the gendered, queer, and trans identitarians, viewing them as accomplices of whiteness. We are back in the infernal spiral of the identitarian drift discussed in the previous chapter.

Referring to writings by Joseph Massad, a professor at Columbia who was well known on Anglophone campuses for the violence of his anti-West discourse, Sadri Khiari took up an old thematics according to which the West invented binary psychiatric categories of sexuality: normal (heterosexuality) on the one side, deviant (homosexuality) on the other. In other words, according to Massad and Khiari, the form of homosexuality known as "Western" does not exist in the Arab and Muslim worlds, where men are content with hugging and kissing without practicing anal penetration. As for hatred of homosexuals (homophobia), it too is viewed as a colonial importation. According to this way of thinking, then, white Western homosexuals compelled Iranian and Egyptian homophiles to work alongside them to create the conditions for an Islamist repression. In this light, homosexuality is not viewed as a universal phenomenon but as a luxury reserved for a colonial elite, and Islamism is the result of mistreatments inflicted by Western homosexuals on the homophiles of the Arab world. And of course, to articulate such absurdities, Massad made use of Foucault and Said.[31]

Like Khiari, an admirer of Massad, Houria Bouteldja went so far as to declare in 2013: "It would be high time, once and for all, to understand that imperialism – in all its forms – treats indigenous populations as savages: at the Gay International, the societies of the South responded by spewing hatred against homosexuals in places where [such hatred] did not exist, or by a reinforcement of homophobia where it already existed."[32] Thus the homophobia of the dominated is viewed as the positive expression of resistance to white "homoracialism" – another neologism – that is translated by an "identitary virilism." To put it more simply, the two founders of the Indigènes de la République Party justified the most savage expression of Islamic hatred toward homosexuality. To top off the expression of this radicality, after the assassination of Jewish children and others by Mohammed Merah in Montauban, Bouteldja declared: "I am Mohamed Merah; what is worse is that it is true."[33]

In an essay published in 2016, a veritable breviary of anti-republican and identitarian indigenism, Bouteldja established a radical separation between those she called the Whites and the Jews on one side (designated by the pronoun "You") and Indigenous popula-tions on the other (called "We," "Us").[34] To this first separation she added a second, to distinguish between the women and the men in the Indigenous category. This classification allowed her to affirm that the Western world was dead, that the soup kitchens (Restos du Coeur) organized by the French actor Coluche were an abomination, that women should henceforth obey the law of their Muslim fathers and brothers, that White colonialists and anticolonialists were all assassins whose negative power had to be eradicated, and finally that Jews had become partisans of an oppressive whiteness while stoking themselves with the Shoah so as to amplify their discrimination against the Palestinians and to affirm their own "Zionist identity." In so doing, they had renounced what was best about them: Yiddish (for the Ashkenazis) and Arabic (for the Sephardi). This approach made it possible to claim that Zionism had never been a movement

THE SOVEREIGN SELF

of emancipation but rather a movement of identitarian nationalism. As for the Jews of the diaspora, Bouteldja depicted them as mere "Zionists" who had capitulated in the face of an apartheid regime, a way of rejecting their Jewish brothers who had been exterminated by the Nazis. In a few chapters, the author thus fabricated a monument of ignorance that conflated hatred for Jews, Whites, Arabs, and Blacks, and especially for herself. She did all this in the name of a "politics of revolutionary love," with herself as the prophet.

The daughter of a family of Algerian immigrants, Bouteldja did not hesitate to pick up the sinister formula of Jean-Marie Le Pen on intrafamilial preference:

> I belong to my family, my clan, my neighborhood, my race; I belong to Algeria, to Islam. I belong to my history and God willing, I will belong to my descendants. "When you marry, in cha Allah, you will say: '*Ana khitt ou oueld ennass hit*' [I am a wall and the son of the people is a wall]. Then, you will belong to your husband."[35]

And she also declared: "I am not exactly white. I am whitened. I am here because I was thrown up by History. I am here because white people were in my country, because they are still there. What am I? *An Indigenous of the Republic*. Above all, I am a victim."[36]

To the vision of a despised emancipation, Bouteldja thus opposed an ego steeped in victimhood and a phantasmatic return to an imaginary Negro-Arab race that no longer had anything to do with the culture of Negritude cherished by Aimé Césaire. In the face of the racism deployed by the Western powers, it was henceforth a matter, for the Indigenes, of inventing a racism of self-esteem, a protective racism advocating "non-racial-mixing," a hierarchic principle according to which "Whites," whoever they might be, ought to be banned from any experience of life with Blacks, since by essence every white person would be a "dominant."

But in what respect would this "racialized" and debiologized racism be liberating? In what way would this "I am myself" differ from the old familiar racism that had served as the matrix for colonialism and thus for the subjugation of non-European peoples – Africans, Arabs, Asians – who were deemed inferior? In claiming to struggle against racism, the Indigenes of the Republic simply renewed its emblems.

I have never thought that it was better to be wrong with Sartre than to be right with Aron. Neither was right or wrong. Sartre was one of the most widely insulted thinkers of the whole twentieth century, along with Simone de Beauvoir, Sigmund Freud, and many others.

118

I truly admire his work and most of his political commitments. Moreover, I also admire Raymond Aron, a theoretician of democracy who devoted fine pages to the sorrow of loss: "To lose friends," he said with reference to his break with Sartre, "is to lose a part of oneself."[37] How could it then be possible to find it tolerable, without batting an eye, that Houria Bouteldja, a self-proclaimed representative of the formerly colonized peoples, should write these words: "'Shoot Sartre! It's not nostalgia for a French Algeria speaking, it's me, an indigenous woman."[38] One could go on indefinitely listing the mad propositions in her book, where the most sinister stereotypes of the hatred of the other and of separation between the races are reiterated ad nauseum: against Black women who should not bring charges against Black rapists, against homosexuals dismissed as "faggots," against Jews, and so on. Added to all this are racist declarations against the identity labeled "White" as opposed to Black identity.[39]

This is where the identitarian demand leads, in its most extreme form: espousing the discourse of what one is claiming to denounce. Wanting to be "racialized," designating oneself as the enemy of the West, of "whiteness," of the Jews suspected of being "whitened by European imperialism" because they had obtained lands in Palestine, is no different from wanting to shoot not only Sartre but also the greatest artisans of the struggles against colonialism, apartheid, and slavery. Will it one day be necessary to "shoot" Fanon, Césaire, Said, Mandela, and Martin Luther King, to rule in favor of the other "identitarians": supremacists, racists, anti-Semites? And why not shoot François Maspero, Fanon's editor, who, referring to the publication of a book by Fanon against which legal charges were brought, wrote that "the cause of the Algerian revolution is also, in France, the cause of democracy."[40]

It is thus surprising to observe that such a discourse could be so solidly supported by collectives of historians, sociologists, or writers, and not the least significant – among them we find the names of Ludivine Bantigny, Annie Ernaux, Isabelle Stengers, and Christine Delphy – who have dared to compare Bouteldja to Said, Césaire, and Fanon: "She expresses with modesty her feeling of humiliation, her shame as a courageous victim of the Whites," and as a representative of a magnificent "politics of revolutionary love."[41] One has to be insane to characterize the criminal call to "Shoot Sartre!" as "superb." Worst of all, the Indigenes and their decolonial and postcolonial allies now present themselves no longer as heirs to the anticolonialism embodied by Sartre, Said, Césaire, Vidal-Naquet,

Maspero, Fanon, Henri Alleg, Maurice Audin and many others, but as the only true anticolonialists worthy of the name.

In one chapter of her book, Houria Bouteldja recounts a memory of her adolescence. On the occasion of a school trip to New York, she had insisted that her parents, who accompanied her to the airport, remain hidden from her teachers and classmates: "I was ashamed of them. They looked too poor and too much like immigrants, with their Arab faces, as they proudly watched me fly off to the country of Uncle Sam. They did not protest. They hid, and I naively believed that they had taken it all in." And she added:

> "Arabs are the last race after toads," my father would say. A phrase he must have heard on a construction site and made his own through the conviction of the colonized ... I live in France. I live in the West. I am white. Nothing can absolve me. I hate the white good conscience. I curse it. It sits on the Right's left, at the heart of social democracy.[42]

The memories associated with the humiliation experienced by parents or children are always instructive, and I know no one who has not experienced, at least once in a lifetime, a feeling of guilt, either because heroic parents managed to resist oppression and the children were crushed, feeling unable to measure up, or on the contrary because the parents had been submissive, cowardly, or worse – sex offenders, violent, no holds barred ... All literature is woven of such grueling memories in which confessions are mixed with tears. All collective memories and all mythologies include such origin stories. But in Bouteldja's confessions, it is the adolescent who humiliated her own parents by demanding that they step aside, not because they were ashamed of what they were, but because she projected her own shame on them, shame at having been conceived by Arab parents. And instead of making peace with herself, years later, she transformed that shame – her own – into a mad commitment to combat a murderous West.[43]

In 2007, Rokhaya Diallo, a journalist and a militant feminist, rebaptized ten years later as a decolonial intersectional feminist,[44] created an association called the *Indivisibles* in order to offer perceptible support to the same struggles as the Indigenes: opposition to the law that prohibited wearing headscarves in schools, support for the emergence of "racialized," "non-mixed" camps, excluding white men, then white women, purporting to allow the victims of racism and sexism to gather among themselves, in identitarian fashion, in order to denounce a "state racism" fabricated by the indivisible, secular, democratic and social Republic along with the Islamophobia that allegedly stemmed from that racism. Two years later, the association decided to create the "Y'a bon Awards,"[45] anti-prizes very similar to those classically awarded by the far right, for example the Lysenko prize; the new awards were intended to denounce "ethno-racial prejudices, and in particular those persons who denied or denigrated the French identity of non-white French persons."[46] Once again the notions of race and French identity come up in the discourse held by adherents to this "racialized antiracism" that has become the vulgate of Indigenist groups. The prizes have thus been awarded, some to authentic racists and neocolonialists, to be sure, but also to personalities on the secular left known for their commitments against racism, most notably Caroline Fourest and Élisabeth Badinter. To top it off, the association has excoriated the groups SOS Racism and the International League Against Racism and Anti-Semitism, viewed as clubs for white intellectuals.

A Representative Council of Black Associations (CRAN) was founded in 2015 by Patrick Lozès, originally from Benin, an activist against racism and anti-Semitism and a harsh critic of Éric Zemmour and Dieudonné M'Bala M'Bala. CRAN was radically opposed to the Indigenes of the Republic (PIR). To combat discrimination against Blacks of any origin, and to inscribe the memory of slavery into the national patrimony, it modeled its approach on the mobilization of Jewish associations that had fought for acknowledgment of France's responsibility, under the Vichy government, for the deportation of Jews, and it sought to enter into a dialogue with the Representative Council of Jews in France (CRIF). Among the initiators of the movement were Gilles Manceron, a historian of colonialism and a member of France's Human Rights League, Christiane Taubira, Fodé Sylla, a former president of SOS Racism, and Louis-Georges Tin, born in Martinique in 1974, a graduate of the prestigious École normale supérieure and an activist in the homosexual cause. Refusing all forms of segregation along community lines and notions of ethnic classification, CRAN adopted the approach inspired by Albert Einstein's superb essay on race and racism sent to W. E. B. Dubois in 1931:

> It seems to be a universal fact that minorities, especially when their individuals are recognizable because of physical differences, are treated by majorities among whom they live as an inferior class. The tragic part of such a fate, however, lies not only in the automatically realized disadvantage suffered by these minorities in economic and social relations,

THE SOVEREIGN SELF

but also in the fact that those who meet such treatment themselves for the most part acquiesce in the prejudiced estimate because of the suggestive influence of the majority, and come to regard people like themselves as inferior. This second and more important aspect of the evil can be met through closer union and conscious educational enlightenment among the minority, and so emancipation of the soul of the minority can be attained.

The determined effort of the American Negroes in this direction deserves every recognition and assistance.[47]

A new actor in French political and intellectual life, CRAN brought together more than 50 associations that were trying to bring out not a Black identity but a "Black consciousness," a desire to be recognized in history and in memory, in a space beyond Negritude, with Nelson Mandela as the tutelary figure.[48] For these groups, it was not only a question of radically challenging the proposal to teach the "positive aspects of colonization," but also to establish a connection with CRIF. In the political world, the initiative met with a mixed reception: some feared the effects of a new communitarianism, while others judged the initiative "useful."

Two years later, CRAN assembled a governing board under the direction of Michel Wieviorka, with the historian Pap Ndiaye among its members. During several colloquia, discussions developed in particular over the question of the so-called "ethnic" or "diversity" statistics. Their partisans, including Wieviorka, saw them as a way of measuring with precision the discriminations of which minorities were the victims, whereas their opponents, for example Hervé Le Bras, emphasized on the contrary that they risked aggravating the retreat into communitarianism. Despite these seemingly irreconcilable positions, and contrary to the views of elected officials on the political left on secularism, the two trends managed to come together by organizing a number of meetings with scholars from different countries, including Russia, Brazil, and the United States: "We were in agreement," Wieviorka has emphasized, "about avoiding any national census of populations on ethnic grounds, but we were in favor of private studies, not financed by the government, that could shed light on generational itineraries while mentioning origins. At no time were we paralyzed by identitarian tendencies."[49]

The most successful initiative of this new association was the organization, in 2010, of a colloquium bringing CRAN and CRIF together, on the condition that no political representative of the state of Israel or any member of the Palestinian Authority would

THE LABYRINTH OF INTERSECTIONALITY

be present. And to avoid any awkward confrontation, the organizers settled on a theme apt to suit all the participants: "Faces: The Encounter with the Other." Needing to find a "neutral" venue, they chose the Collège des Bernardins, a property belonging to the Catholic Diocese of Paris, where high-level debates and lectures were regularly held under the leadership of Father Antoine Guggenheim, a theologian and a teacher well versed in the human sciences, including philosophy, psychoanalysis, and the history of religions. The tone was set at the start, and the opening text is worth citing in full:

Whether it is a question of anthropometric technologies to "detect" Jews in France during the dark years, the racial profiling that often targets Blacks and Arabs, tattoos or scarifications, the canons of advertising or plastic surgery, reproduction rights, or the Islamic headscarf or burqa, the face is often at the heart of the political stakes of our country. Can one see, can one represent, the face of God? The face of man? And the face of woman? What faces do the media show today? And what is the face of our Republic today? What do philosophers, art historians, anthropologists say about it? What do the human sciences in general have to say? What are the political questions that confront our contemporary conscience? In the debate over full face covering, how can religious freedom be articulated with the freedom of women? By relying on figures like Aimé Césaire or [Emmanuel] Levinas, how can we build a new foundation for an ethics of the relation to the other, an ethics that would also be a politics respecting the dignity of all, male and female alike? In short, what will be the face of our common future?[50]

Among the participants, in addition to Richard Prasquier, president of CRIF, Patrick Lozès, Louis-Georges Tin, and Michel de Virville, the head of the Collège des Bernardins, Father Laurent Lantieri gave a masterful presentation on total face transplants.

After the departure of Patrick Lozès, in 2011, CRAN took a different, much more identitarian tack under the influence of Louis-Georges Tin, who was himself engaged in struggles against homophobia and transphobia, and later in favor of a policy of material reparations connected with the period of slavery. Not only did the group's new president preside over a battle concerning historical recognition of the crimes of the slave trade, he also sought to defend the financial interests of all the descendants of slaves and to require the state to restore objects that had been looted from former colonized countries. "How are we to think about the transfers and appropriations, here and there? What status will these sacred

123

and royal objects that have become 'museum fetishes' have when they are returned?" And to support this undertaking, he denounced the "impostures" of universalism, rechristened "uniformalism," an avatar of the "hegemonic thought dissimulated behind alleged republican values."[51] Yet another neologism! It brought an end to the original ambitions of the association as Patrick Lozès had conceived them.

"Je suis Charlie"

On January 7, 2015, in Paris, seven journalists working for the satirical weekly newspaper *Charlie Hebdo* – Stéphane ("Charb") Charbonnier, Jean ("Cabu") Cabut, Elsa Cayat, Philippe ("Honoré") Honoré, Bernard Maris, Bernard ("Tignous") Verlhac, and Georges ("Wolin") Wolinski – were killed, along with others, by members of Al-Qaida. In the aftermath, French graphic artist Joachim Roncin, steeped in popular culture, created a slogan that was to spread around the planet: *Je suis Charlie*, "I am Charlie." Adopted quickly throughout France, the image resembled a plain formal card announcing a death: against a rectangular black background, "Je suis" appeared in white letters, followed by "Charlie" in grey letters, slightly larger than the white ones. The author took inspiration from a famous comic strip, "Où est Charlie?" (Where's Wally?), but also, probably less consciously, from at least three other declarations: "Je suis Spartacus," "Ich bin ein Berliner," and "Nous sommes tous américains."

The first was from the film *Spartacus*, produced in 1960 by Stanley Kubrick. After the defeat of the slaves, Crassus promised to let them live if their leader gave himself up. At the very moment when Spartacus identified himself, all his companions stood up and shouted "I am Spartacus." The second declaration was made by US President John F. Kennedy during a visit to West Berlin in 1963: it offered a virtual promise of reunification. The third was a call to support the victims of the September 11, 2001, attacks; it appeared on the front page of the newspaper *Le Monde*. The first two cases celebrated freedom from oppression; the third was a challenge addressed to Osama bin Laden, who had struck not only a major emblem of American power, but also some 3,000 individuals, about 300 of whom were of other nationalities, thus "non-Americans."

I have always viewed the hashtag #JeSuisCharlie as a hymn to freedom of expression, to be sure, but especially as the assertion of a subjectivity – I am myself, period: that is, perfectly independent, not identified as belonging to any group or any territory. And this is no doubt why it was spontaneously adopted by crowds that came together in multicolored marches, with demonstrators carrying placards that reproduced Roncin's original design.

But at the same time, and for the same reason, it was also rejected by all those who wanted nothing to do with that declaration: identitarians of all stripes. Starting with Jean-Marie Le Pen, who quickly asserted "Je ne suis pas Charlie," but rather "Je suis Charlie Martel,"[52] explaining that the attack against *Charlie Hebdo* was the result of a plot fomented by the French secret services: "I'm not saying that the French authorities are behind this crime, but that they might have allowed it to take place."[53] And immediately afterward, Dieudonné declared that he was neither Charlie nor Charles Martel, but rather "Charlie Coulibaly," using the last name of one of the assassins.

If the slogan "Je suis Charlie" resounded like a deterritorialized ideal, its antonym "Je ne suis pas Charlie"[54] became a worldwide expression of the rejection of the French model of republican secularism, which was accused of favoring blasphemy and discriminating against Muslims. From this standpoint, the *Charlie Hebdo* journalists were criticized for having published caricatures hostile to religion in general, and more particularly to Islam; they had made themselves guilty of offending the religion of the most underprivileged group. And among those who proclaimed "Je ne suis pas Charlie," one found not only collectives protesting Islamophobia, but also intellectuals and academics, some of whom were protesting against the presence, at the large demonstration held on the Place de la République in Paris, of heads of state responsible in their own countries for various forms of discrimination.[55]

Among the multiple positions on the part of the "Je ne suis pas Charlie" faction, let us look at that of Virginie Despentes, who firmly believed that the terrorists deserved the praise usually reserved for resisters fighting against dictators or criminals:

> I was also the guys who went in with their weapons, those who had just bought Kalashnikov rifles on the black market and had decided, in their way, the only way available to them, to die standing rather than to live on their knees. I also loved those who made their victims stand up and give their names before aiming at their faces. ... I loved them in their awkwardness – when I saw them, weapons in hand, sowing terror while yelling "We have avenged the Prophet!"[56]

THE SOVEREIGN SELF

These irresponsible statements can be contrasted to Jean-Luc Godard's searing intervention: "Everybody says, like imbeciles, 'Je suis Charlie'; as for me, I prefer to say 'Je suis Charlie' using the verb *suivre* [to follow], and I have followed Charlie for forty years." The filmmaker was in fact a faithful reader of the newspaper, and in 2012 the cartoonist Luz had produced a caricature of him in the act of filming Mohammed, his rear end up in the air, adapting as caption the famous question Brigitte Bardot asked Michel Piccoli in the film *Le mépris*: "And my butt? You like my butt?"

We cannot help but observe that in the eyes of a good number of academics from the English-speaking world, the French republican model, with its old universalism, its separatism and its anticommunitarianism, confirmed on this occasion that it was stubbornly rejecting cultural diversity, owing to its colonial past. As evidence, we can look at the way the excellent historian Robert Gildea presented, in 2018, the story of the attack against *Charlie Hebdo*.[57] He did not name the journalists who had been murdered, but dwelled instead on the misfortunes of the murderers, Amedy Coulibaly, Chérif and Said Kouachi, all three sons of the suburbs, "victims of (postcolonial) discrimination." He must have forgotten that "Je suis Charlie" embodied an idea that no power, even one armed to the teeth, could ever eradicate.

Iconoclastic rage

After 2015, the identitarian evolution of "studies" took a political turn with the appearance of major punitive campaigns orchestrated by groups adopting the classifications developed in the heart of academic institutions. By going out into the streets, these "studies" ended up providing support for what is called cancel culture, another widespread practice on social networks; all this took place against a background of increasing racism, (American) supremacism, and terror of Islamism. This "culture" consists in pointing fingers, for the purpose of ostracism or elimination, at a person, an association, or an institution whose statements, mores, acts, or habits are judged "offensive" toward one minority or another.

The culture of public denunciation, always dangerous for democracy, whatever its good or bad intentions may be,[58] goes hand in hand with other forms of counterattack, like those targeting "cultural appropriation." Both practices are supported, in France, by the sociologist Éric Fassin, who himself became the target of the

Indigenes of the Republic; they accused him of not having the right, as a White person, to lead an anti-racist struggle. This is a fascinating Pandora's box open to all winds: anyone can accuse someone else of the worst misdeeds and vice versa, since every identitarian position is experienced as persecution.[59]

Taking up on their own account the metaphor of the "Cannibalist manifesto" (eating the other), the subscribers to this "intersectional" approach reject all ideas concerning the universalization of artistic expression; only Blacks would have the right to conceptualize "blackitude," only Jews to conceptualize "Jewry," Whites "whititude," and so on. In the name of that theory, Pablo Picasso would be guilty of racism because he had been inspired by tribal arts, as would all the painters, poets, writers, and artists between 1905 and 1907 who left behind the canons of Western art to invent a new art – Negro art – starting from studies of African statues and masks (even though these had been considered by the colonialists as fetishes originating in a barbaric obscurantism).

From the point of view of the decolonials engaged in cancel culture, André Breton, Claude Lévi-Strauss, Michel Leiris, and many authors would thus be merely the representatives of an aesthetic racism, a racism of appropriation, which henceforth ought to be eradicated on the grounds that it is only the expression of the Western gaze on subalternized cultures. After Sartre had been gunned down, it would now be the turn of all the great artisans of anticolonialism. It is in the name of such a doctrine that Madonna was accused, in 2018, in social media, for having had the audacity to wear traditional Berber dress to celebrate her 60th birthday in Marrakesh: "Berber queen my ass ... You mean queen of cultural appropriation."[60]

But it is always by virtue of the same logic that any person with a "handicap," that is, with a condition henceforth assimilated to an identity – mental illness, autism, obesity, deafness, blindness, and so on – can demand to be hired in theaters or in film productions to interpret roles that have generally fallen to professional actors. And similarly, we are supposed to acknowledge, in the name of "representative diversity," that only a homosexual is qualified to interpret the role of a homosexual, a Jew the role of a Jew, a transgender person a transgender role, and so on. This would mean, *a contrario* and by the same logic, that a Black singer could no longer interpret the classic repertory – Mozart or Verdi – and that a White would no longer have the right to sing the blues or perform in jazz groups.

Among hundreds of demonstrations hostile or favorable to the theses of cultural appropriation, let us look at the misadventures

THE SOVEREIGN SELF

that befell the Canadian playwright Robert Lepage over the creation of *Kanata* in 2018.[61] The play retraces the history of the gradual elimination of Amerindian peoples by the English colonizers in the nineteenth and twentieth centuries. It challenges the government's strategy of assimilating and then marginalizing the descendants of the colonized peoples.

The controversy bore neither on the content of the play nor on the representations of "New France" following the foundation of Quebec in 1608, nor did it concern either the English or French colonial imaginary. It had to do, rather, with the fact that the actors were all Whites: this provoked the anger of the indigenous peoples, who called for the play to be banned: "The spectacle is a cultural appropriation," wrote Janelle Pewapsconias.

> I find it very problematic that a White or a colonizer should attempt to tell our story ... A white person cannot understand the implications of slavery, of the indigenous genocide, of the oppression against mixed-race persons ... We have many educated and talented people, but the Canadian government does not work with indigenous peoples, Blacks, or people of color.[62]

Refusing to give in to this pressure, Ariane Mnouchkine decided to invite Lepage to stage his play at the Théâtre du Soleil and to include the controversy in the scenario. In a communiqué that deserves to be cited at length, the two playwrights responded to all their detractors in the following terms:

> Not considering itself subjected to any laws but those laws of the Republic adopted by the elected representatives of the French people and not having had, in the present case, any occasion to challenge those laws or to demand their modification, thus not being legally or, more especially, morally obliged to submit to other injunctions, however sincere, and still less to yield to attempts at ideological intimidation in the form of culpabilizing articles or accusatory maledictions, most often anonymous, on social media, the Théâtre du Soleil has decided, in agreement with Robert Lepage, to pursue with him the creation of their play and to present it to the public on the dates announced.[63]

And they added:

> After a deluge of legal charges each more insulting than the next, they cannot and must not agree to submit to the verdict of a multitudinous and self-proclaimed jury that, stubbornly refusing to examine the

THE LABYRINTH OF INTERSECTIONALITY

one and only piece of evidence that counts – that is, the work itself – declares it harmful, culturally blasphemous, expropriative, specious, vandalizing, voracious, and politically pathological, even before it has been born.

Reading these declarations, one regrets that they were not heard by the responsible parties in all those French and international institutions that have not ceased – especially since 2015 – to yield to all the "multitudinous and self-proclaimed juries," that is, to the culture of denunciation now well known as "naming and shaming." For such is, in reality, the true problem raised by the acts of identitarian minorities. Why have those responsible for plays, lectures, exhibits, or teaching regularly given in to such threats? What are they really so afraid of that they never dare to defend freedom of expression?

It is the same fear concerning "security," in the face of demonstrators threatening to show up in large numbers, that led the authorities at the University Paris-Sorbonne in March 2019 to cancel the performances of Aeschylus's *The Suppliants*. The director, Philippe Brunet, was accused of racism by the national student union (UNEF), because he had had white actors wear black-colored masks, a variant of the age-old practice of blackface in which actors used makeup to look like black people. Hence the following declaration: "Blackface is in essence a racist practice originating in a colonial past in which caricatures of black people were frequently used to entertain a white public, caricatures generally representing these persons as savage, bestial, stupid. The use of this practice is discriminatory, racist, and inscribed today in a context of cultural and institutional racism that still holds sway."[64] Not only did the authors of this motion call for canceling the presentation, they also demanded public apologies from the university administration for having authorized the expression of such racism on university premises. Two days later, in a press release, two government ministers strongly condemned the unprecedented attack on freedom of creation and promised that a new performance of *The Suppliants* would be put on in the Sorbonne's large amphitheater.[65] This took place on May 21, before an impressive crowd and a number of ministers and ambassadors in the audience, marking the revenge of the dramatic arts against censorship.

In that play, there was no trace of racism, only the placing of the director within a tradition linked to classical Greek theater, in which all the actors wore black or white masks.

Regretting the act of censorship, the historian Laure Murat nevertheless took the side of the censors in their criticisms of the staging,

129

insisting that Brunet should have taken into account the warnings offered by Louis-Georges Tin, the president of CRAN: Tin had called for a boycott of the play, in order to turn the dramaturgy of the masks into an authentic debate. Brunet, Murat said, should have challenged "the more or less unconscious or perverse survival of orientalism and of the contemporary injurious practices of slavery ... in order to leave Europe-centered ideology behind" and get beyond the "tensions and excesses of decolonial thought."[66] It was in the name of such an argument that Ariane Mnouchkine, as we have seen, had refused to yield to threats, while adding a chapter titled "La controverse" (The Controversy) to the performance of *Kanata.*

Manifestly, all these collective denunciations are only the resurgence of the rites of lynching and witch hunting that aim to put to death, symbolically or socially, an adversary deemed dangerous: this is the opposite of democratic debate, which is based on speech. If we are to believe the partisans of cancel culture, this practice has become the most innovative tool in a protest emanating from minorities and from the American radical left, outraged by the impunity of ever more repressive, racist, homophobic, transphobic, and sexist power. The culture of public denunciation comes, according to Murat, in a direct line from the old struggles in favor of civil rights and the emancipation of oppressed minorities.[67] To justify that position, Murat invokes the actions of the Black Lives Matter movement, which appeared in 2013 in the Afro-American community, a community that has been relentlessly persecuted by endemic racism and in which the riots in the summer of 2020 originated after the murder by a white policeman of George Perry Floyd, a former petty criminal who had become a truck driver after having successfully returned to society.

How is one to confront this recurring argumentation, traces of which are found among the indigenists, the decolonials, the neofeminists known as the "dégommeuses" (roughly, "the smashers") and other fans of intersectionality? For my part, I am inclined to say that these movements are taking advantage of the disastrous situation of the victims of racism to situate themselves squarely in the line of an obscurantist counterrevolution that echoes uncannily the identitary and nationalistic discourses of the extreme right. Hostile to the Enlightenment and to reason, they aim, as we have seen, to eradicate the very idea that there was such a thing as Western anticolonialism, and they make it their project to destroy markers of history in acts such as toppling statues, changing street names, and so on. Thus they strive less to struggle in favor of true emancipation, in a straight line from Martin Luther King, than to substitute phantasmatic and binary

THE LABYRINTH OF INTERSECTIONALITY

hagiographies for the history they repudiate – the cult of slavery, the justification of male domination. Such extravagances and such spontaneous fanaticism, which claim to escape the rule of law, have the worst outcomes, since the fight against racism is then transformed into an apologia for (racialized) race, while queerness, established as a norm, serves to deny anatomical or biological difference – all this against a background of physical and verbal violence.

What is most astonishing, moreover, is that this return to the "debiologized" notion of race by the very persons who were its victims coincides chronologically with the debate in France that concluded with the decision by the National Assembly to remove (at last) the word "race" from the Constitution. In the revised Article 1, in the place of "without distinction of origin, race, or religion," we read that France ensures that all citizens are equal before the law "without distinction of sex, origin, or religion."[68]

Since race does not exist scientifically, it was logical to remove the word from the Constitution. This does not mean, of course, that it is eliminated from the French linguistic corpus. However, the legislative decision was contested primarily by representatives of critical race studies, decolonialists, and other indigenists, eager to reclaim its "beneficial" use in the form of racialized identity, and so on. And the same groups demanded that the word "sex" be removed from Article 1, which would then read "without distinction of gender, origin, religion, or race." This formulation is all the more incoherent in that it was accompanied by a nonsensical statement according to which racism is not universal.

This thesis, which ran counter to the positions of Césaire, Fanon, Lévi-Strauss, and all the others who thought seriously about antiracism and anticolonialism, was supported most notably by the sociologist Éric Fassin. In his view, in fact, the only racism that existed was anti-Black racism, since for the social sciences anti-White racism could not be found. What social sciences? The author hardly answers that question, but he asserts that the State itself is the initiator of a "principle of race" that allows it to distinguish between "foreign features" and "French features." The French state, in this view, has instituted "systemic racism." Fassin offers "statistical proof" by showing that police identity checks involve 20 times as many Arab or black men as white men. But how would the acknowledged observation of racist behavior of this sort be the consequence of a law that, on the contrary, aims to combat racism by the elimination of the major signifier of the racialist theory that preaches the existence of races? Sartre had made "antiracist racism" a dialectical moment

131

in the history of the abolition of race, and now we find the users of a new way of conceptualizing antiracism claiming to reactivate its discriminatory power.

Thus we would have to admit, for the greater good of a de-Westernized humanity, that there exists "racism without race" and "racism without racists." But how can we accredit a sociological approach that proposes to explain that the elimination of the word "race" from the French constitution would only reactivate state racism and that the use of the word "race" by the practitioners of racialization would be the ultimate weapon in the antiracist combat, because only white humanity is racist? And to justify such absurd reasoning, Fassin invokes Foucault, who of course never said any such thing.[69]

Such then is henceforth the distinguishing feature of the great labyrinth of racialized antiracism that would be the laughing stock of the authentic racists on the far right: the antiracism of racialized identitarians is a form of racism, they would say. To this renewal of racism, converted into a racialized antiracism, Tania de Montaigne, the author of an essay on the dangers of identitarian attributions, opposes a flat denial: "The word 'racialized,'" she says, "validates the idea that race exists. I find it sad that people immobilize themselves in a group whose criteria are those defined by slaveholders and Nazis. They could have chosen to say 'I am a victim of racism' instead of 'racialized.'"[70]

It is in the name of the practice of denunciation and effacement that enraged collectives from now on attack statues, old buildings, art exhibits, and celebrities, tracking down the ideal guilty party, even if it means denouncing with equal vigor the old slaveowners and their sworn enemies. They go after men suspected of harassment as zealously as they pursue criminal rapists and predators. Similarly, they feed a generalized and reciprocal group hatred: gays versus lesbians, Whites versus Blacks (or "racists" versus "antiracists"), Jews versus Arabs (or "racists" and "Islamophobes" versus "anti-Semites," "Islamists," or "anti-Zionists"), and so on. Fanon and others have sufficiently dismantled this infernal spiral of oneself as a king against the other, so that no more needs to be said about it.

In search of repentance, reparations, or revenge, the identitarians have thus turned themselves into judges presiding over popular tribunals. Conscious of this drift, the writer Alain Mabanckou, a professor of Francophone literature at UCLA and a great admirer of the Harlem Renaissance, the magnificent Afro-American movement of the 1920s and 1930s, has made these observations:

THE LABYRINTH OF INTERSECTIONALITY

If a statue that reminds people of something horrible and unjust is torn down, how am I to give my son some perspective on that event? I was asked a while back whether *Tintin in the Congo* should be modified because the book was deemed too colonial and because it presented native populations in caricatural forms. No, we must look on the colonial period with objectivity. As for myself, I need to read the *Code noir*, just as I have to read *Mein Kampf* to sharpen the reasons for my indignation. By wiping out the traces of Colbert and the *Code noir*, we also wipe out those of the resisters, of the Blacks and the Whites who have fought that person and have spoken out against that code. Reading history should not be guided by emotion ... I do not have to display rancor in order to assert my identity.[71]

It would be hard to put it more clearly.

There is nothing new about this iconoclastic fury; every revolution produces its own. From the destruction of the churches, crosses, and relics in 1793 through the uprising of October 1917 and the Paris Commune all the way to the Spanish Civil War, it was always a matter of abolishing the signs of tyranny and announcing a glorious future. Insurgents follow insurgents, and at each stage the symbols of the despised regime are destroyed and its promoters are eliminated. In Budapest in 1956, the crowd toppled an effigy of Stalin, and that gesture was repeated more or less everywhere in the countries of Eastern Europe after the fall of the Berlin Wall, to such an extent that figures of Marx, Lenin, Stalin, and all the major symbols of a communism that had become totalitarian were put in the same basket.

On each occasion, the same action is repeated, as if, to bring about a better world, it were necessary to destroy the signifiers of the old one. The statues come down, and the persons held responsible for the misfortunes of the past are executed, legally or not. But these acts, which always arouse the indignation of group against group, are generally carried out during riots and liberating battles. They are produced at the very moment when action is necessary to institute a new political order.

In the case of the identitarian rebellions, one has the impression that the act of destruction is being infinitely extended, is bound by no limit and is produced blindly, as the expression of an impulsive and anachronistic rage. The actors start in Boston, by cutting off the head of a statue of Christopher Columbus, accused of the genocide of Amerindians; they throw the statue of Cecil Rhodes, a pure representative of English racism and colonialism, into the Thames; they lash out against General Robert E. Lee, commander-in-chief of the

133

THE SOVEREIGN SELF

Confederate Armies during the War of Secession, who is known for his opposition to mistreatment of slaves but who has become, 150 years after his death, the icon of American neo-Nazis; they deface the statue of Winston Churchill with paint, retaining only his racist remarks and his unfailing support for British imperialism. In Martinique, statues of Victor Schoelcher are trampled because he is judged guilty of having appropriated, as a White, the abolitionist decree of which he was merely the initiator.[72] Finally, it is in the name of a radically identitarian and fanatically religious Islamism that such actors blow up not symbols of a despised epoch but works of art, the patrimony of all humanity. This happened most notably to the Buddhas of Baminyan in central Afghanistan, which were destroyed by dynamite in March 2001 by the Taliban.

Still, one must not believe, as certain French polemicists do, that all American thinkers and writers have become barbaric censors. Quite to the contrary, the more the culture of denunciation develops in the United States, the more it is subject to condemnation by progressive intellectuals hostile to such tactics. As evidence, we can note the opinion piece drafted by the writer Thomas Chatterton Williams and signed by 150 intellectuals, progressive antiracist activists, including Mark Lilla and Margaret Atwood.[73] They all denounce cancel culture, insults, and the collective pressures that aim to destroy freedom of expression, and they all support the Black Lives Matter movement, without needing to resort to neologisms or obscure language: "Left-wing ideas," they say, "are dominant within cultural institutions, the media, and universities. These institutions have considerable prescriptive power to establish what social norms are deemed acceptable. The propagation of intolerance in these milieus thus has to be of concern to us, for this phenomenon could turn up tomorrow in the political debate."[74]

The real question raised by these upheavals that keep on poisoning the relations between interest groups, historians, and political authorities is the question of constructing a shared memory. We know perfectly well that the enraged advocates of repentance, reparation, and punishment will never succeed in healing the suffering of the children of immigrants who turn toward fanaticism, some of whom disavow the history of their own parents. Rather than liberating those children, they only exacerbate their difficulties by thrusting them into the traps set for them by obscurantism.

The duty of truth must never be converted into a duty of identity. And this is why, as Benjamin Stora emphasizes, political power must always recognize in an official way, even if belatedly, the crimes

134

THE LABYRINTH OF INTERSECTIONALITY

that have been committed in the name of the state or the Republic, without ever forgetting to refer, in France, to the Enlightenment, the Revolution, and the anticolonialist tradition, a triple reference on which colonized peoples have drawn for their struggles of liberation, whatever the indigenists, the Islamists, and their allies of all stripes may think of it.[75] Such could be the French path toward the institution of a secular and republican culturalism inherited from Lévi-Strauss and detached from the ideals of identitarian self-enclosure. For it is as futile to claim to be shedding an abstract model of citizenship in favor of valuing individual particularities as it is to establish those particularities as a model of universality.

— 6 —

GREAT REPLACEMENTS

Oneself against all

In a work cited earlier devoted to the identitarian left, Mark Lilla pointed out that the adjective "identitarian" initially brought to mind protesters with shaved heads, dressed in black leather, tossing pigs' heads at mosques or hunting down migrants while brandishing banners decorated with *fleurs-de-lis*.[1] This obviously has nothing to do with the shifts whose history I have traced in the preceding chapters. And yet, from one political extreme to another, "identitarianism" is present: identity versus identity. Since the fall of the Berlin Wall and the global triumph of liberalized capitalism based on the cult of the individual, left-wing movements linked to identity politics are in search of a new model for society, one that would be respectful of differences, attentive to equality, well-being, and care.[2] Ecologist in orientation and supportive of the cause of the weakest, working to protect nature, animals, and oppressed minorities, these generally generous-spirited movements seek to "repair" the world, and to that end they denounce injustices, colonial wars, and racism. But, through a gradual reversal, some of them have made themselves advocates of a narcissism of small differences, to the extent of locking themselves into the deadly logic of the chameleon. Yet no matter how far such movements may drift toward intransigence, they are still motivated by an ideal of emancipation that could eventually regain the upper hand, although the price of such a reversal would be the renunciation of the follies that accompany the hypertrophy of the self.

Just as they have gone astray by cultivating the certainty that they embody the ideal of the sovereign good, so they will be challenged tomorrow by their heirs, who will reject – are already rejecting – their commitments. This can be observed in the many articles of protest published in the press. Why, after all, would the victims of discrimination agree to obey new injunctions of submission inviting them to return to the hell of dependency on a clan, whether that clan is gendered, racialized, or "queerized"?

Worst of all, for the extremists among them, is that by dint of defending Muslims against the rejection of which they are victims, and by using the term Islamophobia indiscriminately, they have ended up denying, whatever they may claim, the dangerous nature of the Salafist drift of Islam and its calls for jihad.[3] Believing they were supporting the wretched of the earth, they reached the point of no longer differentiating between the victims of racism, Muslim or other, and the militants of a religious obscurantism that draped itself in the virtues of an allegedly moderate Islam. Nothing is more aberrant in fact than claiming to defend the religion of the "poor" – the Muslims who experience discrimination – while frequenting Tariq Ramadan and other "brothers" or collectives of the same orientation who promote hatred of women, homosexuals, Jews, Arabs, and the many Muslims who accept secularism.

As I have said, these "identitarians" have renounced the Enlightenment and progress, have insulted Sartre and twisted the thinking of their elders, including Fanon, Said, Foucault, Césaire, the surrealists, Beauvoir, and distinguished anthropologists. In short, in the name of a postmodernity that has aged badly, they have locked themselves into radical criticism of everything they have inherited. And the worst of it is that they have rejected the philosophy of the Enlightenment on the pretext that the partisans of colonization took their inspiration from that philosophy so as to ensure their domination over peoples of color. Might they have forgotten that the anticolonialists emerging from the colonized world turned the principles of 1789 against their oppressors?

And, similarly, they no longer want to pay attention to what happened in 2011 on the occasion of the "Arab spring." Not a word about the mobs that rose up in the name of an ideal of freedom to put an end to plagues and cholera, condemning dictatorships as well as jihadism. This desire for revolution was borne by young people and by women of all ages from all over the planet, against all those who dreaded the return of *les lendemains qui chantent*, the "rosy future" promised by French socialists in the aftermath of the Second World War. This aspiration can be stifled, but it will never be extinguished: to borrow a formulation attributed to Victor Hugo, "no army is as powerful as an idea whose time has come." And rather than spending

137

THE SOVEREIGN SELF

their time supporting those who want to shoot Sartre, these extremist identitarians would do better to condemn in no uncertain terms the fans of decapitation, for example Sheik Issam Amira of the Al-Aqsa mosque in Jerusalem: "When a Muslim of Chechnian origin decapitated an infidel who slandered the Prophet Muhammed, people called it terrorism. ... Well, it is a great honor for him and for all Muslims. That young man defended the Prophet Mohammed. He is like the men and women throughout history who have defended the Prophet, his sanctity and his honor. All these terms will be rethought, once the word of Allah reigns supreme over the word of the infidels."[4] The Arab-Islamic world, too, is traversed by a war of identities that is, as Fethi Benslama emphasizes, nothing but a war of Muslims among themselves, a consequence of the collective rejection of the Enlightenment. To characterize this enterprise of self-destruction, Benslama points to four figures of voluntary death, figures that make the possible entry of Islam into historical time a moot point: jihadism (a parody of heroic engagement), the cult of the human bomb (based on a valorization of the dismembered body), immolation by fire (an act of despair), and finally the practice of *harraga* (drowning at sea with loss of identity, orchestrated by mafias). Muslims will eventually have to find their way out of this hell and stop lashing out at an imaginary West, even though certain European countries do in effect treat them as rubbish. And this is why Benslama suggests that they adopt the principles of secularism and stop losing themselves in a pathological subjectivity that condemns them to shout against blasphemers and obey fatwas.[5] Let me add that they will one day have to take inspiration from the culture of the other to define themselves rather than repeatedly setting off in Theseus's ship.[6]

When it is a matter of the identitarian right – fanatic, nationalist, populist,[7] racialist – which has been reactivated during the same period and, like Islamism, under the sway of globalized capitalism, the question takes a different form. In this case, no awakening is possible, no transformation of an ideal into its opposite can come about. There is thus no direct symmetry between the misguided tendencies of the identitarians on the left – the most serious intellectually – and the pre-established conviction of those on the right – the most dangerous politically – even if they reinforce each other.

Those known as "Identitarians," that is, a loose nebula of groups situated to the right of the right and proclaiming an ideology of lineage (*souche*) – "Génération identitaire," "Français de souche," national-populists, neo-reactionaries of all sorts[8] – have not recently *become* identitarians following a slow drift in that direction. Obsessed

138

with a project of segregation, they are heirs of a tradition shared by neo-Fascists, conspiracy theorists, neo-imperialists, supremacists, and nativists. They also have in common the determination to bring about a worldwide counterrevolution based on the rejection of elites, the University, the "system," and democracy, inasmuch as the latter does not allow representation of the "true" people. Dominated by the death drive, they always seek the destruction of the other, and their calls to war nourish mad dreams of murderous prophets, subscribers to white supremacy. Among them: Anders Behring Breivik, responsible for massacres in Oslo and Utoya in 2011; Brenton Tarrant, assassin of some 50 Muslims in New Zealand in 2019; and Patrick Crusius, a killer of "Latinos" the same year. Convinced that the Hispanic "invasion" was a reality, Crusius traveled over 600 miles to execute some 20 people in a shopping center in El Paso: "America is rotting from the inside out, and peaceful means to stop this seem to be nearly impossible," he had declared in a manifesto he published online before committing his act.[9]

Very divided among themselves, but never allied with traditional conservative positions, the Identitarians lash out pell-mell against the tyranny of repentance, against the "Islamo-leftists," against "political correctness," against the partisans of homosexual marriage, against "victimary" feminism, against antiracist associations (deemed racist) and against all leftists in general, who are responsible, as they see it, for the decadence of a West they define as white, Christian, Greek, Orthodox, Judeo-Christian, patriarchal-heterosexual, but also, henceforth in France, secular and republican; these decadent groups are seen as about to be replaced by godless and lawless barbarians – gendered, queered, colorized, mixed, tribalized, delinquent, Salafized. And the Identitarians often cultivate a grandiloquent national narrative on the Maurrassian model of an opposition between the "real" country and the country as defined by law.

In France, they bring ancient ideals back on stage: virilism, hero worship after the fashion of the high-drama French historical theme park Puy-du-Fou, or anti-Islam gatherings in the guise of meet-ups for drinks after work. Appropriating images from the French film tradition, they see themselves as heirs of Jean Gabin, Jean Renoir, or Jacques Becker, of *La grande illusion* and the *Casque d'or*, when in fact they are often only the recipients of a story straight out of their old schoolbooks, a moving story, to be sure, but lacking the savor of the old days. Thus they extol the glory of references that have been disrupted by the epoch, such as the Family, the Army, the Nation, the Church, the Republic, all in capital letters, without understanding that all these institutions evolve without necessarily risking disappearance. The fathers continue to exist, and so do the heroes, the mothers, the family genealogies, the borders, the beauty of the world, the village churches, and the patriotic spirit.

All these figures of the Republic and, of course, of the old France, all these entities, these patrimonial traces, continue to be transmitted and to populate collective memory. As Mark Lilla emphasizes:

> The reactionary has a thousand faces. He is Proteus. The revolutionaries, whatever doctrinal quarrels they may have, whatever their foolish and contradictory utopias may be, concentrate on a common objective: a more just future. The reactionaries, so disgusted by the present that they have difficulty imagining the future, refer rather, for their part, to an idealized past ... The reactionary is not a student of history, he is an idolater of the past. In order to live, he needs a story that explains how the intolerable present is the necessary result of a historical catastrophe that can be imputed to very specific dark forces.[10]

Since the collapse of the bipolarized world, these Identitarians – as they call themselves – have succeeded in injecting their ideas into public opinion in the Western countries. And we can understand why. The leaders of the liberal democracies had mistakenly thought that after the implosion of the communist regimes and the liquidation of the colonial empires, the aspiration of peoples to individual freedom would end up winning out. They had believed that their world and their mores were so desirable that the formerly oppressed peoples would be eager to take them as models for their lives.

After 1989, there was thus an expectation of a great turn toward happiness. But in fact, to the contrary, many of the formerly communist regimes have regressed toward authoritarianism, at the price of taking an anti-progressive stance, that of the "great replacement," according to which the civilized societies are threatened on all sides by barbarians external to the body of the nation, but also by a cult of the individual that views the infringements made on the structures of collective belonging without compassion.

In this respect, in the Western world, the immense expansion of therapies offering happiness, coaching, personal development, meditation therapies, resilience institutes, and other groups focused on exalting or repairing the self, allied with the growing consumption of psychotropic drugs well beyond the classic psychiatric prescriptions – all this is the sign of a social inability to face up to the question of happiness, a collective and individual ideal, as it had been conceptualized by the Enlightenment thinkers and their heirs, from

Kant to Freud on one side and from Rousseau to Saint-Just on the other. Despite the pessimism that made him think, especially from 1920 on, that human beings are first of all murderers of one another and of themselves, Freud was after all an heir to Enlightenment thinking, French and German together: an Enlightenment at once luminous and somber. Against all the theologies of the Fall – which always nourish the fantasy of the "great replacement" – and even as he adopted for himself the tragic idea of fate dear to the Ancients, Freud gave primacy to feelings, nature, intimacy, and sensitivity, provided, however, that will, reason, and intellect be equally valued. In this sense, instead of joining Kant and his idea of snatching peace from warlike nature, he espoused the ideal of the inventors of liberty so well defined by Jean Starobinski.[11]

Beyond a conception of freedom according to which the self is not master in its own house and thus the subject is never reduced to an identity, Freud thought that the modern nations ought to lay the foundations of a society capable of ensuring the happiness of its citizens. And this is why, in 1930, in *Civilization and Its Discontents*, he reaffirmed that only access to civilization could curb the destructive drive inscribed at the heart of humanity. At bottom, he subscribed tacitly to Hölderlin's prophecy: "Where there is danger, the rescue grows as well."[12]

Now it is indeed an inversion of this advance toward civilization that we are observing today more or less everywhere in the world. In Europe, first of all, with the weakening of progressivism in Poland and Hungary, or in the United Kingdom with Brexit, a nationalist counterstroke in reaction to the loss of a colonial empire, and also in Italy, with populist movements originating in civic society. In addition, we find instability in places that have traditionally been open to policies of social welfare: the Scandinavian countries, or the Netherlands. In Germany and in Greece, we are witnessing a revival of neo-Nazi tendencies. Confronted with strong opposition to the construction of a market-centered Europe, and with a more inward-facing focus, these countries are now crisscrossed by contradictory forces and weakened in their inventiveness, even as they are threatened by new imperial powers. A despot has reigned in Turkey since 2014: Recep Tayyip Erdoğan dreams of reconstituting the Ottoman Empire. Similarly, Russia has become an imperial state again under the reign of Vladimir Putin, who has been in power since 2000, while in India Narendra Modi, the prime minister since 2014, is waging a veritable war, in the name of "Hinduness," against writers, journalists, and intellectuals, while persecuting the Muslim and Christian minorities. As for China, subjected to dictatorship by Xi Jinping since 2008, it promotes a ferocious nationalism, based on what remains of "communism" – a Party that is omnipresent in every act of life – and on an unprecedented exploitation of the masses.[13]

In the United States, the question of "racial" identity does not arise in the same way as it does in the old colonial empires of the Western world, where the ideals of colonialism and anticolonialism are in conflict. The United States has always been constructed according to the principle of multiculturalism, that is, as a nation welcoming all migrations from elsewhere, from Europe and Asia, and the country has drawn its principle of government from the biblical tradition. However, lacking the European "background" of Athens, Jerusalem, or Rome, the country has always considered the color white as a defining characteristic of civilized Americanness, a view that has weighed against the indigenous Indian tribes, gradually massacred; against the Blacks, reduced to slavery; against the Chinese, Japanese, and other Asians; and against the Chicanos (Mexican-Americans and other Hispanics). The racism of white Americans is thus at once biological, patrimonial, cultural, social, and existential.

Founded in 1865, the Ku Klux Klan sect, made up of fanatic southern racists, was also imbued with an archaic anti-Semitism. Its burning crosses and its white tunics made its partisans phantom-like characters; their murderous actions bloodied America for more than a century. And as the demographic evidence began to confirm that racial mixing was the rule and that "racial purity" – whether white or non-white – was simply an illusion, the famous "civilized Whites" felt increasingly deprived of their identity, as the struggle in favor of civil rights advanced – a combat supported moreover by white Americans much more "civilized" and "elitist" than those of the "other America," small-town America between the coasts.[14]

The "white knights" of identitarian America are spread today among a number of different groups: the National Socialist Movement, the Aryan Fraternity, the Proud Boys, the Identitarian Movement, the Identity Evropa/American Identity movement, Vanguard America, the Patriotic Front, the Oath Keepers, and finally QAnon, a conspiracy-theory network that arose in 2017 and now has some three million enthusiasts convinced that there is a worldwide cabal of Satan-worshipping pedophiles who control the media, Hollywood cinema, and the international political elites.

It is in this context, equally marked by the expansion of the various "studies" in American universities, by the destruction of the World Trade Center, and by the emergence of a deadly Islamism, that the identitarian anxieties of non-elite Whites have increased, under a growing conviction that the other half of America – racially mixed, intellectual, university-based – is taking away their "white privilege," that is, their Americanness. And that is why, in 2016, this class of non-elite Whites elected Donald Trump to the presidency: probably not primarily for economic reasons but rather owing to the effect of his "racial identity," and against his predecessor Barack Obama, who was seen as the embodiment of a Black elitist and therefore odious America. The slogan "Make America Great Again" thus became the cry of rage of millions of Americans who hoped to see the re-establishment of the old order of which they had been "dispossessed." "Contrary to what a certain number of specialists have asserted," Sylvie Laurent declares, "it was not economic vulnerability that had aroused their feeling of racial dispossession. The mechanism was reversed. Without perceiving themselves consciously as racist, those Americans appealed for a politics of white identity aiming to restore a policy of racial precedence that they took to be evanescent but from which, in reality, they had never ceased to benefit."[15]

It was, then, not by chance that, confronted with a murderous White racism nourished by the fear of displacement, Black American groups also began to evolve, around 2013, shifting from the struggle in favor of civil rights to often violent demands for a right to the "identity" attached to their status as descendants of former slaves. Hence the adoption of the slogan that caught on widely: "Black Lives Matter." Riots, uprisings, urban battles, destruction of statues were thus multiplied at the heart of the major American cities, sometimes developing into insurrectional situations. And of course, mirroring this existential demand, a "White Lives Matter" movement emerged in 2015, made up of various supremacist groups, heirs of the old Ku Klux Klan and the neo-Nazis, all convinced by the doctrine of the "great replacement." A similar "Blue Lives Matter" slogan, referring to the police, developed during the same period.

The worst of it is that the very people who had fought religious obscurantism and struggled in favor of antiracism and the abolition of discrimination against Blacks now felt discriminated against by "Black Privilege" or assimilated to racists within the far-right cluster. Thus in May 2020, Charles Negy, a professor of the University of Central Florida and a transcultural psychotherapist, was the victim of a campaign of denigration for having studied the way Whites felt themselves to be victims in turn, shamed for being White.[16] In a tweet reproduced thousands of times, he had criticized the procedures of affirmative action and noted that real opprobrium now weighed on white professors, who were ordered to justify themselves for crimes committed by "white culture."[17]

With the help of social networks, groups from the nationalist-identitarian cluster use impoverished peoples to their advantage in propagating their regressive ideas. They share with their extremist enemies on the other side an absolute hatred for progressivism and the left, but for different reasons. They are resolutely attached to the anti-Enlightenment tradition that has been very well described by the historian Zeev Sternhell, a tradition according to which subjects exist only in and through communities, and individuals only in and through their particularities. From this perspective, identity is always separatist. Let us recall how Joseph de Maistre countered Montesquieu on this point, in 1796: "The Constitution of 1795, like its predecessors, was made for *man*. But there is no such thing as *man* in the world. In my lifetime I have seen Frenchmen, Italians, Russians, etc. ... But as for *man*, I declare that I have never in my life met him; if he exists, he is unknown to me."[18]

What the nationalist-identitarians fear now is "mixing," as if one could preserve peoples and territories from all contact, as if individuals should protect themselves against the excesses of globalization, not by regulations, laws, or border protections, but by walls and barbed wire. They label everything other than themselves "totalitarian": they feel that they have been shipwrecked, impoverished, "replaced," excluded, and they see liberalism, communism, Jacobinism, communitarianism, and multiculturalism as responsible for their misfortunes. Thus they see themselves as the last guardians of a civilization threatened by modernity: a wax museum, a portrait gallery, a collection of objects forever fixed in time immemorial. They believe in the purity of the nation, of the culture, convinced that nothing should be mixed: they cannot envision either the "too close" or the "too far apart."

And through an inversion of the stigmata, they designate themselves in turn, all tendencies taken together, as the victims of a dominant ideology that has taken control of the bastions of knowledge, the press and the universities. They see themselves everywhere as poor Whites vanquished by transgendered and decolonialized barbarians, like "natives" deprived of their identities. In France, they affirm that they are being compelled to repent, and to lower their standards. They often develop an "unfortunate identity" syndrome when they observe what they call the "great deculturation" of their country, linked to "replacement immigration."[19] And they often manifest a primitive anti-Americanism[20] by blaming "American campuses," at the very time when, across the Atlantic, Donald Trump and his partisans attack France as a "delinquent" people. Is it necessary to recall that anti-Americanism is no better than Francophobia? No particular identitarian nationalism is preferable to any other.

And, of course, like the identitarians on the other side, their "persecutors," the nationalist-identitarians proclaim their indignation without ever bringing the slightest "solution" to the problem of identitarian tendencies, unless it is the elimination from their territories of alleged foreign "packs" who would be threatening to supplant the good native-born citizens. But where can these purebred natives be found except in identitarian fantasies? For the nationalist identitarians are in no way victims.

The terror of invasion

The theory that a given people could be replaced by another dates back to the late nineteenth century. It first appeared in texts by Édouard Drumont; Maurice Barrès later picked up the theme in the wake of new republican laws passed in 1889 decreeing that children born in France to foreign parents would become French upon reaching majority. Drumont's *La France juive*, published in 1886, is undoubtedly the most abject anti-Jewish book ever written.[21] Haunted by the terror of replacement, Drumont claimed to be retracing in six parts, in an objective fashion, a truth that had constantly been hidden: the history of the destruction of the civilized peoples of Europe by the Jews. As proof of his thesis, he adopted the whole conspiracy theory of Christian anti-Judaism, which accused the Jews of propagating the plague, polluting the waters, committing ritual crimes, carving up children, and so on. But Drumont also included the history of that conspiracy in the long epic death struggle over the centuries between the Semites and the Aryans. He concluded that the greatest victory won by the Aryans against the Semitic scourge was the expulsion of the Jews from France and the confiscation of their property by King Charles VI in 1394. Between that date and the French Revolution, he asserted, in effect, that France, "thanks to the elimination of that venom, had finally become a great European nation, before entering into a period of decadence."[22]

Like Drumont, Barrès never used the term "replacement," but he evoked the "new Frenchmen" who had infiltrated the instincts of the common people and imposed a primitive sensibility on them: "They contradict our own civilization. The triumph of their way of seeing

145

would coincide with the real ruin of our fatherland. The name of France might well survive; the special character of our country would be destroyed, however, and the people installed in our name and on our territory would proceed toward destinies in contradiction with the destinies and needs of our land and of our dead."[23]

Throughout the first half of the twentieth century, up to the Nazi genocide, various theses according to which European populations were under constant threat flourished in the works of numerous writers, Georges Mauco in particular. A psychoanalyst, pedagogue, and demographer, Mauco published a book in 1932 that met with considerable success: *Les étrangers en France: Leur rôle dans l'activité économique*.[24] The author propounded racist and nationalist theses about the "hierarchy of ethnic groups," and he argued that certain foreigners could not be integrated: prominent among these were the Levantines, the Africans, and the Asians.[25] The book was acclaimed by the right, attuned to its inegalitarian bias, and by certain demographers who found it a welcome source of material supporting the hypothesis of a link between immigration and national identity. During the Occupation, Mauco shifted from racism to anti-Semitism while collaborating with Georges Montandon on the journal *L'Ethnie française*, a key organ for the Vichy regime's anti-Semitic propaganda; every article in the journal aimed to denounce the "Jewish type" according to the criteria adopted by Nazism. Mauco published two articles in which he claimed to be mobilizing psychoanalysis to bring to light a "Jewish neurosis."

The idea according to which certain foreigners would be more acceptable than others haunts the work of many writers in this period. In 1939, for example, Jean Giraudoux considered that "the Anglo-Saxon, Scandinavian, and Germanic races" along with "our Swiss and Belgian brothers" could very well benefit from a demographic policy consistent with the French race, a "fusion of diverse ethnic elements," but in no case could it encompass the Arabs, the Asians, or the Blacks. He repeatedly emphasized the extent to which French civilization was threatened by those "teeming hordes" that profited from the population decline to settle into Pantin or Grenelle.[26] The same was true for the "Askenasis" (*sic*) who had escaped from Polish ghettos, and other Poles, plus Czechs and Italians. Giraudoux recommended that foreigners be accepted only if they were healthy, vigorous, and without mental defects.[27]

Numerous works of the period invoked the decline or "disappearance" of the white race, the twilight of the Western nations, or the impossibility for the white race to defend its identity in the face of huge waves of peoples from Asia, Africa, and the colonial empire. A slogan popularized in Germany in 1895, the "Yellow Peril," became synonymous with a phantasmatic invasion of Europe, no longer by the hordes of Ghengis Khan but by small "ants" with slanted eyes coming from China and Japan. To defend the archangel Gabriel and Christian Europe, one had to resist Buddhism and all the polytheist religions. To these terrors another was added: the Red Peril, symbolized by the figure of a disheveled Bolshevik with bulging eyes holding a blood-spattered knife between his teeth.

Starting in 1945, with the notion of race subjected to critique, the terror of subversion was expressed in a different form, as the colonial empires were breaking apart. The fear of migrants – Blacks, mixed-race, Arabs – replaced the fear of Jews, while the term "ethnic group" tended to be generalized, as the word "race" was banished in the social sciences in favor of the notion of "cultural differences." As we have seen, the word "race" was later reappropriated by partisans of identity politics and other decolonialists, in the form of the adjective "racialized." As for the concept of "ethnic group," the term took hold in anthropology and ethnology to define a human population – or group – that shared a common bloodline, a history, a language, a religion, a way of life: in other words, an identity constructed as much by the scholars who observed its mechanisms as by the subjects that composed it. "Ethnicity" was thus henceforth linked to a common cultural heritage, and the use of the prefix "ethno" made it possible to distinguish transcultural disciplines: ethnopsycho-analysis, ethnopsychiatry, ethnohistory, and so on. As for the adjective *ethnique*, borrowed from the English "ethnic," it came to be used in all sorts of identitarian contexts through marketing strategies that had a communitarian connotation: artisanal clothing, folkloric objects, exotic foods,[28] and so on.

During these same years, the theory of substitution and the theme of peril continued to spread in the discourse of the far right and a small portion of the right, to such an extent that, confronted with decoloniz-ation and the debates over Negritude, those who were nostalgic for the old colonial empire that had been defeated on the battlefield and replaced by "Yankee" armies invented new combinations. For many of them, the defense of the European West ought, from that period on, to pass through an identitarian alliance between white prole-tarians and capitalists, both groups being threatened, beyond their class oppositions, by "colored" majorities everywhere on the planet. Hence the appearance of an ideology linking anti-American imperi-alism, the anti-Coca-Cola version, to a sort of egalitarian vision of

THE SOVEREIGN SELF

peoples. All peoples, they said in effect, had a right to their own "vital space," but it was still necessary for them to remain enclosed within well-defined borders – a thesis very different from that of integration, on the one hand, and that of multiculturalism on the other, since it presupposes the institution of a watertight barrier between subjects or groups defined by their identitarian affiliations.

From this perspective, which condemned "mixed" marriage and dual nationality, the Jews were no longer openly designated as agents of destruction of other peoples characterized as the "original" populations, since they themselves were threatened with replacement by Arab migrants, Blacks and others, coming from an extra-European world that was on a path toward Islamization and thus hostile to Judeo-Christianism.

All the identitarian movements that have grown out of the old European far right, small neo-Nazi groups and others, Christian or pagan, ultimately adopted the idea of genocide, accusing progressives as well as anticolonialists of favoring the "civilizational decline" of the West. These groups are charged, by virtue of their utopianism or their cowardice, with encouraging a process of extermination of white populations, or even a "capitalism of forced racial mixing." Thus mixed-race men, and especially mixed-race women, were designated as responsible for the supreme destruction, organized over time, by the armies of the Prophet: "Systematic racial mixing is nothing but slow genocide"; furthermore, "the Arab world, supported this time by African mobs, risks exploding into a direct form of expansionism that recalls the first Islamic attacks mounted by the Prophet's faithful followers during seven centuries in Spain, and during two centuries in Sicily and along the Garigliano river in Italy, where they controlled Tarento and Bari."[29]

This thematics came up again in 1973 in Jean Raspail's *Le Camp des Saints* (*The Camp of the Saints*).[30] The book attracted little attention when it was published, but some 30 years later it achieved phenomenal success among all the nationalist identitarians, and even more among American white supremacists. A long-distance voyager, a paradoxical royalist, a fierce defender of Louis XVI, a fervent Catholic attached to the ideals of "each to his own," Raspail was fascinated by extreme geographies and exceptional experiences. An admirer of mercenaries passionate about their faith, he declared himself the Consul General of Patagonia after writing a fictionalized biography of Antoine de Tounens, a nineteenth-century French adventurer who settled in the territory of the Mapuche people in Auricania and established a kingdom there.[31]

148

Judged insane in 1862 by the Supreme Court in Chile, Tounens was sent back to France, still believing himself to be the sovereign of this imaginary kingdom. And Raspail, identifying with his protagonist, declared himself to be Patagonian because, he claimed, in that country every man can declare himself king. Thus it is in the light of these proclamations – "oneself as a king" and "each to his own" – that Raspail's 1973 novel must be interpreted. The author described the submerging of Western civilization by the immigration of a million wretched castaways who had come from the Ganges Delta and washed up on a beach on the Côte d'Azur.

The entire classic thematics of replacement unfolds: the conscription, by a Belgian priest in the city of Calcutta, of children to be adopted and sent to the West; mobs of starving Indians, piled up in hideous boats; an unfortunate migrant nicknamed "coprophage" hauling up his deformed child to send him toward Europe; Soviet troops prepared to fight the Chinese who were invading Siberia; and finally, the cherry on top: the total subversion of the white West, whose inhabitants are compelled to share their lodgings with godless and lawless dark-skinned strangers. In conclusion, the narrator reveals that he was relating this epic story from his Swiss chalet, the last bastion of a Western civilization that had already been engulfed.

Criticized when it first came out by the right-wing press, *Le Figaro* in particular, the work became a best-seller two years later, initially in the United States. Over the years, it was translated into numerous languages, while in France it gathered a steady audience among far-right journals: *Valeurs actuelles, Minute, Rivarol, Aspects de la France*. With every new edition, the author added "new proofs" of the veracity of his tale, which was no longer, in his eyes, a work of pure fiction. He expressed his humiliation at the fact that neither *Le Monde* or *Le Nouvel Observateur* had reviewed his book even once.[32]

Raspail finally convinced himself that his name was on a blacklist established by partisans of generalized racial mixing in his lovely French fatherland. And then, on February 19, 2001, he had the ultimate revelation that France was doomed to disappear, when reality, he claimed, proved he was right: from his villa, overlooking the terrifying scene on his cherished beach at Boulouris (that of *The Camp of the Saints*), he witnessed the arrival of a thousand savages emerging from the sea after a shipwreck. And when he read the dispatch from Agence France-Presse, he became certain that the journalist had copied the first three paragraphs of his novel: the monsters were really there, and there to stay.

149

THE SOVEREIGN SELF

The reality, however, was quite different. That day, a rusty old bulk freighter, the *East Sea*, flying a Cambodian flag, unloaded 900 Kurdish refugees on the Boulouris beach; half of them were children floundering in a heap of refuse. Abandoned by a team of smugglers who had extorted their property, these boat people in rags were the first refugees from Iraq and Syria to land on French shores. Several days later, two-thirds of them left France to seek asylum in the United Kingdom, in Germany, or in the Netherlands. These, then, were the "invaders" so feared by Jean Raspail.

"Big Other: From Boulouris to *La Campagne de France*

For the reprinting of his novel in 2011,[33] Raspail wrote a preface titled "Big Other," in homage to George Orwell's *1984*[34]; needless to say, Orwell himself had nothing to do with this strange hallucinatory tale. More and more in harmony with the trend toward conspiracy theories that was on the rise in France, Raspail mocked the laws of the Republic by listing all the racist, anti-Semitic, and negationist passages in his novel that constituted statutory offenses under laws that he deemed grotesque. This book he said, could not have been published for the first time in 2011: it would be "unpublishable without serious amputations."[35] The author was mistaken. Since the book was a novel, not an essay or a personal journal, it did not risk being brought before the courts.

Rather than lambasting the unfortunate migrants, who were reduced to a dung heap, in this multiform text Raspail went after the corruption of the public authorities, the weakening of the army, the blindness of the clergy, and France as a whole, which had become, in his eyes, the most cowardly nation on the planet. According to Raspail, France was condemned to go under for having dared to decapitate a king and repudiate the true religion. Hence the book's title, taken from a passage in the Book of Revelation (the Apocalypse of John) in which Satan calls all nations to come together for the final battle against the "camp of the saints" before they are vanquished for all eternity by divine fire (Revelation 20:9). In 2011, Raspail explained that he had written his book at Boulouris, near Saint-Raphaël, in a state of mystic exaltation without knowing "what he was thinking."

Who is "Big Other"?[36] At that point, Raspail apparently had no idea what such a term might signify in the human sciences that he was so ferociously attacking, denouncing pell-mell "the whole

150

pack – media, showbiz, artists, human-rights types, sociologists, academics, teachers, the literary set, activist groups, spin doctors, legalists, bishops, leftist Christians, technocrats, shrinks, militant humanitarians, mutualists, community organizers, and I could keep right on going ..."[37] Feeling like a castaway in his own country, he accused all the scientific institutions (EHESS, ENS, CNRS[38]), all the universities, and all the psychoanalytic associations in France of being responsible for the country's identitarian anguish, owing to their tolerance for foreigners. He saw the eye of a Lacano-Orwellian Big Other everywhere, surveilling him and slipping into his neurons: "Big Other is watching intently. Big Other has a myriad of eyes, ears, and voices all around. It's the Only Begotten Son of the Prevailing Orthodoxy, the way Christ is the Son of God and proceeds from the Holy Spirit."[39] And of course, at the heart of Raspail's defense of the Burgundians, the Vikings, and the Visigoths, there arises the specter of a mixed-race France, destroyed by Islamized extra-Europeans.

This is how, relayed by a mad book academically constructed by an author nostalgic for Hugues Capet and the colonial empire, the thesis of replacement has made its way not only inside the cluster of far-right Identitarians, but also, gradually, into the ranks of the most honorable republican right, then into those of a republican left haunted by an Islamization of France by way of American campuses. Until his death, Jean Raspail was honored in the press as a writer of stature, one of the first to have denounced the migratory peril that no one wanted to see.

This thesis was taken up again by Michel Houellebecq in 2015, in another futuristic novel, *Submission*[40]; in a glacial, hyperrealist style the book describes the rise to power of an Islamist party in France. A perfect emblem of the identitarian anxieties of the cultivated far right, signed by an author fascinated by abjection and writing in a style completely devoid of affect, published on the very day the cartoonists of *Charlie Hebdo* were assassinated, the novel achieved worldwide success: it was received by all the press, on the right and the left alike, as a literary masterpiece.

In this connection, I should point out that, like their sworn enemies, the Identitarians on the far left also had their fetish authors, selected from among the greatest writers of world literature, whose works they reinterpreted in outrageous ways. Thus George Orwell, a ferocious anticolonialist, a former fighter in the International Brigades of the POUM (Workers' Party of Marxist Unification), an empiricist pamphleteer, proponent of a morality of "common decency," a radical antifascist, hostile to all abstract universalism and an anti-Stalinist from the outset, became – 65 years after his death – a sort of conservative anarchist, opposed to "deconstructivism," to "structuralism," to all sociological thought, to liberalism, and thus, ultimately, to the American academic scene, the importers of "queerness" and intersectionality.[41]

Similarly, these critics took Philip Roth – a powerful writer of modernity, an enlightened conservative along Freud's lines, capable of making fun of all the identitarian drifts in the purest New-York-Jewish style – and turned him into the embodiment of a radical anti-progressivism. In fact, in a sumptuous novel published in 2000, *The Human Stain*, Roth told the story of Coleman Silk, a classics professor near the end of his career.[42] Persecuted by antiracist activists because of his use of the word "zombie," Silk chose to resign rather than to reveal his secret life: of mixed race, he had passed as white and as a Jew, even as he maintained a guilty relationship with a university custodian who for her part was being persecuted by her ex-husband, a Vietnam veteran. The book is thus an indictment of conformist and puritanical America, the very America that was behind the attacks on Bill Clinton during the Monica Lewinski affair in 1998.

Despite the legislative arsenal developed from the 1970s through the turn of the century forbidding the direct expression of racism, anti-Semitism, and negationism, the myths of peril continued to prosper in France among the identitarian right, paralleling the phobias emerging from the identitarian politics on the left. The structure can be found in all the manifestations of hostility to laws favorable to homosexual marriage and assisted procreation, since the far-right Identitarians consider that such laws promote the process of abolishing the structure of the family along with the anatomical differences between the sexes.

It must be noted that, starting in the early 1980s, in reaction to the events of May 1968 and to a real advance of individual rights in favor of women, foreigners, and minorities (a movement that prospered under the socialist governments in France pursuant to the election of François Mitterrand to the presidency), several currents of thought were launched with some success toward the reconquest of the intellectual field that had been dominated by the left for years. This was the case in particular of Alain de Benoist and his Group of Research and Study for European Civilization (GRECE), and several journals, including *Éléments*, *Nouvelle École*, and especially *Krisis*. Founded in 1989, this latter journal was presented as offering high-level support apt to attract intellectuals from all horizons, provided that they were open to self-questioning, through "constructive dialogue" on national identity, modern art, and the misdemeanors of antiracism and cosmopolitism.[43] Unquestionably, during that period, several ultrareactionary movements – mutually incompatible tendencies, moreover – found new vigor in the encounter between Catholic integralism, the defense of a shattered West, the mockery of modern art, or the overt neopaganism that purported to follow an extravagant interpretation of the thinking of Georges Dumézil.[44] They tried to restore the ideals of an earlier world, Aryan-Greco-Latin for some, Judeo-Christian for others, against a background of sovereignism, anti-Americanism, and antiglobalism.

In response, in 1993 some 40 intellectuals, teachers and scholars – including Jean-Pierre Vernant, Yves Bonnefoy, Georges Duby, Umberto Eco, François Jacob, Pierre Bourdieu, Jacques Derrida, Michelle Perrot, Jean Pouillon, Françoise Héritier, Jacques Revel, Arlette Farge, and Michel Deguy – published an opinion piece initiated by Maurice Olender appealing to intellectuals to refuse to collaborate with the efforts of this new far right whose protagonists claimed to have changed: "Read between the lines, these signatures obviously accredit the idea that the so-called change is a reality ... By dint of these involuntary complicities, we fear that we shall see in our intellectual life the everyday presence of discourse that must be combated because it threatens both democracy and human lives."[45]

The well-aimed article succeeded in hitting its mark. That year, in fact, Paul Yonnet, a sociologist of sports, had just published, under the auspices of the journal *Le Débat*, *Voyage au centre du malaise français*, a book that incorporated the discourse of the new far right word for word.[46] Yonnet simultaneously denounced the market, the degrading of the ideals of French identity, the claim to hegemony of the partisans of "human-rightsism," and especially "neoantiracism," the antiracist struggles that he regarded as a manifestation of the extinction of French identity. Worse still, he deplored the reduction of the French national story to the history of the Second World War, that is, to the question of the extermination of the Jews. And of course he targeted the NGO SOS Racism and the so-called "caviar" or Mitterrandian left, although that part of the left, as we know, in no way prefigured the decolonialist positions: antiracism was not only more worrying concerning racism, Yonnet insisted, it was more harmful. This thesis was also supported by Pierre-André Taguieff, a highly reputed scholar specializing in racism.

In short, Yonnet brandished the fantasies of racial mixing, replacement, and invasion. Widely criticized, most notably in

THE SOVEREIGN SELF

Libération and *Le Nouvel Observateur*, and seeing himself as the victim of a cabal, he responded in an obscurantist text larded with neologisms, many including the prefixes "neo-" and "pan-":

> Let us posit the following reasoning, which is also a tautology: if the assimilation of immigrants who wish to become French is achieved, it will be against the neo-antiracist utopia of a regeneration of French society through its transformation into a pan-racial, pan-ethnic, pan-communitarian society, against the feverish propagation of a pan-racial vision of social relations, against the proclaimed will to destroy the mechanisms of assimilation after having declared them deadly, it will be against the myth of the dissolution of French culture and nationality into the universality of the rights of man, against the myth of the achievement of the reduction of the so-called 'white" man, against the political program of neo-antiracism, which is to oppose by all possible means the will to control migratory flows.[47]

The difficulty, in this affair, is that back then no one among Paul Yonnet's "enemies" subscribed to such a "pan-racial" program or anything like it. Twenty years later, on the contrary, his theses had won over part of the intelligentsia and were taken up by the right-wing press against the "invasion" of decolonial thought.

Unlike Raspail, Renaud Camus, the inventor of the "great replacement," came from the avant-garde literary milieu; a contributor to the journal *Le Gai Pied*, he was close to Roland Barthes and Marguerite Duras. A militant in the homosexual cause, a left-wing socialist and ecologist, Renaud began his career by publishing stories in which he related the details of his amorous relations in the most literal terms. One of these stories, *Tricks*, was published with a preface by Barthes, and nothing hinted that this affable Proustian dandy would trigger one of the biggest literary, editorial, and media quarrels of the early twenty-first century. His *La Campagne de France: Journal 1944*, published in 2000, prompted over a hundred articles, petitions, and opinion pieces. The book was withdrawn from circulation so that the anti-Semitic passages could be suppressed; the reception of the new edition was raucous.[48] The affair is so well known, has been so thoroughly analyzed and explained by the protagonists and the commentators that I shall not go back over it here.[49] However, it is important to recall that the book actually included an accounting of ethnico-religious identities, at a time when the famous laws contested by Jean Raspail applied not to literature but to the direct expression of opinions and judgments.

154

Criticizing a particular program broadcast on France Culture, Camus indulged, in his *Journal*, in a stylistic exercise on the motif of "too much" and "not enough." According to him,

[t]he Jewish collaborators of "Panorama" went a little too far, nonetheless: on the one hand, they were about four out of five in each program, or four out of six, or five out of seven, which, on a national and almost official station, constituted a clear overrepresentation of a given ethnic or religious group; on the other hand, they managed to have at least one program a week devoted to Jewish culture, the Jewish religion, Jewish writers, the State of Israel and its politics ...

Camus went on to wonder what the listener would feel if, among the journalists gathered around the microphone,

there were four homosexuals out of six, or five out of seven ... Wouldn't one say that these homosexuals were going a little too far? Now, there were in France many more homosexuals than Jews (at least I think there were). There were also many more Arabs. And the Arabs, for their part, are virtually unrepresented in "Panorama," except, from time to time, by a *Christian* Franco-Lebanese.[50]

It is hard, reading this text now, to avoid comparing it to the famous classifications that have come out of the cultural/colonial/gender studies that Camus subsequently attacked. But, a few pages further on, the author embraced the terror of subversion, with the difference that the Jews were "replaced" by the Arabs, the Muslims, the "colored," the foreigners, and above all, once again, the mixed-race populations. The former had been successfully integrated, while the latter were condemned to fail:

I think the mixed-race society is going to win, has already largely won ... Just as the Jews have gradually and more or less happily become integrated, so will the Muslims, the Arabs, and the Blacks. But they will not become integrated with the pureblood French, and the purebloods will not be integrated with them: all will be integrated together into a society and perhaps a civilization that is being born before our eyes, and that we see at work already in the suburbs, the high schools, the discotheques, and television commercials.[51]

From one page to the next, Camus thus went from "too many Jews" to "too many Arabs." But in the first case, he said, integration had been possible, whereas in the second it was doomed to fail. In other words, he was accurately noting the evolution that had taken

THE SOVEREIGN SELF

place in France since the 1990s. Officially, in the discourse of the anti-Semites, the Jews were no longer cast as scapegoats, so long as they did not put their Jewishness on display. They had been replaced in that status by the Arabs, who for their part would never be able, it was said, to become pureblood French persons. It was through this delirious logic of the hierarchy between good and bad races that anti-Semitic discourses mutated, in the work of Camus and his ilk, into a philo-Semitic discourse, still on the hunt for a hateworthy alterity: the Arab, a specter of the Jew. Such is the infernal spiral of the doctrine of the "great replacement": another in the place of another who is replacing yet another. Once the circle has been completed, it is always the Jew, the original kin, who comes back to the forefront: the Jew "too many," the Jew of France Culture's "Panorama," the one who exaggerates, the one who goes too far.

It is on this fertile ground that Camus, an old hand at the rhetoric of "replacementism," began to fetishize the lost paradise of an original language, the good French of the old textbooks, to which it suited him to add an original territory: a castle in the Gers region, at Plieux, acquired in 1992 and transformed into a place of resistance to the Islamization of the planet.[52]

From his ramparts of another age, where he receives his guests and writes his blog, the former activist in the homosexual cause tries to survive in an alternative world that is destined to be replaced one day in its turn. From his lofty vantage point he is witnessing the global triumph of his theory of the "great replacement," adopted by all the identitarian clusters throughout the world and by the fans of *In-nocence retrouvée* (Rediscovered In-nocence), the name he has given to the political party he founded in 2012 with the aim of presenting himself as a candidate for the presidency. But most notably, it was from Colombey-les-Deux-Églises,[53] on November 9, 2017, that Renaud Camus, identifying himself with Charles de Gaulle, decided to launch his appeal for the decolonization of Europe. Immigration, he declared, had become "invasion" and, henceforth, population transfers would lead ineluctably to the Black and Arabic Islamization of Europe as a whole.

These theses have been adopted today not only by the galaxy of the far right but also by the parties and the media troubled by the identity question, a question repeatedly raised by the decolonialists and other intersectionals who boycott books and performances. Reinforcing this tendency, Camus advocates revising the legislation governing birthright citizenship and banning medically assisted procreation outright. In addition, he has embraced the thematics of "remigration" that is

156

being spread by many "pureblood-ist" Identitarians, proposing the adoption of a law that would subsidize non-Europeans who agreed to return ("remigrate") to their country of origin.

Renaud Camus has been one of the most active protagonists of the "great replacement" theory, to be sure. But the thesis would never have acquired a national audience comparable to Édouard Drumont's following in the late nineteenth century without the arrival on stage of a polemicist to whom the complacent media offered an exceptional podium: Éric Zemmour. Born in 1958 in Montreuil into a Jewish family originally from Algeria, he attended a Catholic school where he came to abhor the ritual of morning prayers. Raised by a diabetic homemaker mother and an ambulance-driver father who was a regular at casinos and ready to punish his son's disobedience with his belt, Zemmour became convinced very early that he was a pure product of French secularism, and he never tires of saying that one becomes a real man only when one confronts a "real" father and can "kill the father."[54] Obsessed by the question of the "Name-of-the Father,"[55] this young man prided himself on his knowledge of psychoanalysis, Lacanian by preference. In 2017, at the time of Emmanuel Macron's victory in the French presidential election, Zemmour insisted on the fact that that "Peter Pan" did not want to be a father, which was why he had married a powerful mother who treated him as a "mama's boy." And he cited Lacan in cutting terms: "Love is giving something one doesn't have to someone who doesn't want it."[56]

Disappointed at having failed the entrance examination for the prestigious National School of Administration (ENA), Zemmour decided to take up a career in journalism, shifting from print media to radio and then television, where he began to make himself known for his misogyny and his hatred for Jews, homosexuals, and Arabs. Moreover, in order to ward off any threat of being identified with the Arabness he despised, he asserted that he was a "Berber Jew," one way of claiming the status of "pureblood French." "One cannot be French and Algerian at the same time," he declared. Although obsessed with his origins and detesting religious rituals, he never severed himself fully from them, as if he felt compelled to avow again and again an identity he had denied: "At the synagogue I am Moses, but in civil society my name is Éric Justin Léon." The fact remains that Justin-Léon professes a holy revulsion toward immigrants who give their children foreign first names. He rails against all the Mohameds and Rachids, all the Zhoras and Hapsatous, claiming that it was a disaster for France when it abandoned the requirement of referring to the calendar of saints for naming a child, since the change allowed children of immigrants to retain traces of their countries of origin.

Thanks to the energetic Catherine Barma, and in the overall context of an evolution of public opinion against the "elites," Zemmour secured a comfortable place for himself on a public television channel, despite several condemnations for inciting racial hatred. Subsequently he was entrusted with a daily chronicle on C-News, a continuous news channel in the Canal+ group. Thus every evening, at prime time, he realizes his dream: he receives a guest, preferably an intellectual, to debate his major fixation: France is no longer France.

Beginning in 2010, Zemmour set about transforming himself into a high-level identitarian historian for the purpose of clearing France of its elites, who had sold out to globalization. And it was from this standpoint that he composed a sort of trilogy devoted to the French decline: *Mélancolie française*, *Suicide français*, and *Destin français*.[57] The series is built around the thematics of the "great replacement": France is dying and men are being deprived of their penises and of their ancestral right to dominate the weaker sex. As for the pureblood French, they are being driven out of cities, neighborhoods, and villages so they can be replaced by African, Arab, and Asian populations who transform churches into mosques. And Justin-Léon denounces the vast bordello of a France stuffed with burkinis, niqabs, turbans, lucky charms, prayer rugs, halal meat, transgenders on a spree, served by an army of left-wing academics directed by the Indigenes of the Republic, themselves financed by bizarre and not very French banks.

Carefully constructed on the model of *La France juive*, with lists of names, dates, titles of books recycled helter-skelter in a work resembling a vast witches' cauldron, *Le suicide français* sets forth a frightening picture of the 40 years that, following the events of May '68, have purportedly led France to the threshold of irreversible death throes. But, to try to save his country from succumbing, Justin-Léon makes bold to "deconstruct the deconstructors" by ever so proudly invoking Antonio Gramsci, with his notion of "cultural hegemony," and Fernand Braudel, whom he takes as a nationalist theorist of French identity.

He then draws up an impressive list of those responsible for the suicide, all thinkers whose works he evidently has not read: Sartre, Simone de Beauvoir, Derrida, Bourdieu, Deleuze, Foucault, Guattari, Rosanvallon, Bernard-Henri Lévy, and Claude Lanzmann (whom he reproaches for having privileged the history of the Shoah to the detriment of other genocides). As for Lévi-Strauss, Zemmour criticizes him for having sought to impose a communitarian system on France. Naturally, he mocks all so-called "modern" literature, making an exception for Patrick Modiano, whom he takes to be an admirer of Philippe Pétain. And he does not forget to signal those who, in his eyes, are endangering national cohesion: the homosexuals, and most notably Pierre Bergé and Yves Saint Laurent, guilty of having "masculinized" women by dressing them as men. Finally, he delivers an apologia for Pétain, stressing that the head of the French state could have avoided the deportation of the French Jews by turning the foreign Jews over to the Nazis. Consequently, he denounces the work of Robert Paxton, the better to rehabilitate the Vichy regime.[58]

Four years later, in *Destin français*, purporting to connect his own genealogy with that of his "fatherland," Zemmour revisits "his history of France," from Clovis to de Gaulle, and from the Crusades to the jihad. And this is how, in a burst of acute Drumontism, he accuses the Rothschild family of being responsible for Napoleon's defeat in Russia and at Waterloo: "The Frankfurt brotherhood made its fortune by supporting the struggle against Napoleon. Everything about the emperor displeased them. He refused all indebtedness and scorned those who supplied war materiel."[59]

Is it really necessary to linger over this nonsense and these abject propositions? If a historian of the stature of Gérard Noiriel thought it worth his while to devote an entire book to Zemmour, it was precisely because the latter has played a crucial role in the spread and normalization of identitarian theses that one might well have thought would never be rehabilitated. And yet it is actually in France that this has happened. Received with a volley of criticism by news outlets, *Le suicide français* quickly became a best-seller, with nearly 400,000 copies sold. As for the author, he is viewed as a restorer of the true French values that have been trampled not only by barbarian hordes but also by the greatest thinkers of the second half of the twentieth century, from Sartre through Lévi-Strauss to Césaire, authors who have been translated, read, and discussed throughout the world, to France's honor. Finally, Zemmour is regularly invited by several political parties and other moral rearmament movements that have emerged from a right wing in search of authority.

Gripped with a great surge of hatred, Houria Bouteldja wrote to Zemmour:

> It couldn't be worse: you're not only a Jew but you're also an Arab (or Berber, but it's the same thing). You pile it on. It pains me to see you. You're called Zemmour when others are called Klugman, Klein,

THE SOVEREIGN SELF

Finkelstein. You didn't even have the courtesy to be born Aryan! And in your hatred for us, Muslims and other scum, it's detestation for your own race that you're expressing. *As a Jew and as an Arab.* First of all, you hold it against us that we have resisted the assimilationism that the Republic imposes on us, whereas you and your family have given in ... Our headscarves, our ostentatious beards, our mosques, our halal meat recall too closely the sacrifice of identity to which you have had to submit.[60]

The reader of such an outburst will not be surprised that Zemmour has been joined in this putrid swamp by yet another polemicist, equally adored by the declinist media: Michel Onfray. After accusing Freud, in 2010, of being a fascist, an anti-Sémite, an incestuous brother-in-law, and a bird of prey, he went on to insult Sartre; finally, preferring the good Proudhon to the bad Marx (born to a Jewish tribe), the libertarian philosopher now wants to be seen as the spokesman for the good people of France. Converted to a Zemmourized imaginary realm, he has become in his turn an ardent critic of the structuralist-Islamist-left-wingers and thus of the French Theory he deems responsible for an unprecedented degrading of the French nation. "That theory singles out the centers as well as the margins," he writes:

homosexuals, transgenders, women, Blacks, North Africans, immigrants, Muslims, but also – these are Foucault's favorite subjects – prisoners, madmen, hermaphrodites, criminals, if not – these are Deleuze's heroes – drug addicts or schizophrenics. From here on, members of the proletariat are no longer the actors of History, they are ordered to yield their places to the minorities: they will go console themselves for this eviction, theorized by Terra Nova, among the Le Pens.[61]

And it is by listening to such poppycock that a not-inconsiderable fringe of the French media sphere has adopted the firm belief, while ignoring all or almost all of the decolonial-queer galaxy, that the figures truly responsible for the misfortunes of French identity are called Sartre, Foucault, Derrida, Césaire, Fanon, Deleuze, and, further back in history, Rousseau, Robespierre, Danton, Saint-Just, the Terror, May 1968. Not a week goes by without the appearance in the media of insults of that sort, relayed by thousands of websites in search of conspiracies.

160

EPILOGUE

What will become of these identitarian tendencies? Are they the symptom of a breakdown of subjectivities, connected with a particular moment in world history, or, on the contrary, are they going to persist to the point of replacing other forms of individual and collective engagement?

One thing is certain, at least: the Identitarians of the far right and the reactionary right keep harping on the same themes, with some minor variations – the terror of otherness, the obsession with the "great replacement," hatred of the present, fetishization of a fantasized past. Their discourse is not about to fade away. But it only becomes dangerous when it is massively disseminated by complacent intermediaries or when it feeds into the programs of political parties carried away by the populist wave.

When it comes to the drifts of gender, originating in a movement of emancipation turned into its opposite, it is appropriate, in the framework of a state based on law, to impose serious limits, quite simply because the law cannot be the translation of a desire expressed by a subject, whatever motive is invoked: suffering, for example, when it is caused by a deficient or delirious relation to oneself. The role of the state is to protect citizens from all discriminatory acts, including those that result from a desire to do oneself harm. From this perspective, it is right to oppose any project that would abolish the anatomical and biological difference between the sexes – as would a proposal by the most fanatic proponents to institute a "neuter" gender and inscribe it in civil law. All the more so if, by the same token, such a measure were to be imposed on disturbed prepubescent children, subjecting them to hormonal or even surgical treatments that could be viewed as medical malpractice.[1]

EPILOGUE

As for the identitarian drifts tied to religious obscurantism, the segregationist re-establishment of the idea of race, the destruction of statues, the boycott of certain lectures or instructional material or performances, these already run into limits and sanctions in the legal framework in France, when they are instrumentalized for a terrorist project or when they stem from misdemeanors or criminal acts. And it must never be forgotten, in the face of the claims from the two opposing fringes of extremism, that the strength of French republicanism has rested, since 1789, on a double contract: on one side, the refusal to grant religion any political power in civil society and, on the other, the acceptance of the distinctive identities, religious or other, granted to all citizens on an individual basis. All members of society can thus freely cultivate their own identities, provided that these are not set up as principles of domination.[2]

Moreover, the state must not play the role of censor in claiming to regulate the freedom to debate and to teach. It has no business taking sides in favor of one thesis or another. As for the intellectuals, no doubt it behooves us to set an example, supporting some ideas and combating others: taking sides, then, without ever yielding to insult or invective, a practice too often encouraged in contemporary debates.

NOTES

Notes to preface

1   See Myriam Revault d'Allonnes, *L'homme compassionnel* (Paris: Seuil, 2008).
2   This neologism was created by Serge Doubrovsky in 1977, in connection with his novel *Fils*, to designate a literary genre inherited from Proust that includes the expression of the unconscious in the story of the self without reducing it to a confessional outpouring centered on the suffering of the self in question.
3   Gérard Noiriel, "Patrick Boucheron: Un historien sans gilet jaune," blog, February 11, 2019: https://noiriel.wordpress.com/2019/02/11/patrick-boucheron-un-historien-sans-gilet-jaune/. [Here and elsewhere, translations not otherwise attributed or identified as (anonymous) translations from the French are my own. – *Translator's note.*]
4   Cf. Paul Ricoeur, *Oneself as Another*, trans. Kathleen Blarney (Chicago: University of Chicago Press, [1990] 1992). [The French title of this book, *Soi-même comme un roi* (literally Oneself as a King), echoes Ricoeur's *Soi-même comme un autre*. – *Translator's note.*]
5   Arthur Rimbaud, "Lettre du voyant," to Paul Demeny, May 15, 1871, in *Lettres du voyant: 13 et 15 mai 1871* (Geneva: Droz, 1975).
6   "Je suis Charlie" was widely adopted as an expression of solidarity after the 2015 assassination of several journalists working for the satirical weekly *Charlie Hebdo* in Paris. – *Translator's note.*
7   See Jacques Derrida, *The Monolinguism of the Other, or The Prosthesis of Origin*, trans. Patrick Mensah (Stanford, CA: Stanford University Press, [1996] 1998).
8   According to the lovely formula offered by Michel Serres in an opinion piece titled "Faute" (*Libération*, November 18, 2009).
9   Guy Sorman characterizes this attribution as an "identitarian horror": "Finissons-en avec cet odieux discours réactionnaire!" *Le Monde*, October 1, 2016.
10 *Indigènes de la République* (Indigenes of the [French] Republic) is the name of a movement described by its founders in 2005 as antiracist and decolonial; it became a political party in 2008. – *Translator's note.*

163

NOTES TO PP. 1–6

Notes to chapter 1

1 See the proceedings in Chawki Azouri and Élisabeth Roudinesco, eds., *La psychanalyse dans le monde arabe et islamique* (Beirut: Presses de l'université Saint-Joseph, 2005). The participants included Souad Ayada, Jalil Bennani, Fethi Benslama, Antoine Courban, Sophie Bessis, Christian Jambet, Paul Lacaze, and Anissé el-Amine Merhi.

2 The French concept of *laïcité*, or secularism, is a constitutional principle ensuring the separation of public institutions from the influence of religious organizations, most notably the Catholic Church. – *Translator's note.*

3 Cf. article 1 of the Constitution of October 4, 1958: "France shall be an indivisible, secular, democratic and social Republic. It shall ensure the equality of all citizens before the law, without distinction of origin, race or religion. It shall respect all beliefs. It shall be organized on a decentralized basis. Statutes shall promote equal access by women to elective offices and posts as well as to position[s] of professional and social responsibility." https://www.constituteproject.org/constitution/France_2008.pdf?lang=en.

4 Fernand Braudel, *The Identity of France*, trans. Siân Reynolds, vol. 1 (Paris: Flammarion, [1986] 1992), p. 15.

5 Of these communities, 12 are Christian (Maronite, Greek Orthodox, Greek Catholic, Armenian Orthodox, Armenian Catholic, Syrian Catholic, Jacobite, Chaldean, Nestorian, Latin, Protestant, and Copt). Of the five other communities, one is Israelite and four are Muslim (Sunni, Shia, Druze, and Alawite). See Fredrik Barth, "Les groupes ethniques et leurs frontières," in Philippe Poutignat and Jacelyne Streiff-Fenart, *Théories de l'ethnicité* (Paris: Presses universitaires de France, 1995), pp. 203–49.

6 On this issue, see Catherine Kintzler, *Penser la laïcité* (Paris: Minerve, 2014).

7 Élisabeth Roudinesco, "Le foulard à l'école, étouffoir de l'altérité," *Libération*, May 27, 2003. I testified in favor of the law before a commission convoked in July 2003 by Bernard Stasi. I also spoke out in favor of prohibiting niqabs in public spaces, because the existence of democratic freedoms presupposes that subjects do not conceal their faces and that they can be identified for what they are.

8 Sélim Abou, *La "République" jésuite des Guaranis (1609–1768) et son héritage* (Paris: Perrin/Unesco, 1995), and *De l'identité et du sens: La mondialisation de l'angoisse identitaire et sa signification plurielle* (Paris and Beirut: Perrin/Presses de l'université Saint-Joseph, 2009). Roland Joffé, in his 1986 film *The Mission*, did an excellent job of retracing the history of the fight of the Jesuits and the Guanari people of Paraguay against Spanish and Portuguese colonialism. Abou restated Tocqueville's famous paradox according to which the more a situation improves, the more the gap between the current situation and the ideal is felt subjectively as intolerable by the very people who benefit from the improvement. See Alexis de Tocqueville, *Democracy in America*, trans. Arthur Goldhammer, vol. 2 (New York: Library of America, [1840] 2004), book 2, chapter 13.

9 I examined this issue in *La famille en désordre* (Paris: Fayard, 2002).

10 Charles de Secondat, baron de Montesquieu, *Mes pensées*, anthology established by Catherine Volpilhac-Auger (Paris: Gallimard, 2014). Abou's citation combines *pensées* (thoughts) 350 (p. 143) and 741 (p. 153).

164

NOTES TO PP. 7–12

11 Christopher Lasch, *The Culture of Narcissism: American Life in an Age of Diminishing Expectations* (New York: W. W. Norton, 1979). A bestseller in the United States, the book was greeted in France as a critique of left-wing progressivism.
12 Christopher Lasch, *The Minimal Self: Psychic Survival in Troubled Times* (New York: W. W. Norton, 1984), p. 15.
13 Michel Foucault, "Je suis un artificier," in Roger-Pol Droit, *Michel Foucault: Entretiens* (Paris: Odile Jacob, 2004), pp. 111–12. The interview by Roger-Pol Droit was recorded in June 1975. For the transcript, see https://foucault.info/documents/foucault.entretien1975.fr/.
14 Mark Lilla, *The Once and Future Liberal* (New York: HarperCollins, 2017), pp. 11–12.

Notes to chapter 2

1 The first volume was published by Gallimard in June 1949 and the second in September. It has been published in English translation in a single volume: see Simone de Beauvoir, *The Second Sex*, trans. Constance Borde and Sheila Malovany-Chevallier (New York: Alfred A. Knopf, 2010), p. 283.
2 On this topic, see Robert Stoller, *Sex and Gender: On the Development of Masculinity and Femininity* (New York: Science House, 1968), and Heinz Kohut, *The Analysis of the Self: A Systematic Approach to the Psychoanalytic Treatment of Narcissistic Personality Disorders* (New York: International Universities Press, 1971). See also Thomas Laqueur, *Making Sex: Body and Gender from the Greeks to Freud* (Cambridge, MA: Harvard University Press, 1990); and Lynn Hunt, *Family Romance of the French Revolution* (Berkeley: University of California Press, 1995).
3 Alfred C. Kinsey, *Sexual Behavior in the Human Male* (Philadelphia: W. B. Saunders, 1948). The first volume of this survey, devoted to male sexuality, had just appeared in French translation.
4 Laqueur, *Making Sex*.
5 Plato, *The Symposium*, trans. M. C. Howatson (Cambridge: Cambridge University Press, 2008). See also Jean-François Rey, "L'épreuve du genre: Que nous apprend le mythe de l'androgyne?," *Cités*, no. 44 (2010): 13–26.
6 See Sigmund Freud, "On the universal tendency to debasement in the sphere of love," in Sigmund Freud, James Strachey, Anna Freud, and Angela Richards, *The Standard Edition of the Complete Psychological Works of Sigmund Freud* (London: Hogarth Press, [1912] 1966), vol. 11, p. 189. In French translations of Freud, the German "die Anatomie ist das Schiksal" is sometimes rendered as "le destin c'est la politique," or "destiny is politics."
7 During a meeting with Goethe in Erfurt on October 2, 1808, the Emperor evoked the tragedies of fate that, according to him, revealed a somber period and a bygone past: "'Why, today, do they keep giving us destiny?' he said. 'Destiny is politics'" (see Shannon Selin, "When Napoleon met Goethe," October 7, 2016: https://shannonselin.com/2016/10/napoleon-met-goethe/). I discussed this statement in *La famille en désordre* (Paris: Fayard, 2002), in the opening chapter, "Les femmes ont un sexe."

165

NOTES TO PP. 13–18

8 On gender studies in France, an interesting overview can be found in a report to the National Assembly coordinated by Maud Olivier and registered on October 11, 2016: "Rapport d'information fait au nom de la délégation aux droits des femmes et à l'égalité des chances entre les hommes et les femmes, sur les études de genre, par Mme Maud Olivier, Députée" (https://www.assemblee-nationale.fr/14/rap-info/i4105.asp). See also Juliette Rennes, ed., *Encyclopédie critique du genre* (Paris: La Découverte, 2016).

9 See especially Laurent Dubrueil, *La dictature des identités* (Paris: Gallimard, 2019), and Éliane Elmaleh, "Les politiques identitaires dans les universités américaines," *L'Homme et la société*, no. 149 (2003): 57–74.

10 In Greek mythology, Hermaphrodite is a young man born of the union between Hermès and Aphrodite. Hermaphroditism is a biological phenomenon by virtue of which an individual is both male and female (today we use the terms "intersexuality" and "intersex" individuals); it has nothing to do with androgyny, which refers to a different myth. Hermaphroditism is found in one to two percent of births today. The genetic makeup of a female includes two XX chromosomes, while that of a male includes one X and one Y chromosome. Hermaphroditism can take various forms. In one, which is very rare, women have XY chromosomes and men have XX; the external sex organs are reversed and atrophied. The other – pseudo-hermaphroditism, which is much more frequent – stems from a congenital anomaly without chromosomic modification in which both sets of reproductive organs are found in a single individual; one set or the other may be atrophied.

11 John Money, "Hermaphroditism, gender and precocity in hyperadrenocorticism: Psychologic findings," *Bull. Johns Hopkins Hosp.*, 96, no. 6 (1955): 253–64. See p. 258: "Apparently, a person's gender role as boy or girl, man or woman, is built up cumulatively through the life experiences he encounters and through the life experiences he transacts."

12 On John Money's thought, see Jean-François Braunstein, *La philosophie devenue folle: Le genre, l'animal, la mort* (Paris: Grasset, 2018), pp. 27–73.

13 See, for example, Harry Benjamin, "Transvestism and transsexualism." *International Journal of Sexology*, 7 (1953): 12–14.

14 The best French study on the subject is by Claire Nahon: "Destins et figurations du sexuel dans la culture: Pour une théorie de la transsexualité," Ph.D. thesis in fundamental psychopathology and psychoanalysis, directed by Pierre Fédida and Alain Vanier, University of Paris 7, 2004.

15 Some authors distinguish homophilia from homosexuality as a way of distinguishing abstainers from practitioners.

16 The authors of the *Diagnostic and Statistical Manual of Mental Disorders* (American Psychiatric Association, Committee on Nomenclature and Statistics: Washington, DC [1952] 2013) invented the notion of "gender dysphoria" to characterize transgenderism.

17 On the genesis of this expression, which was well-intentioned at the outset, see Jacques Derrida and Elisabeth Roudinesco, *De quoi demain ... Dialogue* (Paris: Fayard/Galilee, 2001). The critique of political correctness came initially from a conservative movement that sought to represent American scholars working in the areas of feminism, structuralism, anti-racism, and so on, as censors. The expression was then taken up again and given a positive connotation by the very academics who had been designated pejoratively by that label.

166

NOTES TO PP. 18–22

18 Founded in 2009 by Caroline De Haas, a political militant and trade unionist. The movement has been joined by many other collectives including "La Barbe" and "Les Dégommeuses."

19 The most emblematic case is that of the film director Roman Polanski, accused of rape and abuse after the fact even though the statute of limitations had gone into effect well before the testimony was offered.

20 In October 2017, 93 women, including many famous actresses, publicly declared that they had been victims of sexual aggression and blackmail by the producer Harvey Weinstein. Charged and found guilty, Weinstein received a stiff sentence from the American justice system in a fair trial. As for Jeffrey Epstein, a billionaire businessman and sexual predator who had been involved in numerous fraudulent schemes, he succeeded in escaping the justice system for 20 years, despite devastating testimony by his numerous victims. And it was thanks to the #MeToo movement that he was finally caught and incarcerated; he committed suicide in his jail cell on August 10, 2019, in order to avoid a trial. His companion Ghislaine Maxwell, an accomplice in all his sex trafficking crimes, was tried and convicted in 2021.

21 Fleur Burlet, "A New York, une pétition s'élève contre un tableau de Balthus érotisant une très jeune fille," *Les Inrockuptibles*, December 8, 2017: https://www.lesinrocks.com/actu/new-york-une-petition-seleve-contre-un-tableau-de-balthus-erotisant-une-tres-jeune-fille-125792-08-12-2017/. Mia Merrill, a New York entrepreneur, circulated a petition asking the Met either to remove the piece from the exhibit or to provide more context in the painting's description (Mia Merrill, "Metropolitan Museum of Art: Remove Balthus' suggestive painting of a pubescent girl, Thérèse Dreaming," posted November 30, 2017, on Care2 website. https://www.thepetitionsite. com/157/407/182/metropolitan-museum-of-art-remove-balthus-suggestive-painting-of-a-pubescent-girl-th%C3%A9r%C3%A8se- dreaming/?taf_ id=46585122&cid=fb_na#bbfb=809455636). [Although Merrill ultimately collected over 11,000 signatures, the Met refused to remove the painting, explaining its decision as an "opportunity for a conversation" in a statement to *artnet News*: https://news.artnet.com/art-world/met-museum-responds-to-petition-calling-for-removal-of-balthus-painting-1169105. – *Translator's note.*]

22 Alexiane Guchereau, "L'American Library Association a dévoilé lors de la semaine nationale des bibliothécaires la liste des 11 livres les plus censurés aux États-Unis en 2018," *Livres Hebdo*, April 12, 2019. https://www.livreshebdo.fr/article/etats-unis-les-11-livres-les-plus-censures-en-2018.

23 Laure Murat, "*Blow-Up* revu et inacceptable," *Libération*, December 12, 2017. And see Serge Kaganski's response: "Faut-il brûler *Blow-Up*, le chef d'oeuvre d'Antonioni?" *Les Inrockuptibles*, December 15, 2017.

24 On the critique of the evolution of American psychiatry, see Élisabeth Roudinesco, *Pourquoi la psychanalyse?* (Paris: Fayard, 1999); see also Stuart Kirk and Herb Kutchins, *The Selling of DSM: The Rhetoric of Science in Psychiatry* (New York: A. de Gruyter, 1992), and Herb Kutchins and Stuart Kirk, *Making Us Crazy. DSM: The Psychiatric Bible and the Creation of Mental Disorders* (New York: Free Press, 1997).

25 See Henri Ellenberger, *The Discovery of the Unconscious: The History and Evolution of Dynamic Psychiatry* (New York: Basic Books, 1970), and

167

NOTES TO PP. 22–26

Ian Hacking, *Rewriting the Soul: Multiple Personality and the Sciences of Memory* (Princeton, NJ: Princeton University Press, 1995).

26 The seventeenth-century French playwright Molière (born Jean-Baptiste Poquelin) is known for his biting satirical comedies, including *Le malade imaginaire* (The Imaginary Invalid), which mocked the medical practices and practitioners of his day. – *Translator's note.*

27 Mark Moran, "Spitzer issues apology for study supporting reparative therapy," *Psychiatric News*, published online June 15, 2012: https://psychnews.psychiatryonline.org/doi/full/10.1176/pn.47.12.psychnews_47_12_1-b.

28 See George Orwell, *1984: A Novel* (New York: New American Library, [1949] 1983).

29 Allen Frances, "The new crisis of confidence in psychiatric diagnosis," *Annals of Internal Medicine*, 159, no. 3 (August 6, 2013).

30 The French branch of this militant political association was formed to fight HIV/AIDS in 1989; a declaration issued on November 12, 2008, describes the group: "We, women and men, militants, seropositive, seronegative, hetero, homo, bi, trans, we have been fighting from within Act Up-Paris for many years; we campaign with our bodies. Our ruined bodies, in some cases; wounded bodies, bodies on the line in public actions, bodies brought together in demonstrations, rallies and at all our meetings; it is through our bodies and public images of our bodies that we manifest our strength. Our bodies, which sometimes escape us: diseased bodies surviving precariously until 1995, we have now become survivors marked by the side effects of treatment. In this performance society, we hold our own thanks to the many devices and displays that we stage, for we shall never abdicate." https://fr.wikipedia.org/wiki/Act_Up-Paris#cite_note-36.

31 A performative statement is one that brings something into existence by the very fact of stating it (as when an officiant says "I now pronounce you man and wife"). Gender is thus inscribed in a social space by the way one says who one is – hence the possibility of an absolute negation of the assignment of a so-called "natural" sex at birth. See J. L. Austin, *How to Do Things with Words* (Cambridge, MA: Harvard University Press, 1962).

32 Eve Kosofsky Sedgwick, "Queer and now," in Eve Kosofsky Sedgwick, *Tendencies* (London: Taylor & Francis Group, 1994), p. 8.

33 The flag appeared for the first time in 1978 at a march in favor of gay and lesbian rights. In its definitive six-color version (1979), it represented various aspects of political and sexual identities; red for life, orange for healing, yellow for sunlight, green for ecology, blue for art, violet for spirit.

34 The term "queer theory" was forged in 1990 by Teresa de Lauretis, an American academic of Italian origin who was influenced by the French structuralist and post-structuralist thought of the 1960s and 1970s, especially that of Jacques Derrida, Michel Foucault, and Jean Laplanche. On the first use of the term, see David M. Halperin, "The normalization of queer theory," *Journal of Homosexuality*, 45, nos. 2/3/4 (2003): 339–43.

35 The same developments occurred in France some ten years later.

36 Anne-Claire Rebreyend, "Quand la médecine fait le genre," *Clio: Femmes, genre, histoire*, no. 37 (2013): 251–4. https://journals.openedition.org/clio/11110.

37 Anne Fausto-Sterling, *Sexing the Body: Gender Politics and the Construction*

168

NOTES TO PP. 26–29

of Sexuality (New York: Basic Books, 2000), p. 21. See also Braunstein, *La philosophie devenue folle*, pp. 72–3.

38 According to her, intersex individuals represent 1.7% of total births and not 0.018%, or even 1%. But to reach such a figure, she has to annex all children afflicted with various disorders that have nothing to do with hermaphroditism: she includes Turner syndrome (a genetic disorder of the X chromosome that affects only females) and Klinefelter syndrome (an anomaly involving an extra S chromosome in males).

39 On the history of hermaphroditism, see Alice Domurat Dreger, *Hermaphrodites and the Medical Invention of Sex* (Cambridge, MA: Harvard University Press, 1998). Dreger's book explores the relations between hermaphrodites and their doctors in the late nineteenth century. The tragic fate of hermaphrodites has been described magnificently in *Herculine Barbin: Being the Recently Discovered Memoirs of a Nineteenth-Century French Hermaphrodite*, with a preface by Michel Foucault, trans. Richard McDougall (New York: Pantheon Books, [1978] 1980). This was the first volume in a series titled *Vies parallèles* (Parellel Lives). In describing his project, Foucault explains: "This would be like the opposite of Plutarch's: lives so parallel that nothing can bring them together." https://www.decitre.fr/livres/herculine-barbin-dite-alexina-b-9782070299607.html.

40 Vincent Guillot, "Intersexes: Ne pas avoir le droit de dire ce que l'on ne nous a pas dit que nous étions" (Intersexes: Not having the right to say what we have not been told that we were), *Nouvelles questions féministes*, 27, no. 1 (2008): 37–48. It is hard to assess the number of declared homosexuals, but the statistics show that the figure always lies between around 5 to 10 per cent of the population of a country. The percentage is constant. Homosexuals have nothing in common with intersexuals except as militant allies.

41 "Faut-il opérer les enfants intersexués?" *Le Monde*, July 5, 2019, p. 25.

42 See the fine documentary film by Floriane Devigne, *Ni d'Ève ni d'Adam: Une histoire intersexe* (2018), which argues for the abolition of surgical interventions.

43 Pauline Machado, "L'histoire émouvante de Lilie, 'née dans un corps de petit garçon.'" *Terrafemina*, September 11, 2020.

44 See Sébastien Lifshitz's documentary film *Petite fille*, shown on the Arte channel in France on December 2, 2020.

45 See Vanessa Springora, *Le consentement* (Paris: Grasset, 2020). The author describes how, when she was 14 years old, the writer Gabriel Matzneff exercised a form of sexual control over her that rendered her complicit in her own annihilation.

46 See Rachel Cooke, "Tavistock trust whistleblower David Bell: 'I believed I was doing the right thing,'" *The Guardian*, May 2, 2021. https://www.theguardian.com/society/2021/may/02/tavistock-trust-whistleblower-david-bell-transgender-children-gids.

47 Marcus Evans, cited in a personal communication from Dany Nobus, October 21, 2020. And see Jamie Doward, "Governor of Tavistock foundation quits over damning report into gender identity clinic," *The Guardian*, February 23, 2019.

48 "La justice britannique met des conditions aux transitions des mineurs

NOTES TO PP. 30–34

transgenres" (British Justice sets conditions on transitions by transgender minors), *Le Monde*, December 1, 2020. https://www.lemonde.fr/societe/article/2020/12/01/la-justice-britannique-met-des-conditions-aux-transitions-des-mineurs-transgenres_6061808_3224.html.

49 Judith Butler, *Gender Trouble: Feminism and the Subversion of Identity* (New York: Routledge, 1990). The term "borderline state," borrowed from psychiatry and psychoanalysis, designates personality disorders that are on the border between neurosis and psychosis. This borrowing shows that Butler never completely rejected the psychiatric/psychoanalytic vocabulary of her era.

50 This is also the position of the American historian Joan W. Scott, who considers that the French model of secularism (originating in a law passed in 1905 designed to reduce the role of the Catholic Church in public life) has been "instrumentalized" by those who banned Islamic headscarves from schools in a "racist" manner "in order to exclude a minority. Moreover, inequality is at the very heart of our secular states, starting with the inequality between men and women that justifies racial and religious inequality" (Joan Scott, interviewed by Marie Lemonnier, *L'Obs*, September 7, 2018). See also Joan W. Scott, *The Politics of the Veil* (Princeton, NJ: Princeton University Press, 2007). Scott's position is debatable at the very least, since there is nothing "racist" in the French model of republican secularism.

51 Judith Butler, "Can one lead a good life in a bad life?" *Radical Philosophy*, no. 176 (November–December 2012): 9–18.

52 Hans Riebsamen, "Heftiger Streit um Adorno-Preisträgerin" (Fierce Dispute over Adorno Prize Winner), *Frankfurter Allgemeine Zeitung*, August 28, 2012.

53 Judith Butler, *Parting Ways: Jewishness and the Critique of Zionism* (New York: Columbia University Press, 2012), especially pp. 41–9 and 60–1.

54 "Reject transphobia, respect gender identity: An appeal to the United Nations, the World Health Organization and the states of the world," April 1, 2009. I signed that appeal, as did Élisabeth Badinter, Michelle Perrot, and many others. See https://outrightinternational.org/sites/default/files/238-1.pdf.

55 Richard von Krafft-Ebing (1840–1902) was an Austrian psychiatrist who founded sexology; he was the author of the famous *Psychopathia sexualis, with Especial Reference to Contrary Sexual Instinct: A Medico-legal Study*, trans. Charles Gilbert Chaddock (Philadelphia: F. A. Davis, [1886] 1893).

56 Raphaëlle Maruchitch, "Changer de sexe, un long parcours chirugical," *Le Monde*, May 28, 2019.

57 Serge Hefez, "Familles en transition," *Libération*, October 6, 2020. I have changed the names.

58 Émilie Brouze, "Garçon ou fille, à l'enfant de choisir!" *L'Obs*, October 25–31, 2008. See also Thierry Hoquet, *Sexus nullus, ou l'égalité* (Donnemarie-Dontilly: Éd. iXe, 2015). From the scientific standpoint, "human biodiversity" does not exist any more than "race"; this is yet another invention of identity politics.

59 Gary L. Albrecht, Jean-François Ravaud, and Henri-Jacques Stiker, "L'émergence des *disability studies*: État des lieux et perspectives," *Sciences sociales et santé*, 19, no. 4 (December 2001): 43–73. The term disability

170

NOTES TO PP. 34–40

signifies incapacity or handicap (the latter term has fallen out of favor in English but has been adopted in French). All health policy is now based on the notion of disability, which makes it possible to liquidate pluridisciplinary approaches. This is especially true of autism, which is becoming "an opportunity for human biodiversity," even as it is assimilated to a neurodevelopmental illness. With regard to this reductionism, it is worth reading Edith Scheffer, *Asperger's Children: The Origins of Autism in Nazi Vienna* (New York: Norton, 2018).

60 Andrew Solomon, *Far from the Tree: Parents, Children and the Search for Identity* (New York: Scribner, 2012).

61 Solomon, *Far from the Tree*, p. 702.

62 The Council of Paris is a governing body for the municipality and the department of Paris. –*Translator's note*.

63 The French terms *seigneur* (lord) and *saigneur* (blood-letter) are homonyms. – *Translator's note*.

64 Alice Coffin, *Le génie lesbien* (Paris: Grasset, 2020), pp. 39, 228, and 230. Coffin has never been disavowed by her party, even though remarks like these clearly indicate that she cannot claim to represent voters of the male sex in her functions as an elected official of the Republic.

65 Valerie Solanas, *SCUM Manifesto* (London: Verso, [1967] 2001). SCUM is an acronym for Society for Cutting up Men. A French translation was published in 1998 with a postface by Michel Houellebecq, and reprinted in 2021 with a preface by Manon Garcia and a postface by Lauren Bastide. See also the excellent article by Éric Loret, "L'homme couvert d'infâme," *Libération*, May 28, 1998. Let us note that Avital Ronell, a student of Jacques Derrida, wrote a fine preface to the English re-edition of *SCUM Manifesto* (London: Verso, 2006).

66 Solanas, *SCUM Manifesto*, pp. 35 and 45.

67 Michel Houellebecq, postface in Valérie Solanas, *Scum Manifesto*, trans. Emmanuèle de Lesseps (Paris: Mille et Une Nuits, "Les Petits Libres," 2005).

68 Agence France Presse, "Des élèves transgenres américains dénoncent la 'guerre des toilettes,'" *L'Express*, May 26, 2016.

Notes to chapter 3

1 Claude Lévi-Strauss, *Race and History*, translated from the French (Paris: UNESCO, 1952). UNESCO, the United Nations Educational, Scientific and Cultural Organization, was founded on November 16, 1945.

2 Hannah Arendt, *The Origins of Totalitarianism* (New York: Harcourt Brace Jovanovich [1951] 1994), Part One, "Antisemitism," p. 117.

3 See Élisabeth Roudinesco, *Retour sur la question juive* (Paris: Albin Michel, 2009).

4 Paul-Éric Blanrue, *Le monde contre soi: Anthologie des propos contre les Juifs, le judaïsme et le sionisme* (Paris: Blanche, 2007). Withdrawn from circulation, the book was later republished by Alain Soral.

5 On this topic, see Élisabeth Roudinesco, "Se poser en victime d'un complot de l'extrême droite, le tour de force de Yann Moix," *Le Monde*, September 1, 2019.

NOTES TO PP. 40–45

6 See Claude Lévi-Strauss, *The Elementary Structures of Kinship*, ed. Rodney Needham, trans. James Harle Bell, John Richard von Sturmer, and Rodney Needham (Boston: Beacon Press, [1949] 1969).

7 Structuralism is a current of thought that originated in Ferdinand de Saussure's *Course in General Linguistics*, translated by Wade Baskin (New York: Columbia University Press, [1916] 2011). The early structuralists proposed to study language and systems of thought as an arrangement in which each element (sign, symbol, myth, and so on) is defined by the relations of equivalence or opposition that it maintains with other elements, the whole thus forming a "structure." This current has been criticized for its formalism, its antihistoricism, and its dogmatism.

8 Lévi-Strauss, *Race and History*, p. 6.

9 Ibid., p. 12.

10 Claude Lévi-Strauss, *Tristes tropiques*, trans. John Russell (New York: Atheneum, [1955] 1963).

11 See Frédéric Keck, "Le sacrifice des insectes: Caillois entre Lévi-Strauss et Bataille," *Littérature*, no. 170 (2013): 21–32.

12 See Patrick Simon, "Pour lutter contre le racisme, il ne faut pas invisibiliser la question de la 'race,'" *Le Monde*, June 12, 2019.

13 Voltaire (François-Marie Arouet), "Of the discoveries of the Portuguese," in *The [Prose] Works of M. de Voltaire: Additions to the Essay on General History*, trans. T. Smollett, T. Francklin, et al. (London: J. Newbery et al., 1763), vol. 22, p. 227.

14 Voltaire (François-Marie Arouet), *The Philosophy of History*, translated from the French (Glasgow: Robert Urie, [1756] 1766), p. 27 (the spelling has been modernized). *Cafre* was the term used by Arabic slave merchants to designate the indigenous peoples from the lands extending from the Mozambique trading post to the Cape region of South Africa. The term "science of man" is used to characterize the naturalist approach to human types that was developed between the late eighteenth century and the end of the nineteenth. See the excellent doctoral thesis in the history of science and philosophy by Antoine Lévêque, "L'égalité des races en science et en philosophie (1750–1885)," Sorbonne-Paris-Cité University (prepared at Paris-Diderot University under the direction of Justin Smith, public defense held January 27, 2017): https://www.academia.edu/40729847/The_se_LEVEQUE_04.

15 Regarding this question and the genesis of the infernal pairing of Aryans and Semites, invented from whole cloth by German and French philologists, see Maurice Olender, *Les langues du paradis. Aryens et Sémites: Un couple providentiel* (Paris: Gallimard/Seuil, coll. "Hautes études," 1989). I commented on this work in *Retour sur la question juive*.

16 Ernest Renan, cited in Olivier Le Cour Grandmaison, *La République impériale: Politique et racisme d'État* (Paris: Fayard, 2009), p. 7. And see Jules Ferry, "Discours devant la Chambre des députés," July 28, 1885: https://www2.assemblee-nationale.fr/decouvrir-l-assemblee/histoire/grands-discours-parlementaires/jules-ferry-28-juillet-1885.

17 Georges Clemenceau, "Discours à la Chambre des députés," July 30, 1885.

18 Published in English as *The Wretched of the Earth*, trans. Richard Philcox, with forewords by Homi K. Bhabha and Jean-Paul Sartre (New York: Grove Press, 2004), p. xlvii.

NOTES TO PP. 45–48

19 Victor Schoelcher (1804–1893), a politician and a journalist, helped craft the definitive abolition of slavery in France by a decree signed by the provisional government of the Second Republic on April 27, 1848. The first decree abolishing slavery had been passed by the Convention on February 4, 1794, before being abrogated by Napoleon Bonaparte in 1802.

20 The principle of colonization was developed well before the colonial conquests. Without going all the way back to the colonization of Gaul by the Romans, we can recall that it was against "British colonization" that Ireland fought for its independence.

21 Victor Hugo, in a speech given to a party of French Radicals celebrating the abolition of slavery in the French colonies, cited in translation from the French in "Hugo reading the future: The visions of a visionary," *The New York Times*, June 2, 1879, p. 3.

22 Especially on the site of *Mediapart*: see Marc Mvé Bekale's blog, "Victor Hugo: Le blanc a fait du noir un homme," in *Mediapart*, April 22, 2019 (https://blogs.mediapart.fr/marc-mve-bekale/blog/220419/victor-hugo-le-blanc-fait-du-noir-un-homme). Appeals are launched periodically to pull down street signs bearing Hugo's name. Aimé Césaire himself expressed indignation, wrongly, about statements by Hugo.

23 Victor Hugo, *Jargal*, translation of *Bug-Jargal* by C. E. Wilbour (New York: Carleton, [1826] 1866).

24 See C. L. R. James, *The Black Jacobins: Toussaint L'Ouverture and the San Domingo Revolution* (New York: Vintage Books, 1963).

25 For the history of the slaves' revolt, see Aimé Césaire, *Toussaint-Louverture* (Paris: Présence africaine, 1961). See also an excellent article by Pierre Laforgue, "*Bug-Jarval*, ou de la difficulté d'écrire en 'style blanc,'" *Romantisme*, no. 69 (1990): 29–42. UNESCO has established August 23 as the International Day for the Remembrance of the Slave Trade and its Abolition.

26 Victor Hugo was presumably familiar with the antislavery novel by Joseph Lavallée, *Le Nègre comme il y a peu de Blancs*, published in English translation as *The Negro Equalled by Few Europeans* (Dublin: P. Byrne et al., [1789] 1791). – *Translator's note.*

27 Hugo, *Jargal*, pp. 281–2.

28 See Léon-François Hoffmann, "Victor Hugo, les Noirs et l'esclavage," *Francofonia*, 16, no. 31 (1996): 47–90.

29 Victor Hugo, *Choses vues: Souvenirs, journaux, cahiers 1830–1848* (Paris: Gallimard, 1997), p. 671.

30 Lévêque, "L'égalité des races," p. 45.

31 René Depestre, "An interview with Aimé Césaire," in Aimé Césaire, *Discourse on Colonialism*, trans. Joan Pinkham (New York: Monthly Review Press, [1950] 2000), p. 89.

32 Léopold Sédar Senghor, *Liberté*, vol. 1, *Négritude et humanisme* (Paris: Seuil, 1964), p. 202. Senghor was widely attacked for this statement, most notably by Abdouaye Wade, president of the Republic of Senegal from 2000 to 2012. Wole Soyinka made fun of it: "The tiger does not proclaim his tigritude: he pounces" (*Time Magazine*, November 17, 1967). Senghor's response: "The zebra cannot shed his stripes without ceasing to be a zebra; similarly, the Negro cannot shed his Negritude without ceasing to be a Negro" ("Négritude," in Wikipédia, https://en.wikipedia.org/wiki/N%C3%A9gritude).

173

NOTES TO PP. 49–53

33 Aunt Jemima, the brand name for a pancake mix introduced in the late nineteenth century in the United States, was depicted as a caricatural "Mammy" figure on the box and in advertising. The name was discontinued and the produce rebranded as Pearl Milling Company in 1921. – *Translator's note.*

34 Laurence Proteau, "Entre poétique et politique: Aimé Césaire et la 'négritude,'" *Sociétés contemporaines*, no. 44 (Presses de Science Po, December 2001): 15–39.

35 Léopold Sédar Senghor, ed., *Anthologie de la nouvelle poésie nègre et malgache de langue française*, with a foreword, "Orphée noir," by Jean-Paul Sartre (Paris: Presses universitaires de France, [1948] 1969).

36 Jean-Paul Sartre, "Black Orpheus," trans. John MacCombie, *The Massachusetts Review*, 6, no. 1 ([1948] Autumn 1964–Winter 1965): 13–52. https://www.massreview.org/sites/default/files/Sartre.pdf.

37 Jean-Paul Sartre, "The Republic of Silence," translated from the French, in *The Republic of Silence*, ed. A. J. Liebling (New York: Harcourt, Brace [1944] 1947), p. 499.

38 Sartre, "Black Orpheus," p. 35.

39 Ibid., p. 18. This is the same movement of reversing stigmata that led homosexuals to identify themselves as gay (joyous), and then trans persons as queer (shady). See also Ozouf S. Amedegnato and Ibrahim Ouattara, "'Orphée noir' de Jean-Paul Sartre: Une lecture programmatique de la négritude," *Revue d'études africaines* (April 2019): 23–50.

40 Sartre, "Black Orpheus," p. 18.

41 Césaire, *Discourse on Colonialism*, p. 36. The first French version, in 1950, had a preface by Jacques Duclos; the second in 1955, included comments on Lévi-Strauss's *Race and History*.

42 Césaire, *Discourse on Colonialism*, p. 31.

43 Gilbert Meynier and Pierre Vidal-Naquet, review of Olivier Le Cour Grandmaison, *Coloniser, exterminer: Sur la guerre et l'État colonial* (Paris: Fayard, 2005), in *Études coloniales*, May 10, 2006. http://etudescoloniales. canalblog.com/archives/2006/05/10/2311101.html.

44 https://fresques.ina.fr/de-gaulle/fiche-media/Gaulle00311/discours-de-brazzaville.html.

45 Robert Gildea, *Empires of the Mind: The Colonial Past and the Politics of the Present* (Cambridge: Cambridge University Press, 2019), p. 68.

46 Especially the form practiced by the major Béké (white Creole) families, who held most of the wealth in the Antilles.

47 Aimé Césaire, *Resolutely Black: Conversations with Françoise Vergès*, trans. Matthew B. Smith (Cambridge: Polity, 2019), p. 8. [For a probing discussion of the challenges of translating terms related to race, see Smith's "Note on the translation," pp. vi–xi. – *Translator's note.*]

48 "Je redoute autant la recolonisation sournoise que le génocide rampant!" "Discours à l'Assemblée nationale, November 3, 1977," in *Écrits Politiques, 1972–1987* (Paris: Jean-Michel Place, 2018), pp. 163–7.

49 See the speech Césaire gave at the Sorbonne in Paris on April 27, 1938, in *Commémoration du Centenaire de l'abolition de l'esclavage* (Paris: Presses Universitaires de France, 1948), pp. 30–1. Césaire paid homage to Schoelcher on several occasions, describing him as the primary inspiration for Césaire's own Brazzaville speech.

NOTES TO PP. 53–55

50 Promulgated by Louis XIV in 1685 after the death of Jean-Baptiste Colbert (1619–1683), who had been one of its initiators, the Code noir (Black Code) was a legal document consisting in 60 articles that defined the rules governing the management of slaves by their masters. This code was the result of a policy carried out by Henri IV and Cardinal Richelieu in a world dominated by slavery. Slaves were defined as *êtres meubles*, essentially living pieces of furniture, deprived of all rights, the property of their masters – who nevertheless had to feed them and baptize, educate, marry, and bury them in the Catholic religion. No marriage was tolerated without the master's authorization, although the master was not supposed to compel an unwilling slave to marry. Several articles of the Code were devoted to concubinage and to marriages between masters and slaves. There was thus a contradiction at the heart of the Code between the definition of human beings as pieces of furniture and the obligation to incorporate them into the Catholic religion. In cases of rebellion, slaves were subject to the worst tortures: whipping, amputation of limbs, even beheading. The very first article of the Code also contained this notice: "Let us bid all our officers to drive out of our islands all Jews who have established residency there."

51 All peoples who have practiced slavery, including Africans and peoples of the Arab-Islamic world, as well as the three great monotheistic religions, have been its active accomplices. But the triangular slave-trafficking arrangements between Europe, Africa, and America represented slavery in its most massive form. The idea of abolition has always existed, but the abolitionist project became an ideological current in Western societies starting in the eighteenth century. The first abolition of Black slavery in all French colonies was adopted by law in the Convention of February 4, 1794.

52 The term "third world" was invented in 1952 by Alfred Sauvy, with a nod to the Third Estate of the French Revolutionary period, to designate the most disadvantaged countries of the planet, those that belonged neither to the developed capitalist West nor to the Soviet bloc. Deemed degrading, "the third world" has been replaced by "developing countries," although the old term has not completely disappeared.

53 In English, Frantz Fanon, *Black Skin, White Masks*, trans. Charles Lam Markmann (London: Pluto Press, [1952] 1986).

54 See Jacques Lacan, "The mirror stage as formative of the *I* function as revealed in psychoanalytic experience," in *Écrits*, trans. Bruce Fink with Héloïse Fink and Russell Grigg (New York: W. W. Norton & Co., [1940] 2006), pp. 75–81.

55 Fanon, *Black Skin, White Masks*, p. 112. We may be reminded here of a remark Jean Genet included as an epigraph to his 1958 play *The Blacks: A Clown Show* (*Les Nègres, une clownerie*), trans. Bernard Frechtman (New York: Grove Press, [1958] 1960): "But what exactly is a black? First of all, what's his color?" (p. 3). One can contest the claim that Fanon is a sort of structuralist Lacan before Lacan, as has been suggested by some postcolonialist Lacanians inspired by Homi Bhabha in his preface to the English edition of Fanon's book. When Fanon published *Black Skin, White Masks*, he was offering a phenomenological reading of Lacan's theory; Lacan was not yet a structuralist.

56 Octave Mannoni, *Prospero and Caliban: The Psychology of Colonization*, trans. Pamela Powesland (New York: Praeger, [1950] 1964). The 1984 French

NOTES TO PP. 55–60

edition included Mannoni's "The decolonization of myself," first published in English in *Race*, 7, no. 4 (1966): 327–35. Never before had a book of this sort aroused so much controversy and spawned so many reprintings.

57 Roudinesco citing Mannoni, in "La décolonisation de soi: Un souvenir d'analyse," in *Psychanalyse et décolonisation: Hommage à Octave Mannoni*, ed. Anny Combrichon (Paris: L'Harmattan, 1999), p. 103.

58 The Malagasy uprising, accompanied by massacres of French colonizers, was put down by the French army in a bloodbath.

59 Among the dozens of articles devoted to this book, let me mention in particular the well-documented essay by François Vatin, "Octave Mannoni (1899–1989) et sa psychologie de la colonisation: Contextualisation et décontextualisation," *Revue du Mauss*, 37, no. 1 (2011): 137–78.

60 See Roudinesco, "La décolonisation de soi," p. 104.

61 A major figure in the artistic movement known as the Algiers School, Antoine Porot (1876–1965) based his psychiatric approach on the racist theory of "primitivism." See Frantz Fanon, *Écrits sur l'aliénation et la liberté*, ed. Jean Khalfa and Robert J. C. Young (Paris: La Découverte, 2015), p. 343. This colonial psychiatry conformed to the *Code de l'indigénat* that had been adopted in France in 1881, This "native code" distinguished two categories of citizens: French citizens originating in metropolitan France, and French subjects, who were deprived of most personal liberties and political rights. On the civic level, the latter possessed only their personal status, based on their religious origins or customs. See Gilles Mancerone, *Marianne et les colonies: Une introduction à l'histoire coloniale de la France* (Paris: La Découverte, 2003).

62 Antoine Porot, "Notes de psychiatrie musulmane," *Annales médico-psychologiques*, 74, no. 9 (May 1918): 377–84.

63 Henri Alleg, *The Question*, trans. John Calder (Lincoln: University of Nebraska Press, [1958] 2006).

64 *Les damnés de la Terre* was published in Paris by François Maspéro, a militant anticolonialist himself; the book was banned for endangering the security of the state.

65 Fanon, *Wretched of the Earth*, p. 151. The awakening of Islam Fanon speaks of here has little to do with the political Islamism of the late twentieth and early twenty-first century.

66 Frantz Fanon, *The Political Writings from Alienation and Freedom*, ed. Jean Khalfa, Robert J. C. Young, and Steven Corcoran, trans. Robert J. C. Young (London: Bloomsbury, 2020), pp. 134–5.

67 Frantz Fanon, letter to François Maspero, April 7, 1961: "Ask Sartre to preface me. Tell him that I think of him each time I sit down at my desk. He has written things that are so important for our future ..." (Fanon, *Political Writings*, p. 155).

68 Fanon, *Wretched of the Earth*, foreword, p. lix.

69 Ibid., foreword, p. lv. Sartre completed his preface in September 1961.

70 Jean-Luc Einaudi, *La Bataille de Paris, 17 octobre 1961* (Paris: Seuil, 1991). Some 200 Algerians were drowned or massacred during the racist attacks. Sartre was alluding to the demonstrations of May 8, 1945, during which, in Sétif, on the very day the defeat of Nazism was being celebrated, the French army undertook a wholesale massacre of Algerian independentists and nationalists.

NOTES TO PP. 60–64

71 My account of this episode of my life can be found in a book by Catherine Simon, *Algérie, les années pieds-rouges* (Paris: La Découverte, 2011). The secondary school in question is now called the Institut algérien du pétrole (the Algerian Oil Institute).

72 Kateb Yacine, "Toujours la ruée vers l'or" (1988), interview with Mediene Benamar, in *Le poète comme un boxeur: Entretiens 1958–1989* (Paris: Seuil, 1994), p. 132.

73 Kateb Yacine, *Nedjma: A Novel*, trans. Richard Howard (New York: G. Braziller, [1956] 1961).

74 In this sense it is absurd to assert, as the sociologist Éric Fassin did in his Twitter account on October 10, 2018, that antiwhite racism does not exist. And it is even more absurd to claim that it does not exist for the social sciences, a claim that amounts to dissuading researchers from studying the question.

75 Fanon, *Black Skin, White Masks*, p. 122. This warning was repeated on the front page of the newspaper *L'Humanité* on February 18, 2019, accompanied by a photograph of Simone Veil, in the context of a call to action against the proliferation of anti-Semitic acts during the Yellow Vest demonstrations.

76 William F. S. Miles, "Caribbean hybridity and the Jews of Martinique," in Kristin Ruggiero, ed., *The Jewish Diaspora in Latin America and the Caribbean: Fragments of Memory* (Brighton, UK/Portland, OR: Sussex Academic Press, 2005), pp. 139–62.

77 Aimé Césaire, *Notebook of A Return to the Native Land*, ed. and trans. A. James Arnold and Clayton Eshleman (Middletown, CT: Wesleyan University Press), [1939] 2001), p. 12.

78 Aimé Césaire, "Inauguration de la place de l'Abbé-Grégoire, à Fort-de-France," December 28, 1950, in *Écrits politiques*, vol. 2. 1935–1956, ed. Édouard de Lépine (Paris: Jean-Michel Place, 2013), p. 236.

79 Aimé Césaire, cited in the catalog of the exhibit in his honor organized by UNESCO in Martinique in 1998.

80 Personal communication from Jean Khalfa, September 16, 2020. See also "Le conflit israélo-arabe," *Les Temps Modernes*, special issue (July 1967).

81 André Schwartz-Bart, *The Last of the Just*, trans. Stephen Becker (London: Secker & Warburg, [1959] 1981).

82 André Schwartz-Bart, *A Woman Named Solitude*, trans. Ralph Manheim (New York: Atheneum, [1972] 1973). [The French title, *La Mûlatresse Solitude*, makes the protagonist's background explicit. –*Translator's note.*]

83 Simone Schwarz-Bart, interview with Annick Cojean, *Le Monde*, October 11–12, 2020. See also the excellent article by Francine Kaufmann, "L'oeuvre juive et l'oeuvre noire d'André Schwarz-Bart," *Pardès*, no. 44 (2008): 135–48.

84 *Marrons* (in English, literally "brown people") was the term used for fugitive slaves who were pursued by their masters' dogs.

85 André Schwarz-Bart, *A Woman Named Solitude*, p. 179.

86 The General's son, also named Alexandre (1802–1879), was famous for historical novels such as *The Count of Monte Cristo* and *The Three Musketeers*. – *Translator's note.*

87 Such a call has been issued by Frédéric Potier, interministerial delegate to the struggle against racism, anti-Semitism, and anti-LGBT hatred, and

NOTES TO PP. 64–69

Claude Ribbe, president of the Association of the Friends of Alexandre Dumas: see "Rétablissons la statue du général Dumas," *Le Journal du Dimanche*, July 4, 2020.

88 Aimé Césaire, "Discours de Miami," *Écrits politiques, 1972–1987* (Paris: Jean-Michel Place, 2018), pp. 519–27.

89 Raphaël Confiant, *Aimé Césaire: Une traversée paradoxale du siècle* (Paris: Écriture, [1993] 2006).

90 Creoles are languages whose grammatical structure is close to that of African languages and whose lexicon is for the most part of European origin, although not exclusively: a certain number of African words remain, depending on the particular Creole. The Creole languages in the world generally have lower status on the social, cultural, and political levels, on the pretext that they result from mixing. However, French, English, Portuguese, and many other languages also result from mixing. French is a Romance language derived from Latin blended with Gallic and especially Frankish influences; English originated from a mix of Old German, Latin, Norman, and French.

91 Confiant, *Aimé Césaire*, p. 129.

92 Édouard Glissant, *Introduction à une poétique du divers* (Paris: Gallimard, [1995] 1996), p. 133. See also Gilles Deleuze and Félix Guattari, *A Thousand Plateaus: Capitalism and Schizophrenia*, trans. Brian Massumi (Minneapolis: University of Minnesota Press, [1980] 1987). Opposing the doctrine of hierarchical authority, the authors use the term "rhizome" (or "polymorphous root") to characterize a structure that evolves in a horizontal fashion. They criticize both Freudian Oedipalism and the Lacanian concepts of "signifier" and "name-of-the-father" as they develop their own theory of subjective multiplicity. Along with Jacques Derrida and Michel Foucault, Deleuze is one of the philosophers most frequently cited by the authors of Francophone, Anglophone, and Hispanophone postcolonial studies.

93 Jean Bernabé, Patrick Chamoiseau, and Raphaël Confiant, *Éloge de la créolité* (Paris: Gallimard, 1989). See also Raphaël Confiant, "La créolité contre l'enfermement identitaire," *Multitudes*, no. 22 (2005): 179–85, and the excellent synthesis by Philippe Chanson, "Identité et altérité chez Édouard Glissant et Patrick Chamoiseau, scripteurs visionnaires de la parole créole," for the Franklin College Conference on Caribbean Literature, "The Caribbean Unbound," Franklin, IN, April 13–16, 2005: https://www.potomitan.info/chamoiseau/identite.php.

94 Confiant, "La créolité contre l'enfermement identitaire," p. 185.

95 Jean-Sylvain Bailly, *Mémoires de Bailly*, vol. 1 (Paris: Baudoin frères, 1821), p. 281. Bailly was reporting statements by Dominique Joseph Garat (1749–1833), a lawyer and future deputy from Gironde. Jean-Sylvain Bailly (1736–1793) was a mathematician, a deputy from the Third Estate to the Estates General, and mayor of Paris; he was guillotined for failing to testify against Marie-Antoinette.

96 The Ligue de défense juive, created in 2000, is the French branch of the Jewish Defense League, an organization on the far right founded by Meir Kahane (1932–1990) in the United States in 1968.

97 The video of this meeting, which took place on June 3, 2005, can be found on YouTube: https://www.youtube.com/watch?v=15PcLLb6Ol0.

178

NOTES TO PP. 69–72

98 The colors of the French flag are customarily named in this order, in contrast to the American "Red, White, and Blue." – *Translator's note.*

99 The full text of Confiant's remarks, never officially published, circulated on the Internet under the title "La faute (pardonnable) de Dieudonné."

100 A professor of philosophy at the Lycée Bainbridge (Guadeloupe) and the author of numerous articles on slavery, Dahomay was a member of France's High Council on Integration from 2002 to 2008. In an interview in 2015, he declared: "There is a form of memory that liberates and a form that emprisons." See Natalie Levisalles, interview: "Jacky Dahomay: 'Il y a une mémoire qui libère et une mémoire qui emprisonne,'" *Libération*, May 22, 2015.

101 Jacky Dahomay, "L'innommable Raphaël Confiant?" *Le Monde*, December 2, 2006; Jean-Charles Houel, "Ce qu'il faut penser de Dieudonné par Jacky Dahomay, philosophe antillais," blog, January 28, 2014: https://louviers-2008.blogspot.com/2014/01/ce-quil-faut-penser-de-dieudonne-par.html; Raphaël Confiant, "Les Noirs, du malaise à la colère," *Le Monde*, December 8, 2006.

102 Patrick Chamoiseau, *Texaco*, trans. Rose-Myriam Réjouis and Val Vinokurov (New York: Pantheon Books, [1992] 1997). The novel won the prestigious Goncourt Prize.

103 Conversation with French linguist Bernard Cerquiglini, July 2, 2020.

Notes to chapter 4

1 Daniel Rivet, "Le fait colonial et nous: Histoire d'un éloignement," *Vingtième siècle*, no. 33 (1992): 129–30, 138.

2 Thus the considerable place occupied by psychoanalysis in this matter, as in all genre studies.

3 Internal colonialism must not be confused with neocolonialism, which focuses on the way the former colonial powers maintain their domination (economic or cultural) over the former colonies that have achieved independence.

4 This is the case to such an extent that, for several years now, people who use this term on French radio or television, even in citing works by Césaire, Genet, or Dany Laferrière, are labeled racist. This tendency reached a peak in 2020, when the heir to Agatha Christie's estate decided to withdraw her celebrated novel *Dix petits nègres* (*Ten Little Niggers*) from the market. The title, judged offensive, had come from a nursery rhyme. And the word *nègre* (used 74 times) had to be removed from the body of the text (a ruling issued in France on August 26, 2020). Why not mandate a change in the title of Césaire's *Nègre je suis, nègre je resterai*? And what can be done about Jean Genet's famous play *Les Nègres*? [In the Christie novel, the term in the original English has been changed to "soldier"; the English-language version of the Genet play is titled *The Blacks*. – *Translator's note.*]

5 With the International League against Racism and Anti-Semitism, founded in 1927, and SOS Racism, founded in 1984.

6 The talk was a shorter and somewhat different version of the published text cited here: Jacques Derrida, *The Monolinguism of the Other; or, The Prosthesis of Origin*, trans. Patrick Mensah (Stanford, CA: Stanford

NOTES TO PP. 72–76

University Press, [1996] 1998), p. 1. A year after the Louisiana talk, on November 6, 1993, Derrida engaged in a dialogue with Édouard Glissant on the same theme, at a meeting of the International Parliament of Writers organized by Christian Salmon for the purpose of creating an international structure that could intervene in favor of victims of persecution in the writers' own countries: Adonis, Édouard Glissant, Pierre Bourdieu, and Salman Rushdie were among the members of the executive board.

7 The degree was named after Adolphe Crémieux, a French-Jewish lawyer and politician who served under the French Government of National Defense as Minister of Justice in 1870–1. The decree granted French citizenship for the first time to most of the Jews born in French Algeria.

8 The Judeo-Romance language derived from Old Castilian and Hebrew; it is the equivalent of Yiddish for Ashkenazy Jews.

9 Derrida, *Monolinguism*, pp. 54–5. See also Marc Crépon, "Ce qu'on demande aux langues (autour du *Monolinguisme de l'autre*)," *Raisons politiques*, no. 2 (2001): 27–40.

10 Derrida, *Monolinguism*, p. 39.

11 See Jacques Derrida, *L'autre cap* (Paris: Minuit, 1991).

12 See Benoît Peeters, *Derrida*, trans. Andrew Brown (Cambridge: Polity, [2010] 2013), pp. 33–4.

13 Jacques Derrida, "The laws of reflection: Nelson Mandela, in admiration," trans. Mary Ann Caws and Isabelle Lorenz, in Jacques Derrida, *Psyche: Inventions of the Other* (Stanford, CA: Stanford University Press, [1986] 2007), vol. 2, p. 73.

14 Derrida, *Specters of Marx: The State of the Debt, the Work of Mourning and the New International*, trans. Peggy Kamuf (London: Routledge, [1993] 2006). See also Élisabeth Roudinesco, "Jacques Derrida: Spectres de Marx, spectres de Freud," in *Un Jour Derrida*, colloquium proceedings, ed. Daniel Bougnous and Peter Sloterdijk (Paris: Bibliothèque publique d'information, 2006), pp. 51–60.

15 Francis Fukuyama, *The End of History and the Last Man* (New York: Free Press, 1992); Samuel Huntington, *The Clash of Civilizations and the Remaking of World Order* (New York: Simon & Schuster, 1996). See also Jean Birnbaum, *La religion des faibles: Ce que le djihadisme dit de nous* (Paris: Seuil, 2018), pp. 138–9.

16 Karl Marx and Friedrich Engels, *Manifesto of the Communist Party* (Moscow: Progress Publishers, 1977), p. 34.

17 Paul Valéry, *Essais quasi politiques*, in Paul Valéry, *Oeuvres* (Paris: Gallimard, coll. Bibliothèque de la Pléiade), vol. 1, [1919] 1957), p. 993.

18 Jacques Derrida and Élisabeth Roudinesco, *De quoi demain ... Dialogue* (Paris: Fayard/Galilée, 2001), p. 168.

19 See *The Combahee River Collective Statement*, https://www.blackpast.org/african-american-history/combahee-river-collective-statement-1977/. For a presentation in French, see "Le Combahee River Collective, pionnier du féminisme noir (April 1977)," *Les Cahiers du CEDREF*, no. 14 (2006): 69–104. Rosa McCauley Parks (1913–2005), a close associate of Martin Luther King, Jr., was an emblematic figure in the struggle against racial segregation. I have a vivid memory of my own participation in the big March for Civil Rights held in Washington, DC, on August 28, 1963, during my first trip to the United States. I was staying with a family of

NOTES TO PP. 76–78

antiracist Jewish intellectuals. The march had been organized by Bayard Rustin, one of King's advisors; Rustin was the object of discrimination both as a Black and as a homosexual.

20 The term "intersectionality" was invented in 1989 by Kimberlé Crenshaw to conceptualize an idea that had grown out of Black American feminism.

21 The word "post" does not mean "after," here; there is no diachrony in the notion of "postcolonialism," but rather a structural "beyond" of colonialism.

22 Thomas Brisson, "Pour une sociologie des critiques postcoloniales: Tu Weiming et le néoconfucianisme nord-américain," *Sociétés contemporaines*, no. 93 (2014): 89. See also Paul Gilroy, *Postcolonial Melancholy* (New York: Columbia University Press, 2005), and Jim Cohen, "De l'Atlantique noir à la mélancolie postcoloniale: Entretien avec Paul Gilroy," trans. Jade Lindgaard, *Mouvements*, 51, no. 3 (2007): 90–101. A British sociologist, Gilroy received the prestigious Holberg Prize in 2019.

23 See Alain Mabanckou and Dominic Thomas, "Pourquoi a-t-on si peur en France des études postcoloniales?" *L'Express*, January 20, 2020, in response to a violent opinion piece by Pierre-André Taguieff and Laurent Bouvet, who were convinced that the artisans of postcolonial studies were "hucksters looking for academic respectability" ("Les bonimenteurs du postcolonial business en quête de respectabilité économique," *L'Express*, December 26, 2019). They neglected to point out that these alleged "hucksters" were all highly credentialed professors teaching in the best universities of the Western world and that they very often claimed to be followers of prestigious figures from the French academic world whose works have been widely translated: Foucault, Bourdieu, Derrida, and so on.

24 For the 2010 census, the Office of Management and Budget required a minimum of five categories; White, Black or African American, American Indian or Alaska Native, and Native Hawaiian or Other Pacific Islander. In the 2020 census, a sixth category was added: Some Other Race. Since the 2000 census, US residents have been allowed to check more than one category, thereby identifying as multiracial. – *Translator's note.*

25 See Éliane Elmaleh, "Les politiques identitaires dans les universités américaines," *L'homme et la société*, no. 149 (2003): 57–74, and Denis Lacorne, *La crise de l'identité américaine: Du melting pot au multiculturalisme* (Paris: Fayard, 1997).

26 Hundreds of articles and dozens of books have been published on this question, and on the reception of the notions of postcoloniality and decoloniality in the humanities and the social sciences. Here are a few of the most representative titles: Sophie Bessis, *Western Supremacy: Triumph of an Idea?*, trans. Patrick Camiller (London: Zed Books, [2001] 2003); Neil Lazarus, ed., *The Cambridge Companion to Postcolonial Literary Studies* (Cambridge: Cambridge University Press, 2004); Marie-Claude Smouts, ed., *La situation postcoloniale: Les "postcolonial studies" dans le débat français* (Paris: Presses de Sciences Po, 2007); Jean-François Bayart, *Les études postcoloniales: Un carnaval académique* (Paris: Karthala, 2010); Thomas Brisson, *Décentrer l'Occident: Les intellectuels postcoloniaux chinois, arabes et indiens, et la critique de la modernité* (Paris: La Découverte, 2018); Romain Bertrand, "La mise en cause(s) du 'fait colonial,'" *Politique africaine*, no. 102 (2006): 28–49; Anne Berger, interview with Grégoire

NOTES TO PP. 78–80

Leménager and Laurence Marie, "Traversées de frontières: Postcolonialité et études de 'genre' en Amérique," *Labyrinthe*, no. 24 (2006): 11–37; Béatrice Collignon, "Notes sur les fondements des *postcolonial studies*," *ÉchoGéo*, no. 1 (2007): 1–9; Yves Lacoste, "Le postcolonial et ses acceptions contradictoires dans trois récents recueils d'articles," *Hérodote*, no. 128 (2008): 143–55. Postcolonial studies exist in all French universities, as do gender studies, but they are in a minority, contrary to the assertions of polemicists alarmed by the terror of a barbarian invasion. Between 2014 and 2019, 665 theses were devoted to postcolonial studies, out of a total of 40,453. And the 665 includes some theses that are critical of the drift toward identitarianism (source: Agence bibliographique de l'enseignement supérieur). French universities are thus not being "ravaged" by a generalized and racist "islamo-leftism" emanating from American campuses, although this does not keep certain polemicists – always the same ones – from seeking to create committees intended to surveil course contents, or from recommending the initiation of parliamentary investigations. On this subject, see the communiqué from the conference of French university presidents in response to Minister of National Education Jean-Michel Blanquer, the day after the assassination of Professor Samuel Paty by a Chechnian Islamist: "No, universities are not places where an ideology that leads to the worst [possible outcome] is constructed ... Research is not responsible for the ills of society, it analyzes them. It is in its essence a space of debate and construction of the critical spirit" (https://www.lemonde. fr/societe/article/2020/10/23/polemique-apres-les-propos-de-jean-michel-blanquer-sur-l-islamo-gauchisme-a-l-universite_6057164_3224.html). See also Soazig Le Nevé, "Les sciences sociales dans le viseur du politique," *Le Monde*, December 3, 2020.

27 Course taught by Fatima Khemilat, "Épistémicides: L'impérialisme m'a TueR [*sic*]," appeared on YouTube in 2015 (https://www.youtube.com/watch?v=zK6hegi_wHE). The author is a lecturer at the School for Advanced Studies in the Social Sciences (EHESS); she has a doctorate from Sciences-Po Aix-en-Provence, and has published numerous articles on the question. See also the many articles and books by Boaventura de Sousa Santos (Portugal), Aníbal Quijano (Peru), Enrique Dussel (Mexico), and Ramón Grosfoguel (Puerto Rico). All these scholars have been welcomed by North American universities and all have been "globalized."

28 The name "French theory" has been given to a corpus inspired by the principal French thinkers of the 1970s – from Foucault through Lacan, Simone de Beauvoir, or Jean-François Lyotard to Derrida; this has allowed polemicists on the right, the far right, and even some on the left to assert that these philosophers were obscurantist imposters responsible for the shift toward identitarianism. I would say, rather, that we are seeing an effect of the globalization of certain critical reflections, reformulated in prestigious American universities. See Razmig Keucheyan, "Le moment américain: Sur la mondialisation des pensées critiques," *Revue française d'études américaines*, no. 126 (2010): 21–32.

29 Edward Said, *Out of Place: A Memoir* (New York: Knopf, 1999), pp. 5–6.

30 Edward Said, *Joseph Conrad and the Fiction of Autobiography* (Cambridge, MA: Harvard University Press, 1966).

31 Joseph Conrad, *Lord Jim* (New York: Oxford University Press, [1899]

NOTES TO PP. 80–85

1999); *Heart of Darkness* (Cambridge: Cambridge University Press, [1899] 2018).

32 See Alexis Tadié, "Edward Said et Joseph Conrad: La critique de l'illusion coloniale," *Tumultes*, no. 35 (2010): 67–80.

33 He received tenure in 1977.

34 Edward Said, *Orientalism* (New York: Pantheon Books, 1978).

35 That is, the Orient in the sense of the Arab Orient, or the Arab or Arabo-Islamic world, whose geographic limits are variable.

36 Said, *Orientalism*, p. 285.

37 Ibid., p. 307.

38 Gustave Flaubert, letter to Louis Bouilhet, March 13, 1850, in *The Letters of Gustave Flaubert*, selected, edited, and translated by Francis Steegmuller (Cambridge, MA: The Belknap Press of Harvard University Press, 1979), pp. 116–17.

39 Said, *Orientalism*, p. 6.

40 Fabienne Dupray, "*Madame Bovary* et les juges: Enjeux d'un procès littéraire," *Histoire de la justice*, no. 17 (2007): 227–45.

41 These were the labels used at the time.

42 Gustave Flaubert, letter to Louise Colet, August 26, 1846, in *The Letters of Gustave Flaubert*, ed. and trans. Francis Steegmuller (Cambridge, MA: The Belknap Press of Harvard University Press, 1979), p. 71. See the excellent thesis by Hassen Bkhairia, "L'inscription littéraire de l'histoire chez Flaubert, des oeuvres de jeunesse à 'Salammbô,'" defended at the University of Bordeaux in 2012. See also the website of the Centre Flaubert de Rouen, https://flaubert-v1.univ-rouen.fr/, and Francis Lacoste, "L'Orient de Flaubert," *Romantisme*, 119 (2003): 73–84.

43 See Guy Harpigny's review of Said's book, in *Revue théologique de Louvain*, fasc. 3 (1981): 357–61. See also Birnbaum, *La religion des faibles*. Henry Laurens, a historian of the Arab world, rightly reproaches Said for refusing to accept the idea of conflict between East and West, and for clinging to the representation of a fixed binarity. See Henry Laurens, "Dans l'Orient arabe toujours plus compliqué," inaugural lesson at the Collège de France, March 11, 2004, published in *Le Monde*, March 12, 2004; and *Orientales*, vol. 1, *Autour de l'expédition d'Égypte* (Paris: CNRS Éditions, 2004). Let us note that, like Michel Foucault, Jacques Derrida, and many others, Edward Said was copiously insulted throughout his career.

44 Georges Perec (1936–1982) was a French writer whose use of lists is among the many innovative techniques to be found in his novels. On the drift toward identity politics, see Laurent Dubreuil, *La dictature des identités* (Paris: Gallimard, 2019); for an essay in English by the same author on the same topic, see "Nonconforming: Against the erosion of academic freedom by identity politics," *Harper's*, 341, no. 2044 (September 2020): 61–6. See also Laurent Dubreuil, "Alter, inter: Académisme et *postcolonial studies*," *Labyrinthe*, no. 24 (2006): 47–61.

45 See Marion Uhlig, "Quand *postcolonial* et *global* riment avec 'médiéval'": Sur quelques approches théoriques anglo-saxonnes," *Perspectives médiévales*, no. 35 (2014): https://doi.org/10.4000/peme.4400.

46 Sonya Faure, "Faut-il utiliser le mot 'race'?" *Libération*, September 25, 2020. See also Maurice Olender, *Race sans histoire* (Paris: Seuil, coll. "Points Essais," 2009).

183

NOTES TO PP. 85–89

47 See Robin DiAngelo, *White Fragility: Why It's So Hard for White People to Talk about Racism* (Boston: Beacon Press, 2018).

48 This is the central thesis developed by the Indian psychologist Ashis Nandy, who took his inspiration from psychoanalytic concepts: *The Intimate Enemy: Loss and Recovery of Self under Colonialism* (Delhi: Oxford University Press, 1983). Nandy's approach closely resembles that of Octave Mannoni. The French version, translated from the English by Annie Montaut, *L'ennemi intime: Perte de soi et retour à soi sous le colonialisme* (Paris: Fayard, 2007), is prefaced by Charles Malamoud and Pierre Legendre; the latter sees a violence in colonialism that spills over onto the condition of the conquerors, "camouflaged victims in an advanced stage of psychological decomposition."

49 I am borrowing this term from Montaigne: "the obscure, ambiguous, and fantastic language of the prophetical jargon": see Michel de Montaigne, *Essays*, trans. George B. Ives (Cambridge, MA: Harvard University Press, 1925), vol. 1, book I, chapter 11, p. 55.

50 Gildea, *Empires of the Mind*, p. 158.

51 Consisting in defining oneself in binary fashion as Muslim or non-Muslim.

52 This encounter is related by Paul Veyne in *Foucault: Sa pensée, sa personne*. Expelled from Iran, Khomeini lived in France from October 6, 1978, to February 1, 1979. Raymond Aron for his part believed, wrongly, that Khomeini would become an ally of the United States.

53 Michel Foucault, "À quoi rêvent les Iraniens" (1978) and "Une poudrière appelée islam" (1979), in *Dits et écrits 3: 1976–1979* (Paris: Gallimard, 1994), pp. 688–98, 759–62. Giesbert rehearsed what he saw as "Foucault's stupidities" ("Récit: Cendrillon au pays des mille et un jours," *Le Point*, December 5, 2003). As for Minc, he did not hesitate to call Foucault an "advocate for Iranian Khomeini-ism, in theoretical solidarity with Khomeini's abuses" ("Le terrorisme de l'esprit," *Le Monde*, November 7, 2001). On this topic, see the excellent clarification by Julien Cavagnis, "Michel Foucault et le soulèvement iranien de 1978: Retour sur la notion de 'spiritualité politique,'" *Cahiers philosophiques*, no. 130 (2012): 51–71. See also Jean Birnbaum, *Un silence religieux: La gauche face au djihadisme* (Paris: Seuil, 2016).

54 Salman Rushdie, *The Satanic Verses* (London: Viking, 1988).

55 A proclamation made on February 14, 2006, by the Fondation des Martyrs, an Iranian governmental entity, cited in Lila Azam Zanganeh, "Salman Rushdie, sous le soleil de Satan," *Le Monde*, September 4, 2006. https://www.lemonde.fr/societe/article/2020/10/23/polemique-apres-les-propos-de-jean-michel-blanquer-sur-l-islamo-gauchisme-a-l-universite_6057164_3224.html.

56 See Antonio Gramsci, *Prison Notebooks*, trans. Joseph A. Buttigieg and Antonio Callari, 2 vols. (New York: Columbia University Press, 2011).

57 See Riccardo Ciavolella, "L'émancipation des subalternes par la 'culture populaire': La pensée gramscienne et l'anthropologie pour appréhender l'Italie d'après-guerre et le tiers monde en voie de décolonisation (1948–1960)," *Mélanges de l'École française de Rome: Italie et Méditerranée modernes et contemporaines*, 128, no. 2 (2016): 431–46.

58 The project of subaltern studies took concrete form with the publication of an 11-volume series between 1982 and 2000 that brought together some

NOTES TO PP. 89–93

50 collaborators. The first ten volumes were published in Delhi by Oxford University Press and the eleventh in New York by Columbia University Press (Columbia professor Gayatri Chakravorty Spivak joined the team in 1985). Naturally, as in all avant-garde movements, the actors in this huge project entered into conflict with one another. It was at the heart of the greatest American universities – Harvard, Columbia, Cornell, and so on – that they clashed and that they crossed paths with thinkers from France or Latin America. See Brisson, *Décentrer l'Occident*. Robert J. C. Young, a specialist in Fanon, was one of the first to characterize postcolonialist theory as a field of study: see his *White Mythologies: Writing History and the West* (London: Routledge, 1990).

59 In addition to the work of Thomas Brisson, see Jacques Pouchepadass, "Les *subaltern studies* ou la critique postcoloniale de la modernité," *L'Homme*, no. 156 (2000): 161–86, and Isabelle Merle, "Les *subaltern studies*: Retour sur les principes fondateurs d'un projet historiographique de l'Inde coloniale," *Genèses*, no. 56 (2004): 131–47.

60 See Brisson, *Décentrer l'Occident*.

61 This theme was taken up by Chinua Achebe (1930–2013), an Anglophone Nigerian writer who taught at Brown University and at Bard College; his novel *Things Fall Apart* (London: Heinemann, 1958), about the loss of African identity upon contact with European colonization, has been translated into some 50 languages. In a lecture given in 1975, he traced Joseph Conrad's "racism" in *Heart of Darkness* from a postcolonialist perspective that had nothing in common with Said's; the latter devoted his narrative to studying the way Kurtz represented Africa.

62 Trans. John and Anne Tedeschi (Baltimore: Johns Hopkins University Press, [1976] 1980).

63 *I, Pierre Rivière, Having Slaughtered My Mother, My Sister, and My Brother: A Case of Parricide in the 19ᵗʰ Century*, ed. Michel Foucault, trans. Frank Jellinek (New York: Pantheon, [1973] 1975).

64 Georges Duby and Michelle Perrot, "Writing the history of women," trans. Arthur Goldhammer, in *A History of Women in the West*, ed. Georges Duby and Michelle Perrot (Cambridge, MA: Belknap Press of Harvard University Press, [1991] 1992–1994), vol. 2, pp. ix–x.

65 Michelle Perrot, *Mélancolie ouvrière* (Paris: Grasset, 2012); Kamel Daoud, *The Meursault Investigation*, trans. John Cullen (New York: Other Press, [2013] 2015); Arlette Farge, *Vies oubliées: Au coeur du XVIIIe siècle* (Paris: La Découverte, 2019); Virginie Despentes, *King Kong Theory*, trans. Stephanie Benson (New York: Feminist Press, [2006] 2010), p. 7.

66 Robert O. Paxton, *Vichy France: Old Guard and New Order 1940–1944* (New York: Knopf, 1972). The book stirred up a scandal and continues to be a target for all the identitarian nationalists.

67 Jacques Derrida, *Of Grammatology*, trans. Gayatri Chakravorty Spivak (Baltimore: Johns Hopkins University Press, [1967] 1976).

68 Cited in Élisabeth Roudinesco, "Lacan and Derrida in the history of psychoanalysis," trans. Richard Hyland, *JEP European Journal of Psychoanalysis*, no. 2 (Fall 1995), http://www.psychomedia.it/jep/number2/roudinesco.htm.

69 Gayatri Chakravorty Spivak, "Can the subaltern speak?" in *Marxism and the Interpretation of Culture*, ed. Cary Nelson and Lawrence Grosberg (Urbana: University of Illinois Press, 1988), pp. 66–111, and later in revised

NOTES TO PP. 93–99

form in *Can the Subaltern Speak? Reflections on the History of an Idea*, ed. Rosalind C. Morris (New York: Columbia University Press, 2010), pp. 21–78.

70 For a thorough treatment of this topic, see Catherine Weinberger-Thomas, *Ashes of Immortality: Widow-Burning in India*, trans. Jeffrey Mehlman and David Gordon White (Chicago, IL: University of Chicago Press, [1996] 1999).

71 As was the case for the ritual of dueling.

72 See Maurice Pinguet, *Voluntary Death in Japan*, trans. Rosemary Morris (Cambridge: Polity Press, [1984] 1993).

73 Catherine Weinberger-Thomas, "Cendres d'immortalité: La crémation des veuves en Inde," *Archives de sciences sociales des religions*, 34, no. 67.1 (January–March 1989): 26.

74 Sigmund Freud, "A child is being beaten: A contribution to the study of the origin of sexual perversions," *International Journal of Psycho-Analysis*, 1 (1920): 371–95.

75 Spivak, *Can the Subaltern Speak?*, p. 50. "Faced with the dialectically interlocking sentences that are constructible as 'White men are saving brown women from brown men' and 'The women wanted to die,' the metropolitan feminist migrant (removed from the actual theater of decolonization) asks the question of simple semiosis – What does this signify? – and begins to plot a history."

76 Dipesh Chakrabarty, *Provincializing Europe: Postcolonial Thought and Historical Difference*, 2nd ed. (Princeton, NJ: Princeton University Press, [2000] 2008); a new preface by the author was included in the second edition.

77 Ibid., p. 16. Let us note that in his inaugural lecture at the Collège de France (October 3, 2019), the historian of African worlds Xavier-François Fauvelle emphasized, in response to Chakrabarty, that it would be preferable to "provincialize the world."

78 Chakrabarty, *Provincializing Europe*, pp. 112–13.

79 On this point, see Matthieu Renault, "Heidegger en Inde: De Jarava Lal Mehta aux *subaltern studies*," *Revue Asylon(s)*, no. 10 (July 2012–July 2014): http://www.reseau-terra.eu/article1293.html.

80 Chakrabarty, *Provincializing Europe*, p. 255.

81 Terry Eagleton, "In the gaudy supermarket," *London Review of Books*, 21, no. 10 (May 13, 1999): 3–6, discussing Gayatri Chakravorty Spivak, *A Critique of Post-Colonial Reason: Toward a History of the Vanishing Present* (Cambridge, MA: Harvard University Press, 1999).

82 Homi Bhabha, *The Location of Culture*, 2nd ed. (London: Routledge [1994] 2004), p. x.

83 Ibid., p. 175.

84 On the difficulties encountered by Homi Bhabha's translators, see Claire Joubert, "Théorie en traduction: Homi Bhabha et l'intervention postcoloniale," *Littérature*, no. 154 (2009): 149–74.

85 Gilberto Freyre, *The Masters and the Slaves (Casa-grande & Senzala): A Study in the Development of Brazilian Civilization*, trans. Samuel Putnam, 2nd English language ed., revised (New York: Knopf, [1946] 1987).

86 Oswald de Andrade, "Cannibalist manifesto," trans. Leslie Bary, *Latin American Literary Review*, 19, no. 38 (July–December 1991): 38–47.

NOTES TO PP. 99–103

87 André Breton, *Manifestoes of Surrealism*, trans. Richard Seaver and Helen R. Lane (Ann Arbor: University of Michigan Press, [1962] 1969).

88 Andrade, "Cannibalist manifesto," p. 38. Bary notes that "Tupi or not tupi" was in English in the original, and that *"Tupi* is the popular, generic name for the Native Americans of Brazil and also for their language, *nheengatu"* (p. 44).

89 Bhabha, *Location of Culture*, p. 29.

90 Ibid., p. 30.

91 Homi Bhabha, cited in Jonathan Rutherford, "The third space: Interview with Homi Bhabha," in *Identity: Community, Culture, Difference* (London: Lawrence and Wishart, 1990), pp. 215–16.

92 See, for example, Joan Copjec, *Read My Desire: Lacan Against the Historicists* (Cambridge, MA: MIT Press, 1994).

93 Slavoj Žižek, *The Sublime Object of Ideology* (London: Verso, 1989).

94 See the excellent analysis by Azzedine Haddour in "Fanon dans la théorie postcoloniale," *Les Temps modernes*, nos. 635–6 (December 2005–January 2006): 136–59.

95 Hannah Arendt, *On Violence* (New York: Harcourt Brace Jovanovich, [1969] 1970). I thank Jean Khalfa for his invaluable help on this point (personal communication, September 6, 2020). See also Jean Khalfa, "Ethique et violence chez Frantz Fanon," *Les Temps modernes*, no. 698 (2018): 51–69.

96 Homi Bhabha, "Framing Fanon," foreword to Fanon, *The Wretched of the Earth*, pp. vii–xli. Judith Butler offered Bhabha her support, adding a "gendered" touch to his undertaking: see "Violence, non-violence: Sartre on Fanon," *Graduate Faculty Philosophy Journal*, 27, no. 1 (2006): 3–24.

97 On December 3, 2016, Thamy Ayouch submitted his thesis for the prestigious post-doctoral degree *Habilitation à diriger des recherches*, which qualifies a professor to direct doctoral theses; it was published as *Psychanalyse et hybridité: Genre, colonialité, subjectivations* (Louvain: Presses universitaires de Louvain, 2018). In its preface, Laurie Laufer wrote: "This book is an essential opening for an epistemological work of a certain psychoanalysis that refuses to retreat, to dogmatize, to pathologize."

98 Thamy Ayouch, "Homosexuel/les marocain/es en postcolonie: Psychanalyse et subalternisation," International Colloquium, "Psychanalyse, études de genre, études postcoloniales, état de l'art," Université Paris-Diderot, December 14–15, 2018.

99 "La pensée 'décoloniale' renforce le narcissisme des petites différences," *Le Monde*, September 25, 2019. And "Panique décoloniale chez les psychanalystes!", *Libération*, October 4, 2019. The first forum was initiated by Céline Masson, a militant supporting a Freudian-republican universalism, and the second by a psychoanalyst of a culturalist bent; she was able to collect signatures from a large number of scholars in postcolonial studies, who had not really grasped the meaning of this nonsensical debate, as I observed in talking to several of them.

100 Jean-Loup Amselle analyzed this drift splendidly in *L'Occident décroché: Enquête sur les postcolonialismes* (Paris: Stock, 2008).

101 Jasbir K. Puar, *Terrorist Assemblages: Homonationalism in Queer Times (Next Wave)* (Durham, NC: Duke University Press, 2007).

NOTES TO PP. 104–110

Notes to chapter 5

1 Nicolas Bancel, Pascal Blanchard, Gilles Boëtsch, Éric Deroo, and Sandrine Lemaire, eds., *Zoos humains: De la Vénus hottentote aux reality shows* (Paris: La Découverte, 2002).

2 Nicolas Bancel, Pascal Blanchard, and Sandrine Lemaire, *La fracture coloniale: La société française au prisme de l'héritage coloniale* (Paris: La Découverte, 2005).

3 On the *Indigènes de la République*, see Preface, note 10.

4 See Pierre-André Taguieff and Laurent Bouvet, "Les bonimenteurs du *postcolonial business* en quête de respectabilité académique," *L'Express*, December 26, 2019.

5 Pascal Blanchard, Nicolas Bancel, and Sandrine Lemaire, *Décolonisations françaises: La chute d'un empire*, preface by Benjamin Stora; afterword by Achille Mbembe (Paris: La Martinière, 2020). See also the fine documentary film by David Korn Brzoza and Pascal Blanchard, *Décolonisations: Du sang et des larmes*, 2020; an interview with co-author Blanchard appeared in *Télérama* on September 30, 2020, pp. 75–7.

6 Malek Bouyahia, "Postcolonialités," in Juliette Rennes, ed., *Encyclopédie du genre* (Paris: La Découverte, 2016), p. 493.

7 Noted by Bernard Cerquiglini in a personal communication, August 7, 2020.

8 Thus Jacques Toubon, a former Keeper of the Seals (roughly equivalent to Lord Chancellor or Attorney General) under Jacques Chirac, has been called an "Islamo-leftist" by far-right militants on the basis of his action in the role of Defender of Rights (2014–20), when he became alarmed about the living conditions in migrant encampments in France. Similarly, today anyone can be called an "Islamophobe" and insulted by extremist groups seeking to institute a law against blasphemy in France. See Simon Blin, "En finir avec l'‘islamo-gauchisme'?" *Libération*, October 23, 2020.

9 Al-Qaida, for example, is an Islamist terrorist organization whose most famous representative was Osama bin Laden. Its rival ISIS, or the Islamic State (known in French as *Daech*), is a terrorist branch of Salafism that advocates the re-establishment of a caliphate. On the strength of Islamism in France, see the excellent study coordinated by Bernard Rougier, *Les terroristes conquis de l'islamisme* (Paris: Presses universitaires de France, 2020).

10 As demonstrated by the statistics I cited in the preceding chapter.

11 In France, Catholic integralism (*intégrisme*) holds that Catholic doctrine should be the basis of civil law and public policy. – *Translator's note*.

12 Christiane Taubira, born in French Guiana, served as a member of the National Assembly from 1993 to 2012 and Minister of Justice from 2012 to 2016.

13 See the annual report of the Observatoire de la laïcité for 2019–20, published online on December 18, 2020: https://www.gouvernement.fr/communique-de-presse-0.

14 Charles Enderlin, "Il est du droit de tout Juif de se déclarer non sioniste," interview with Valérie Toranian, *Revue des Deux Mondes* (October 2020): 36.

188

NOTES TO PP. 111–116

15 Law no. 2005-158 adopted on February 23, 2005, expressing the gratitude of the nation for the contribution to the nation made by repatriated French citizens: https://www.legifrance.gouv.fr/loda/id/JORFTEXT000000444898/. – *Translator's note*.

16 The petition was launched on December 13, 2005; it was widely reproduced in the press. I was among the signatories. https://www.liberation.fr/societe/2005/12/13/liberte-pour-l-histoire_541669/.

17 I had already had the opportunity to discuss the Gayssot law with Jacques Derrida; see Derrida and Roudinesco, *De quoi demain* …, p. 215.

18 This was the slogan of a cereal brand that featured a cartoonish primitive Black figure on its boxes and in its advertisements, comparable to the "Aunt Jemima" figure on an American brand of pancake mix and subject to the same scathing criticisms as reinforcing unacceptable old clichés. – *Translator's note*.

19 Fanon, *Black Skin, White Masks*, p. 230.

20 Aimé Césaire, "Je ne suis pas pour la repentance ou les réparations," *L'Express*, September 13, 2001. https://www.lexpress.fr/culture/livre/aime-cesaire-je-ne-suis-pas-pour-la-repentance-ou-les-reparations_817538.html.

21 Jacques Derrida, in conversation with Michel Wieviorka, "Le siècle et le pardon," *Le Monde des Débats*, December 1999: http://hydra.humanities.uci.edu/derrida/siecle.html. The passage also appears verbatim in Jacques Derrida, *Pardonner: L'impardonnable et l'imprescriptible* (Paris: Galilée, 2012).

22 Benjamin Stora, "Je ne suis pas pour effacer les traces, je suis pour renforcer l'histoire," *La Marseillaise*, June 14, 2020.

23 This movement was to become the Party of the Indigenes of the Republic (PIR).

24 This neologism is used by women who refuse to wear headscarves.

25 See Simone de Beauvoir and Gisèle Halimi, *Djamila Boupacha; The Story of the Torture of a Young Algerian Girl Which Shocked Liberal French Opinion*, trans. Peter Green (London: André Deutsch, 1962).

26 Françoise Vergès, *The Wombs of Women: Race, Capital, Feminism*, trans. Kaiama L. Glover (Durham, NC: Duke University Press, [2017] 2020). Martine Storti has criticized this position in a fine essay, *Pour un féminisme universel* (Paris: Seuil, coll. "La République des idées," 2020).

27 Françoise Vergès, *Un féminisme décolonial* (Paris: La Fabrique, 2019), pp. 83–4.

28 Paul Vergès (1925–2016) was the founder of the Communist Party of La Réunion, deputy and senator under the Fourth and Fifth Republics, son of Raymond Vergès, the French Consul in Siam, and Pham Thi Khan, a Vietnamese schoolteacher. Paul's brother was the celebrated attorney Jacques Vergès (1924–2013). Laurence Deroin (1924–2012) was a militant in the French Communist Party, close to Raymond Aubrac; she was a feminist and a cofounder of the Women's Union of La Réunion.

29 Sara R. Farris, *In the Name of Women's Rights: The Rise of Femonationalism* (Durham, NC: Duke University Press, 2017). Let us note that the Simone de Beauvoir Prize was attributed in 2017, under the direction of Sylvie Le Bon de Beauvoir, to Giusi Nicolini, the (female) mayor of Lampedusa, a combatant for refugee and migrant rights. It is known that, in the boats

189

NOTES TO PP. 116–119

destined to see so many deaths and drownings, women suffer doubly, because they are often raped by their companions in misfortune. Rape is indeed a universal practice, and there are no such things as "good" and "bad" rapists.

30 See Sadri Khiari, *Pour une politique de la racaille: Immigré-e-s, indigènes et jeunes de banlieues* (Paris: Textuel, 2006), and, by the same author, *La contre-révolution coloniale en France: De de Gaulle à Sarkozy* (Paris: La Fabrique, 2009); see also Houria Bouteldja, Sadri Khiari, and Félix Boggio Ewanjé-Epée, *Nous sommes les indigènes de la République* (Paris: Amsterdam, 2012). In English, see Houria Bouteldja, "Party of the Indigenes of the Republic (PIR): Key concepts," trans. Paola Bacchetta, *Critical Ethnic Studies*, 1, no. 1 (Spring 2015): 27–32. Houria Bouteldja resigned from the Parti des Indigènes de la République in October 2020: http:// indigenes-republique.fr/demission-dhouria-bouteldja-communique-du-pir/.

31 See Joseph Massad, *Desiring Arabs* (Chicago, IL: University of Chicago Press, 2007). See also the excellent commentary by Jean Birnbaum, in *La religion des faibles*, pp. 197–8. I had the opportunity to interact with Joseph Massad at a colloquium held in London in 2008; see Joseph Massad, *Islam in Liberalism* (Chicago, IL: University of Chicago Press, 2015), p. 309. Let us note that, by virtue of his conception of a hybridized psychoanalysis, Thamy Ayouch also asserts that the notion of homosexuality does not exist in the Arab-Muslim world: see Thamy Ayouch, *Psychanalyse et hybridité: Genre, colonialité, subjectivations* (Louvain: Presses universitaires de Louvain, 2018), p. 164.

32 Houria Bouteldja, blog, "Universalisme gay, homoracialisme et 'mariage pour tous,'" February 23, 2013: http://indigenes-republique.fr/ universalisme-gay-homoracialisme-et-mariage-pour-tous-2/.

33 Houria Bouteldja, blog, "Mohamed Merah et moi," April 6, 2012: http:// indigenes-republique.fr/mohamed-merah-et-moi/. [Montauban, a commune in southern France, was the site of an Islamist terrorist attack carried out in March 2012 by Mohammed Merah. – *Translator's note*.]

34 Houria Bouteldja, *Whites, Jews, and Us: Toward a Politics of Revolutionary Love*, trans. Rachel Valinsky (South Pasadena, CA: Semiotext(e), [2016] 2017). In this book, capital letters are used systematically: Whites, We, You, Blacks, Indigenous, and so on, as if all these terms designated peoples or nations.

35 Ibid., p. 74.

36 Ibid., pp. 29–30.

37 *L'abécédaire de Raymond Aron*, ed. Dominique Schnapper and Fabrice Gardel (Paris: L'Observatoire, 2019), p. 16.

38 Bouteldja, *Whites, Jews, and Us*, p. 32. On October 3, 1960, 7,000 demonstrators supporting French Algeria had marched down the Champs-Élysées shouting "Fusillez Sartre" (Shoot Sartre). De Gaulle had aligned himself with André Malraux's position: it would be better to let Sartre shout "Long live the FLN!" than to make the mistake of condemning him. It was at this moment that the encounter between Sartre and Fanon took place. See Joseph Mornet, "Commentaire à la préface de Jean-Paul Sartre pour *Les Damnés de la terre* de Frantz Fanon," *Vie sociale et traitements*, no. 89 (2006): 148–53.

39 On the television program "Ce soir (ou jamais!)" (Tonight [or never!])

NOTES TO PP. 119–124

hosted by Frédéric Taddéi on March 18, 2016, in the presence of Bouteldja and her ally, the postcolonial academic Maboula Soumahor, Thomas Guénolé, a left-wing political scientist, tore this book to shreds.

40 Letter from Maspero to Fanon, April 26, 1960, in Fanon, *Political Writings*, p. 149.

41 Ludivine Bantigny et al., "Vers l'émancipation, contre la calomnie: En soutien à Houria Bouteldja et à l'antiracisme politique," *Le Monde*, June 19, 2017. This was a response to a critical opinion piece by Jean Birnbaum, "La gauche déchirée par le 'racisme antiraciste,'" published June 10, 2017, in *Le Monde*.

42 Bouteldja, *Whites, Jews, and Us*, p. 26.

43 In a fascinating book, Fethe Benslama and Farhad Khosrokhavar show that women who choose jihadism invert the values of women's emancipation to endorse a regressive identity based on the rejection of their parents' ideas, since they view their parents as underlings humiliated by colonialism. The task is thus to redeem them by a sacrifice. See Benslama and Khosrokhavar, *Le jihadisme des femmes: Pourquoi ont-elles choisi Daech?* (Paris: Seuil, 2017).

44 Anne-Charlotte Dancourt, "On a parlé féminisme avec Rokhaya Diallo," *Les Inrockuptibles*, January 8, 2017: https://www.lesinrocks.com/actu/on-a-parle-feminisme-rokhaya-diallo-115060-08-01-2017/.

45 The expression comes from the notoriously racist slogan for Banania cereal (see this chapter, note 18). In pidgin French, it is often translated as "It's good"; here, the meaning is closer to "*That's* a good one," said ironically. – Translator's note.

46 The prizes are awarded in a parodic ceremony of rewarding racist statements, those most representative of systemic racism, made by public personalities in the media. For an article describing the first ceremony, see https://www.voici.fr/news-people/actu-people/les-y-a-bon-awards-ou-les-prix-du-racisme-282635.

47 Written at the request of W. E. B. Dubois and translated from the German by Dubois himself for publication in *The Crisis* magazine, the short essay can be found in Albert Einstein, *Einstein on Race and Racism*, ed. Fred Jerome and Rodger Taylor (New Brunswick, NJ: Rutgers University Press, 2005), p. 137.

48 Personal exchange with Michel Wieviorka, September 1, 2020.

49 Personal exchange with Michel Wieviorka, September 1, 2020. See Hervé Le Bras, Michel Wieviorka, Rebecca Lemos Igreja et al., *Diviser pour unir? France, Russie, Brésil, États-Unis, face aux comptages ethniques* (Paris: Éditions de la Maison des sciences de l'homme, 2018). See also Catherine Vincent, "Querelle républicaine autour des statistiques ethniques," *Le Monde*, September 12, 2020.

50 *Le visage et la rencontre de l'autre: Colloque du 10 octobre 2012, Collège des Bernardins* (Paris: Lethielleux-Parole et Silence, 2012), back cover.

51 This was the theme of a colloquium on "Identities through the prism of restitution" held on June 6, 2019, at the Université Paris 5 Descartes. See Louis-Georges Tin, *Les impostures de l'universalisme: Conversations avec Régis Meyran* (Paris: Textuel, 2020). On the fratricidal struggles within CRAN, see Sara Daniel, "Lutte fratricide, soupçons de malversations ... rien ne va plus au Cran," in *L'Obs*, August 18, 2020. In the wake of serious

NOTES TO PP. 125–132

internal differences, Louis-Georges Tin was expelled from CRAN in July 2020.
52 Charles Martel, grandfather of Charlemagne, was a Frankish leader who ruled Francia from 718 until his death in 741. – *Translator's note.*
53 *Libération*, January 16, 2015.
54 Let us note that "Je ne suis pas Charlie" does not mean "Je suis anti-Charlie." The nuance is important, for it authorizes those who make use of this "Je ne suis pas," "I am not," to assert that they nevertheless do not approve recourse to murderous acts.
55 See the set of opinion pieces by sociologists, economists, and historians on the left and the far left: "Ceux qui ne sont pas Charlie," *Le Monde*, January 14, 2015.
56 Virginie Despentes, "Les hommes nous rappellent qui commande, et comment," *Les Inrockuptibles*, January 17, 2015. https://www.lesinrocks.com/actu/virginie-despentes-les-hommes-nous-rappellent-qui-commande-et-comment-102086-17-01-2015/.
57 Gildea, *Empires of the Mind*, pp. 224–8.
58 This became apparent with the hashtag #MeToo, a necessary move toward action but one that cannot be extended indefinitely.
59 Éric Fassin, "L'appropriation culturelle, c'est lorsqu'un emprunt entre les cultures s'inscrit dans un contexte de domination" [Cultural appropriation is when a borrowing between cultures takes place in a context of domination], *Le Monde*, August 24, 2018. See also Sonya Faure, "Un credo pour les antiracistes," *Libération*, June 29, 2018. The same accusation had been made against Pascal Blanchard.
60 "Pourquoi la tenue de Madonna pour son anniversaire fait-elle scandale?" *Elle*, December 31, 2018. https://www.elle.fr/Mode/La-mode-des-stars/Pourquoi-la-tenue-de-Madonna-pour-son-anniversaire-fait-elle-scandale-3714040.
61 Kanata, the name of an Iroquois village, is the source of the word "Canada."
62 Statement made on Radio-Canada, July 17, 2018.
63 "Malgré la polémique, Ariane Mnouchkine et Robert Lepage maintiennent leur spectacle 'Kanata,'" *Le Monde*, September 5, 2018.
64 Appeal by UNEF, March 25, 2019.
65 Press release by Frédérique Vidal, Minister of Higher Education and Innovation, and Franck Riester, Minister of Culture, March 27, 2019.
66 Laure Murat, "'Blackface,' une histoire de regard," *Libération*, April 10, 2019. https://www.liberation.fr/debats/2019/04/10/blackface-une-histoire-de-regard_1720559/.
67 Laure Murat, "La *cancel culture*, c'est d'abord un immense ras-le-bol d'une justice à deux vitesses," *Le Monde*, August 2–3, 2020.
68 French Constitution, July 2, 2018: https://www.assemblee-nationale.fr/connaissance/constitution.asp.
69 Éric Fassin, "Le racisme anti-Blancs n'existe pas," conversation with Elsa Mourgues on the podcast "Les idées claires," France Culture, October 10, 2018. And see his blog "Identités politiques," *Médiapart*, September 29, 2019.
70 Laure Daussy, "Tania de Montaigne: Le mot 'racisé' accrédite l'idée selon laquelle la race existe," *Charlie Hebdo*, June 6, 2018. And see Tania de

192

NOTES TO PP. 133–138

Montaigne, *L'assignation: Les Noirs n'existent pas* (Paris: Grasset, 2018). Tania de Montaigne is a member of the 50/50 collective, which strives to promote the equality of women and men and diversity in film and other audiovisual media.

71 Alain Mabanckou, "Je n'ai pas besoin d'afficher une rancœur pour affirmer mon identité." Interview with Valérie Marin La Meslée and Christophe Ono-dit-Biot, *Le Point*, August 13, 2020: https://www.lepoint.fr/culture/litterature-alain-mabanckou-je-n-ai-pas-besoin-d-afficher-une-rancoeur-pour-affirmer-mon-identite-12-08-2020-2387484_3.php.

72 All these acts took place in 2019 and 2020.

73 See Thomas Chatterton Williams, "A letter on justice and open debate," *Harper's Magazine*, July 7, 2020: https://harpers.org/a-letter-on-justice-and-open-debate/.

74 Thomas Chatterton Williams, "Un espace public corseté par la *cancel culture* ne sert pas les intérêts des minorités," conversation with Marc-Olivier Bherer, *Le Monde*, July 26, 2020. Williams is the author of the autobiographical book *Self-Portrait in Black and White: Unlearning Race* (New York: W. W. Norton, 2019).

75 Benjamin Stora, *La guerre des mémoires: La France face à son passé colonial* (La Tour d'Aigues: Éditions de l'Aube, 2007). And see Jacques Chirac, in a speech delivered on July 16, 1995, during the commemoration of the 53rd anniversary of the *Vel' d'Hiv* roundup: "France, that day, accomplished the irreparable." https://www.lhistoire.fr/discours-de-jacques-chirac-du-16-juillet-1995. [During the night of July 16–17, 1942, in Paris, nearly 14,000 Jews were arrested and taken to the Vélodrôme d'Hiver, a winter cycling rink, pending deportation. – *Translator's note*.]

Notes to chapter 6

1 See Mark Lilla, *The Once and Future Liberal*. [The *fleur-de-lis*, a stylized lily, is a symbol of France's Old Regime. – *Translator's note*.]

2 The philosophy of care originated in the United States in 1982, in reaction to the rise of individualism. In the French context, we find it in Paul Ricoeur's *Oneself as Another*, and it is supported by the philosopher Sandra Laugier: see, for example, *Politics of the Ordinary: Care, Ethics, and Forms of Life* (Leuven: Peeters, 2020).

3 This is most notably the case with Vincent Geisser, author of *La nouvelle islamophobie* (Paris: La Découverte, 2003), who popularized the expression in France while attacking SOS Racism and the French model of secularism characterized as *national-laïcisme*, before wrongly accusing a high-ranking staff member of the CNRS (National Center of Scientific Research) of being an informer charged with monitoring scholars specializing in Islam. In 2009, that scandal inflamed the academic world, for Geisser was supported by 5,000 scholars. I wrote an article on the subject: "Geisser: Une pétition à l'aveuglette," published in *Libération* on June 25, 2009. See also Joseph Illand, "L'honneur d'un ingénieur général: Réponse aux accusations de Vincent Geisser," *Le Monde*, July 9, 2009.

4 Sheik Issam Amira, in a sermon calling for support for the killer of Samuel Paty, delivered November 3, 2020, quoted in *Le Monde Juif*.

NOTES TO PP. 138–144

info, November 2, 2020: https://www.lemondejuif.info/2020/11/silence-assourdissant-de-la-france-un-imam-palestinien-de-la-mosquee-al-aqsa-glorifie-la-decapitation-de-samuel-paty/.

5 Fethi Benslama, *La guerre des subjectivités en Islam* (Paris: Lignes, 2014). On the question of the decapitations staged for dissemination on the Internet, see the magnificent book by Jean-Louis Comolli, *Daech, le cinéma et la mort* (Lagrasse: Verdier, 2016), which shows how the "enemies of the West" use visual effects borrowed from Hollywood action movies.

6 The Athenians, who venerated Theseus's ship, replaced worn-out parts by new ones, to such an extent that philosophers made it the basis for a thought experiment concerning identity: some maintained that the boat was always the same, while others argued that it was a different boat. Plutarch tells this story in his *Lives of the Noble Greeks and Romans*.

7 The term "populism" must be handled with care. I use it here in the sense of a regime of passions and emotions marked by a feeling of abandonment that leads to the construction of narratives that are often conspiratist. See Pierre Rosanvallon, *The Populist Century: History, Theory, Critique*, trans. Catherine Porter (Cambridge: Polity, 2021).

8 In November 2005, the CRAB, a representative council of white associations, was established in France, mirroring the CRAN, although it did not remain active for long. Its message: "For more than 2000 years, France has been white. During the last 40 years, it has been becoming gray and black!!! We do not have to tolerate people who have a religious culture above the laws of the Republic. No to [racial] mixing." (Michel Lucas, head of the political party Rassemblement national in the Loire region, quoted in Quentin Laurent, "Relents complotistes, propos sur l'islam ...," *Le Parisien*, April 21, 2021.

9 Patrick Crusius, "The inconvenient truth," https://randallpacker.com/wp-content/uploads/2019/08/The-Inconvenient-Truth.pdf.

10 Mark Lilla, *L'esprit de réaction*, trans. Hubert Darbon (Paris: Desclée de Brouwer, 2019), pp. 11–12. [The passage cited is from Lilla's preface to the French translation of his *The Shipwrecked Mind: On Political Reaction* (New York: New York Review of Books, 2016). – *Translator's note.*]

11 Jean Starobinski, *The Invention of Liberty, 1700–1789*, trans. Bernard C. Swift (Geneva: Skira, 1964).

12 Friedrich Hölderlin, from the first stanza of the hymn *Patmos*, composed in 1803, trans. Scott Horton, *Harper's Magazine*, July 16, 2007.

13 See Jacques Juillard, "La démocratie en danger," *Le Figaro*, October 5, 2020.

14 On this topic, see Sylvie Laurent, *Pauvre petit blanc: Le mythe de la dépossession raciale* (Paris: Maison des sciences de l'homme, 2020).

15 Ibid., p. 19.

16 Negy was affiliated with the growing field of cross-cultural psychology, which studies the way in which ethnic origin, social class, sex, and so on, play a role in the constitution of personality. Negy specialized in studying and providing therapy for poor Hispanic families. In 2012, after he stated that no proof of the existence of "paradise" existed, he was confronted by a group of extremist students who asserted the superiority of Christianity over the other religions.

17 Charles Negy, *White Shaming: Bullying Based on Prejudice, Virtue-Signaling,*

194

NOTES TO PP. 144–148

and Ignorance (Dubuque, IA: Kendall Hunt, 2020). And see Michael Levenson, "University to investigate professor who tweeted about 'Black Privilege,'" *New York Times*, June 5, 2020.

18 Joseph de Maistre, *Considerations on France*, translated from the French, ed. Isaiah Berlin and Richard A. Lebrun (Cambridge: Cambridge University Press, [1796, 1821] 1994), p. 97. Jean-Marie Le Pen has taken up this model, as has Houria Bouteldja. See also Zeev Sternhell, *The Anti-Enlightenment Tradition*, trans. David Maisel (New Haven, CT: Yale University Press, [2006] 2010).

19 See Alain Finkielkraut, *L'identité malheureuse* (Paris: Stock, 2013). This book was harshly critiqued by Pierre Nora: "The expression 'unfortunate identity' would be just as unfortunate if there were not a single immigrant" ("Malheureuse, oui, mais pourquoi?" *Le Débat*, no. 179 [March–April 2014]): 6. The expression became widely used starting in 2014 to designate "a French malady."

20 On the specifically French form of anti-Americanism, see Philippe Roger, *L'ennemi américain: Généalogie de l'anti-américanisme français* (Paris: Seuil, 2002).

21 Édouard Drumont, *La France juive: Essai d'histoire contemporaine* (Paris: Ernest Flammarion & Charles Marpon, 1886). The first edition in two volumes, totaling 1,200 pages, found 65,000 buyers, and the book went through 150 reprintings. An illustrated edition published in 1887 contained "scenes, views, portraits, maps, and diagrams by our best artists."

22 Ibid., p. 154.

23 Maurice Barrès, "Les études nationalistes au Quartier Latin," *Le Journal*, February 15, 1900.

24 Georges Mauco, *Les étrangers en France: Leur rôle dans l'activité économique* (Paris: Armand Colin, 1932).

25 Patrick Weil and I were the first to retrace Mauco's collaborationist past: the founder of the Claude-Bernard centers, Mauco succeeded throughout his life in passing for a resister and a benefactor of humanity. See Élisabeth Roudinesco, "Georges Mauco (1899–1988): Un psychanalyste au service de Vichy. De l'antisémitisme à la psychopédagogie," *L'Infini*, no. 51 (Fall 1995): 69–84, and Patrick Weil, "Racisme et discrimination dans la politique française de l'immigration, 1938–1945/1975–1995," *Vingtième siècle*, 47 (July–September 1995): 77–102.

26 Pantin is a suburban commune neighboring Paris to the northeast. Grenelle is a district in the southwestern part of Paris. – *Translator's note.*

27 Jean Giraudoux, *Pleins pouvoirs* (Paris: Gallimard, 1939); see especially the chapter titled "La France peuplée," pp. 65–7. See also Jean-Claude Milner, "Entretien," produced by Jean-Claude Poizat, *Le Philosophoire*, 43 (2015): 9–55. Giraudoux did not simply target the unassimilated Jews, he was much more radical: "If the French Republic is a fine nature, then the Jews are excluded from it, whether they were born in France or not" (*Pleins pouvoirs*, p. 47).

28 Personal exchange with Bernard Cerquiglini, November 7, 2020.

29 Gilles Fournier, "La guerre de demain est déjà déclenchée," *Europe-Action*, no. 16 (April 1964): 20–1. See also Pino Rauti, "L'Europa e il terzo mondo," *Ordine nuovo*, 10, nos. 5–6 (June–July 1964), p. 8. For an excellent synthesis of all these positions, see Pauline Picco, "Penser et dire

NOTES TO PP. 148–153

la race à l'extrême droite (France–Italie, 1960–1967)," *Vingtième siècle*, no. 30 (2016): 77–88.

30 Jean Raspail, *The Camp of the Saints*, trans. Norman Shapiro (New York: Scribners, [1973] 1975).

31 Jean Raspail, *Moi, Antoine de Tounens, roi de Patagonie* (Paris: Albin Michel, 1981).

32 Solenn de Royer, "L'épopée des Kurdes de l'*East Sea*: Drame en cinq actes," *Confluences Méditerranée*, no. 42 (2002): 13–21.

33 Jean Raspail, "Big Other," trans. L. F. Mares, in *The Camp of the Saints* (Petoskey, MI: Social Contract Press, [2011] 2018), pp. xxiii–xliii.

34 George Orwell, *1984: A Novel* (New York: New American Library, [1949] 1983). In this book, "Big Brother" is the invisible mustachioed leader of a party that uses cameras to surveil everything done and said by a devastated population.

35 Cited in Pierre Assouline, "*Le camp des saints* pousse à choisir son camp," *Le Monde*, March 24, 2011. In this article, Assouline addresses the conditions surrounding the reprinting of this work, which was never the object of any legal pursuit.

36 "Big Other" is the English translation of the famous concept of *grand Autre* ("*grand A*") developed by Jacques Lacan, a concept familiar to all specialists in the human and social sciences. It designates a symbolic alterity – Law, Language, Unconscious, God – that determines the subject unbeknownst to the subject himself or herself. In this connection, thinking of himself as Orwellian, Raspail thus unwittingly convoked his own unconscious, presumably Lacanian.

37 Raspail, "Big Other," p. xxxii.

38 École des hautes études en sciences sociales, École normale supérieure, Centre national de la recherche scientifique.

39 Raspail, "Big Other," p. xxxiii.

40 Michel Houellebecq, *Submission*, trans. Lorin Stein (New York: Farrar, Straus & Giroux, 2015).

41 See Jean-Claude Michéa, "Orwell, la gauche et la double pensée," postface to Michéa's *Orwell anarchiste tory* (Castelnau-le-Lez: Climats, 2020). https://lesamisdebartleby.wordpress.com/2020/11/11/jean-claude-michea-orwell-la-gauche-et-la-double-pensee/.

42 Philip Roth, *The Human Stain* (Boston: Houghton-Mifflin, 2000).

43 Contributors to *Krisis* included authors who had never subscribed even remotely to the ideas of the new right, for example Jean-Luc Mélenchon, Jacques Julliard, Boris Cyrulnik, and André Comte-Sponville.

44 Georges Dumézil was a linguist, an anthropologist, a philologist, and a theorist of Indo-European mythology and of Indo-European trifunctionality: priests, warriors, farmers. On his affinities with the far right, see Didier Eribon, *Faut-il brûler Dumézil? Mythologie, science et politique* (Paris: Flammarion, 1992).

45 "Appel à la vigilance," followed by an article by Roger-Pol Droit, "La confusion des idées. Quarante intellectuels appellent à une 'Europe de la vigilance' face à la banalisation de la pensée d'extrême droite," *Le Monde*, July 13, 1993. And see Maurice Olender, *Race sans histoire*.

46 Paul Yonnet, *Voyage au centre du malaise français: L'antiracisme et le roman national* (Paris: Gallimard, 1993).

NOTES TO PP. 154–159

47 Paul Yonnet, "Sur la crise du lien national," *Le Débat*, no. 75 (May–August 1993): 131, a response to a fierce critique by Michel Wieviorka in the same issue: "Penser le malaise," *Le Débat*, no. 75 (May–August 1993): 122–7.

48 Renaud Camus, *La Campagne de France* (Paris: Fayard, 2000).

49 I participated in the response to Camus's book, as did Jacques Derrida, Jean-Pierre Vernant, and Claude Lanzmann; on that occasion I received as many insults as when I criticized Michel Onfray for the polemical tract he had devoted to Freud ten years earlier. See Derrida and Roudinesco, *De quoi demain* ... All the documents on the controversy can be found on Renaud Camus's website. See also the account offered for the first time by Olivier Bétourné in his *La vie comme un livre: Mémoires d'un éditeur engagé* (Paris: Philippe Rey, 2020).

50 Camus, *Campagne de France*, p. 48.

51 Ibid., pp. 60–1.

52 Renaud Camus, *Le Grand Remplacement* (Neuilly-sur-Seine: David Reinhart, 2011; 2nd exp. ed., 2012). See also, by the same author, *2017, dernière chance avant le Grand Remplacement: Changer de peuple ou changer de politique? Entretiens avec Philippe Karsenty* (Paris: La Maison d'édition, 2017). Let us note that Kemi Seba, a Franco-Béninois activist, a friend of Alain Soral and of Dieudonné who passed from the anticolonialist far left to the identitarian far right, became a self-appointed spokesperson for reverse remigration, seeking to promote a movement of return of the black populations of Europe to their countries of origin – the only way, as he saw it, to cultivate the purity of "the black race" and separate it from "the white race." His segregationist group Tribu Ka (2004–6) was dissolved on charges of inciting racial hatred. In 2008, converted to Islamism, Seba announced that "the white man is the devil": see *Les Inrockuptibles*, September 16, 2017.

53 Colombey-les-Deux-Églises is a village in northeastern France known as the family home and burial place of Charles de Gaulle. – *Translator's note.*

54 See Ariane Chemin, "Et Zemmour devint Zemmour," *Le Monde*, November 6, 2014, and Gérard Noiriel, *Le venin dans la plume: Édouard Drumont, Éric Zemmour et la part sombre de la République* (Paris: La Découverte, 2019).

55 This concept, widely known in France, was invented by Jacques Lacan in 1953 to designate the signifier of the paternal function.

56 RTL (a French radio station), May 9, 2017. Here Zemmour was relying on a retail psychoanalytic vulgate purporting to explore the unconscious of politicians.

57 Éric Zemmour, *Mélancolie française* (Paris: Fayard/Denoël, 2010); *Le suicide français* (Paris: Albin Michel, 2014); *Destin français* (Paris: Albin Michel, 2018).

58 During every interview, Zemmour adds lists to those he had published in *Le suicide français*; see, for example, the major interview he gave on Radio Courtoisie on October 16, 2014.

59 Murat Lama, "*Destin français* de Zemmour: Le livre le plus antisémite de la Vᵉ République," blog, Médiapart, October 18, 2018: https://blogs.mediapart.fr/murat-lama/blog/111018/destin-francais-de-zemmour-le-livre-le-plus-antisemite-de-la-veme-republique/.

NOTES TO PP. 160–162

60 Houria Bouteldja, "Lettre à Éric Zemmour, l'"israélite,'" blog, June 12, 2014: http://indigenes-republique.fr/lettre-a-eric-zemmour-l-israelite-3/.
61 Michel Onfray, "La gauche acéphale," *Le Figaro Magazine*, June 19, 2020. On Michel Onfray, see Élisabeth Roudinesco, ed., *Mais pourquoi tant de haine?* (Paris: Seuil, 2010), and "Onfray, fin de partie," dialogue between Élisabeth Roudinesco and Guillaume Mazeau, moderated by Gilles Cressani, *Le Grand Continent*, July 2020. Terra Nova, founded in 2008, is a French association with a social-democratic orientation.

Notes to epilogue

1 This would be incompatible with the Universal Declaration of the Rights of the Child (1959): https://www.ohchr.org/EN/Issues/Education/Training/Compilation/Pages/1DeclarationoftheRightsoftheChild(1959).aspx.
2 See Maurice Samuels, "Dès 1789, le républicanisme français s'est montré ouvert au particularisme religieux," *Le Monde*, January 1, 2021.

198

REFERENCES

"Ceux qui ne sont pas Charlie." *Le Monde*, January 14, 2015.

"Faut-il opérer les enfants intersexués?" *Le Monde*, July 5, 2019: 25.

"La justice britannique met des conditions aux transitions des mineurs transgenres." *Le Monde*, December 1, 2020. https://www.lemonde.fr/societe/article/2020/12/01/la-justice-britannique-met-des-conditions-aux-transitions-des-mineurs-transgenres_6061808_3224.html.

"La pensée 'decoloniale' renforce le narcissisme des petites différences." *Le Monde*, September 25, 2019.

"Le Combahee River Collective, pionnier du Féminisme noir." *Les Cahiers du CEDREF*, no. 14 (2006): 69–104.

"Le conflit israélo-arabe." *Les Temps Modernes*, special issue, July 1967.

"Panique décoloniale chez les psychanalystes!" *Libération*, October 4, 2019.

"Reject transphobia, respect gender identity: An appeal to the United Nations, the World Health Organization and the States of the World." April 1, 2009. https://outrightinternational.org/sites/default/files/238-1.pdf.

Abou, Sélim. *De l'identité et du sens: La mondialisation de l'angoisse identitaire et sa signification plurielle*. Paris and Beirut: Perrin/Presses de l'université Saint-Joseph, 2009.

Abou, Sélim. *La "République" jésuite des Guaranis (1609–1768) et son héritage*. Paris: Perrin/Unesco, 1995.

Achebe, Chinua. *Things Fall Apart*. London: Heinemann, 1958.

Agence France Presse. "Des élèves transgenres américains dénoncent la 'guerre des toilettes.'" *L'Express*, May 26, 2016.

Albrecht, Gary L., Jean-François Ravaud, and Henri-Jacques Stiker. "L'émergence des *disability studies*: État des lieux et perspectives." *Sciences sociales et santé*, 19, no. 4 (December 2001): 43–73.

Alleg, Henri. *The Question*, trans. John Calder. Lincoln: University of Nebraska Press, (1958) 2006.

Amedegnato, Ozouf S., and Ibrahim Ouattara. "'Orphée noir' de Jean-Paul Sartre: Une lecture programmatique de la négritude." *Revue d'études africaines* (April 2019): 23–50.

Amselle, Jean-Loup. *L'Occident décroché: Enquête sur les postcolonialismes*. Paris: Stock, 2008.

REFERENCES

Andrade, Oswald de. "Cannibalist Manifesto," trans. Leslie Bary. *Latin American Literary Review*, 19, no. 38 (July–December 1991): 38–47.

Arendt, Hannah. *On Violence*. New York: Harcourt Brace Jovanovich, (1969) 1970.

Arendt, Hannah. *The Origins of Totalitarianism*. New York: Harcourt Brace Jovanovich, (1951) 1994.

Aron, Raymond. *L'Abécédaire de Raymond Aron*, ed. Dominique Schnapper and Fabrice Gardel. Paris: L'Observatoire, 2019.

Assouline, Pierre. "*Le camp des saints* pousse à choisir son camp." *Le Monde*, March 24, 2011.

Austin, J. L. *How to Do Things with Words*. Cambridge, MA: Harvard University Press, 1962.

Ayouch, Thamy. "Homosexuel/les marocain/es en postcolonie: Psychanalyse et subalternisation," International colloquium, "Psychanalyse, études de genre, études postcoloniales, état de l'art." Université Paris-Diderot, December 14–15, 2018.

Ayouch, Thamy. *Psychanalyse et hybridité: Genre, colonialité, subjectivations*. Louvain: Presses universitaires de Louvain, 2018.

Azouri, Chawki, and Élisabeth Roudinesco, eds. *La psychanalyse dans le monde arabe et islamique*. Beirut: Presses de l'université Saint-Joseph, 2005.

Bailly, Jean-Sylvain. *Mémoires de Bailly*. Paris: Baudoin frères, 1821–1822.

Bancel, Nicolas, Pascal Blanchard, Gilles Boëtsch, Éric Deroo, and Sandrine Lemaire, eds. *Zoos humains: De la Vénus hottentote aux reality shows*. Paris: La Découverte, 2002.

Bancel, Nicolas, Pascal Blanchard, and Sandrine Lemaire, eds. *La fracture coloniale: La société française au prisme de l'héritage coloniale*. Paris: La Découverte, 2005.

Bantigny, Ludivine, et al. "Vers l'émancipation, contre la calomnie. En soutien à Houria Bouteldja et à l'antiracisme politique." *Le Monde*, June 19, 2017.

Barrès, Maurice. "Les études nationalistes au Quartier Latin." *Le Journal*, February 15, 1900.

Barth, Fredrik. "Les groupes ethniques et leurs frontières," in Philippe Poutignat and Jacelyne Streiff-Fenart, *Théories de l'ethnicité*, pp. 203–49. Paris: Presses universitaires de France, 1995.

Bayart, Jean-François. *Les études postcoloniales: Un carnaval académique*. Paris: Karthala, 2010.

Beauvoir, Simone de. *The Second Sex*, trans. Constance Borde and Sheila Malovany-Chevallier. New York: Alfred A. Knopf, 2010.

Beauvoir, Simone de, and Gisèle Halimi. *Djamila Boupacha; The Story of the Torture of a Young Algerian Girl Which Shocked Liberal French Opinion*, trans. Peter Green. London: André Deutsche, 1962.

Bekale, Marc Mvé. "Victor Hugo: "Le blanc a fait du noir un homme," blog, *Mediapart*, April 22, 2019 (https://blogs.mediapart.fr/marc-mve-bekale/blog/220419/victor-hugo-le-blanc-fait-du-noir-un-homme).

Benjamin, Harry. "Transvestism and transsexualism." *International Journal of Sexology*, 7 (1953): 12–14.

Benslama, Fethi. *La guerre des subjectivités en Islam*. Paris: Lignes, 2014.

Benslama, Fethi, and Farhad Khosrokhavar. *Le jihadisme des femmes: Pourquoi ont-elles choisi Daech?* Paris: Seuil, 2017.

REFERENCES

Bernabé, Jean, Patrick Chamoiseau, and Raphaël Confiant. *Éloge de la créolité.* Paris: Gallimard, 1989.

Bertrand, Romain. "La mise en cause(s) du 'fait colonial.'" *Politique africaine,* no. 102 (2006): 28–49.

Bessis, Sophie. *Western Supremacy: Triumph of an Idea?,* trans. Patrick Camiller. London: Zed Books, (2001) 2003.

Bétourné, Olivier. *La vie comme un livre: Mémoires d'un éditeur engagé.* Paris: Philippe Rey, 2020.

Bhabha, Homi. "Foreword: Framing Fanon," in Franz Fanon, *The Wretched of the Earth,* trans. Richard Philcox, pp. vii–xli. New York: Grove Press, 2004.

Bhabha, Homi. *The Location of Culture,* 2nd ed. London: Routledge (1994) 2004.

Bherer, Marc-Olivier. Conversation with Thomas Chatterton Williams. "Un espace public corseté par la *cancel culture* ne sert pas les intérêts des minorités." *Le Monde,* July 26, 2020.

Birnbaum, Jean. "La gauche déchirée par le 'racisme antiraciste.'" *Le Monde,* June 10, 2017.

Birnbaum, Jean. *La religion des faibles: Ce que le djihadisme dit de nous.* Paris: Seuil, 2018.

Birnbaum, Jean. *Un silence religieux: La gauche face au djihadisme.* Paris: Seuil, 2016.

Bkhairia, Hassen. "L'inscription littéraire de l'histoire chez Flaubert, des oeuvres de jeunesse à 'Salammbô.'" Ph.D. thesis, University of Bordeaux, 2012. http://www.theses.fr/2012BOR30076.

Blanchard, Pascal. Interview. *Télérama* (September 30, 2020): 75–77.

Blanchard, Pascal, Nicolas Bancel, and Sandrine Lemaire. *Décolonisations françaises: La chute d'un empire.* Paris: La Martinière, 2020.

Blanrue, Paul-Éric. *Le monde contre soi: Anthologie des propos contre les Juifs, le judaïsme et le sionisme.* Paris: Blanche, 2007.

Blin, Simon. "En finir avec l''islamo-gauchisme'?" *Libération,* October 23, 2020.

Bouteldja, Houria. "Mohamed Merah et moi," blog, April 6, 2012. http://indigenes-republique.fr/mohamed-merah-et-moi/.

Bouteldja, Houria. "Universalisme gay, homoracialisme et 'mariage pour tous,'" blog, February 12, 2013. http://indigenes-republique.fr/universalisme-gay-homoracialisme-et-mariage-pour-tous-2/.

Bouteldja, Houria. "Lettre à Éric Zemmour, l''israélite.'" Blog, June 12, 2014. http://indigenes-republique.fr/lettre-a-eric-zemmour-l-israelite-3/.

Bouteldja, Houria. "Party of the Indigenes of the Republic (PIR): Key concepts," trans. Paola Bacchetta. *Critical Ethnic Studies,* 1, no. 1 (Spring 2015): 27–32.

Bouteldja, Houria. *Whites, Jews, and Us: Toward a Politics of Revolutionary Love,* trans. Rachel Valinsky. South Pasadena, CA: Semiotext(e), (2016) 2017.

Bouteldja, Houria, Sadri Khiari, and Félix Boggio Ewanjé-Epée. *Nous sommes les indigènes de la République.* Paris: Amsterdam, 2012.

Bouyahia, Malek. "Postcolonialités," in Juliette Rennes, ed., *Encyclopédie du genre,* pp. 488–510. Paris: La Découverte, 2016.

Braudel, Fernand. *The Identity of France,* trans. Siân Reynolds. Vol. 1. Paris: Flammarion, (1986) 1992.

Braunstein, Jean-François. *La philosophie devenue folle: Le genre, l'animal, la mort.* Paris: Grasset, 2018.

REFERENCES

Breton, André. *Manifestoes of Surrealism*, trans. Richard Seaver and Helen R. Lane. Ann Arbor: University of Michigan Press, (1962) 1969.

Brisson, Thomas. "Pour une sociologie des critiques postcoloniales." *Sociétés contemporaines*, no. 93 (2014): 89–109.

Brisson, Thomas. *Décentrer l'Occident: Les intellectuels postcoloniaux chinois, arabes et indiens, et la critique de la modernité*. Paris: La Découverte, 2018.

Brouze, Émilie. "Garçon ou fille, à l'enfant de choisir!" *L'Obs*, October 25–31, 2008.

Brzoza, David Korn, and Pascal Blanchard. Film. *Décolonisations: Du sang et des larmes*. 2020.

Burlet, Fleur. "A New York, une pétition s'élève contre un tableau de Balthus érotisant une très jeune fille." *Les Inrockuptibles*, December 8, 2017.

Butler, Judith. *Gender Trouble: Feminism and the Subversion of Identity*. New York: Routledge, 1990.

Butler, Judith. "Violence, non-violence: Sartre on Fanon." *Graduate Faculty Philosophy Journal*, 27, no. 1 (2006): 3–24.

Butler, Judith. "Can one lead a good life in a bad life?" *Radical Philosophy*, no. 176 (November–December 2012): 9–18.

Butler, Judith. *Parting Ways: Jewishness and the Critique of Zionism*. New York: Columbia University Press, 2012.

Camus, Renaud, *La Campagne de France*. Paris: Fayard, 2000.

Camus, Renaud. *Le Grand Remplacement*. 2nd exp. ed. Neuilly-sur-Seine: David Reinhart, (2011) 2012.

Camus, Renaud. *2017, dernière chance avant le Grand Remplacement: Changer de peuple ou changer de politique? Entretiens avec Philippe Karsenty*. Paris: La Maison d'édition, 2017.

Cavagnis, Julian. "Michel Foucault et le soulèvement iranien de 1978: Retour sur la notion de 'spiritualité politique.'" *Cahiers philosophiques*, no. 130 (2012): 51–71.

Centre Flaubert de Rouen. https://flaubert-v1.univ-rouen.fr/.

Césaire, Aimé. "Discours à l'Assemblée nationale." November 3, 1977. In *Écrits Politiques, 1972–1987*, pp. 164–7. Paris: Jean-Michel Place, 2018.

Césaire, Aimé. "Discours de Miami." *Écrits politiques, 1972–1987*, pp. 519–27. Paris: Jean-Michel Place, 2018.

Césaire, Aimé. "Inauguration de la place de l'Abbé-Grégoire, à Fort-de-France." *Écrits politiques*, vol. 2, 1935–1956, ed. Édouard de Lépine, pp. 235–42. Paris: Jean-Michel Place, 2013.

Césaire, Aimé. "Je ne suis pas pour la repentance ou les réparations." *L'Express*, September 13, 2001.

Césaire, Aimé. *Discourse on Colonialism*, trans. Joan Pinkham. New York: Monthly Review Press, (1950) 2000.

Césaire, Aimé. Interview with Dieudonné M'Bala M'Bala. June 3, 2005. https://www.youtube.com/watch?v=zK6hegi_wHE.

Césaire, Aimé. *Notebook of A Return to the Native Land*, trans. and ed. A. James Arnold and Clayton Eshleman. Middletown, CT: Wesleyan University, (1939) 2001.

Césaire, Aimé. *Resolutely Black: Conversations with Françoise Vergès*, trans. Matthew B. Smith. Cambridge: Polity, 2019.

Césaire, Aimé. *Toussaint-Louverture: La Révolution française et le problème colonial*. Paris: Présence africaine, 1961.

REFERENCES

Chakrabarty, Dipesh. *Provincializing Europe: Postcolonial Thought and Historical Difference*. Princeton, NJ: Princeton University Press, (2000) 2008.

Chamoiseau, Patrick. *Texaco*, trans. Rose-Myriam Réjouis and Val Vinokurov. New York: Pantheon Books, (1992) 1997.

Chanson, Philippe. "Identité et altérité chez Édouard Glissant et Patrick Chamoiseau, scripteurs visionnaires de la parole créole." Franklin College Conference on Caribbean Literature, "The Caribbean Unbound," Franklin, IN, April 13–16, 2005. https://www.potomitan.info/chamoiseau/identite.php.

Chemin, Ariane. "Et Zemmour devint Zemmour." *Le Monde*, November 6, 2014.

Chirac, Jacques. "Discours de Jacques Chirac du 16 juillet 1995." https://www.lhistoire.fr/discours-de-jacques-chirac-du-16-juillet-1995.

Ciavolella, Riccardo. "L'émancipation des subalternes par la 'culture populaire': La pensée gramscienne et l'anthropologie pour appréhender l'Italie d'après-guerre et le tiers monde en voie de décolonisation (1948–1960)." *Mélanges de l'École française de Rome: Italie et Méditerranée modernes et contemporaines*, 128, no. 2 (2016): 431–46.

Clemenceau, Georges. "Discours à la Chambre des députés." July 30, 1885. https://www.assemblee-nationale.fr/histoire/7ec.asp.

Coffin, Alice. *Le génie lesbien*. Paris: Grasset, 2020.

Cohen, Jim. "De l'Atlantique noir à la mélancolie postcoloniale: Entretien avec Paul Gilroy," trans. Jade Lindgaard. *Mouvements*, 51, no. 3 (2007): 90–101.

Cojean, Annick. "Simone Schwartz-Bart: 'Épouser quelqu'un hors de sa culture, ça dessille votre regard.'" *Le Monde*, October 11–12, 2020.

Collignon, Béatrice. "Notes sur les fondements des *postcolonial studies*." *ÉchoGéo*, no. 1 (2007): 1–9.

Combahee River Collective. *The Combahee River Collective Statement*. http://circuitous.org/scraps/combahee.html.

Comolli, Jean-Louis. *Daech, le cinéma et la mort*. Lagrasse: Verdier, 2016.

Confiant, Raphaël. "Les Noirs, du malaise à la colère." *Le Monde*, December 8, 2006.

Confiant, Raphaël. *Aimé Césaire; Une traversée paradoxale du siècle*. Paris: Écriture, (1993) 2006.

Confiant, Raphaël. "La créolité contre l'enfermement identitaire." *Multitudes*, no. 22 (2005): 179–85.

Conrad, Joseph. *Heart of Darkness*. Cambridge: Cambridge University Press, (1899) 2018.

Conrad, Joseph. *Lord Jim*. New York: Oxford University Press, (1899) 1999.

Cooke, Rachel. "Tavistock Trust Whistleblower David Bell: 'I Believed I Was Doing the Right Thing,'" *The Guardian*, May 2, 2021.

Copjec, Joan. *Read My Desire: Lacan Against the Historicists*. Cambridge, MA: MIT Press, 1994.

Crépon, Marc. "Ce qu'on demande aux langues (autour du *Monolinguisme de l'autre*)," *Raisons politiques*, no. 2 (2001): 27–40.

Crusius, Patrick. "The inconvenient truth." https://randallpacker.com/wp-content/uploads/2019/08/The-Inconvenient-Truth.pdf.

Dahomay, Jacky. "L'innommable Raphaël Confiant?" *Le Monde*, December 2, 2006.

Dancourt, Charlotte. "On a parlé féminisme avec Rokhaya Diallo." *Les Inrockuptibles*, January 8, 2017. https://www.lesinrocks.com/actu/on-a-parle-feminisme-rokhaya-diallo-115060-08-01-2017/.

REFERENCES

Daniel, Sara, "Lutte fratricide, soupçons de malversations ... rien ne va plus au Cran." *L'Obs*, August 18, 2020.

Daoud, Kamel. *The Meursault Investigation*, trans. John Cullen. New York: Other Press, (2013) 2015.

Daussy, Laure. "Tania de Montaigne: Le mot 'racisé' accrédite l'idée selon laquelle la race existe." *Charlie Hebdo*, June 6, 2018.

De Gaulle, Charles. https://fresques.ina.fr/de-gaulle/fiche-media/Gaulle00311/discours-de-brazzaville.html.

Deleuze, Gilles, and Félix Guattari. *A Thousand Plateaus: Capitalism and Schizophrenia*. Minneapolis: University of Minnesota Press, (1980) 1987.

Depestre, René. "An Interview with Aimé Césaire," in Aimé Césaire, *Discourse on Colonialism*, trans. Joan Pinkham, pp. 79–94. New York: Monthly Review Press, (1950) 2000.

Derrida, Jacques. "Le siècle et le pardon." *Le Monde des Débats*, December 1999: http://hydra.humanities.uci.edu/derrida/siecle.html.

Derrida, Jacques. "The laws of reflection: Nelson Mandela, in admiration," trans. Mary Ann Caws and Isabelle Lorenz. In Jacques Derrida, *Psyche: Inventions of the Other*, vol. 2, pp. 63–86. Stanford, CA: Stanford University Press, (1986) 2007.

Derrida, Jacques. *Specters of Marx: The State of the Debt, the Work of Mourning and the New International*, trans. Peggy Kamuf. London: Routledge, (1993) 2006.

Derrida, Jacques. *L'autre cap*. Paris: Minuit, 1991.

Derrida, Jacques. *Of Grammatology*, trans. Gayatri Chakravorty Spivak. Baltimore: Johns Hopkins University Press, (1967) 1976.

Derrida, Jacques. *Pardonner: L'impardonnable et l'impréscriptible*. Paris: Galilée, 2012.

Derrida, Jacques. *The Monolinguism of the Other, or The Prosthesis of Origin*, trans. Patrick Mensah. Stanford, CA: Stanford University Press, (1996) 1998.

Derrida, Jacques, and Élisabeth Roudinesco. *De quoi demain . . . Dialogue*. Paris: Fayard/Galilée, 2001.

Despentes, Virginie. "Les hommes nous rappellent qui commande, et comment." *Les Inrockuptibles*, January 17, 2015.

Despentes, Virginie. *King Kong Theory*, trans. Stephanie Benson. New York: Feminist Press, (2006) 2010.

DiAngelo, Robin. *White Fragility: Why It's So Hard for White People to Talk about Racism*. Boston: Beacon Press, 2018.

Doward, Jamie. "Governor of Tavistock Foundation quits over damning report into gender identity clinic." *The Guardian*, February 23, 2019.

Dreger, Alice Domurat. *Hermaphrodites and the Medical Invention of Sex*. Cambridge, MA: Harvard University Press, 1998.

Droit, Roger-Pol. "La confusion des idées: Quarante intellectuels appellent à une 'Europe de la vigilance' face à la banalisation de la pensée d'extrême droite." *Le Monde*, July 13, 1993.

Drumont, Édouard. *La France juive: Essai d'histoire contemporaine*. Paris: Ernest Flammarion & Charles Marpon, 1886.

Dubreuil, Laurent. "Alter, inter: Académisme et *postcolonial studies*." *Labyrinthe*, no. 24 (2006): 47–61.

Dubreuil, Laurent. "Nonconforming: Against the erosion of academic freedom by identity politics." *Harper's*, 341, no. 2044 (September 2020): 61–6.

REFERENCES

Dubreuil, Laurent. *La dictature des identités*. Paris: Gallimard, 2019.

Duby, Georges, and Michelle Perrot. "Writing the history of women," trans. Arthur Goldhammer. *A History of Women in the West*, vol. 2, pp. ix–x. Cambridge, MA: Belknap Press of Harvard University Press, 1992.

Dupray, Fabienne. "*Madame Bovary* et les juges: Enjeux d'un procès littéraire." *Histoire de la justice*, no. 17 (2007): 227–45.

Eagleton, Terry. "In the gaudy supermarket." *London Review of Books*, 21, no. 10 (May 13, 1999): 3–6.

Einaudi, Jean-Luc. *La Bataille de Paris, 17 octobre 1961*. Paris: Seuil, 1991.

Einstein, Albert. *Einstein on Race and Racism*, ed. Fred Jerome and Rodger Taylor. New Brunswick, NJ: Rutgers University Press, 2005.

Ellenberger, Henri. *The Discovery of the Unconscious: The History and Evolution of Dynamic Psychiatry*. New York: Basic Books, 1970.

Elmaleh, Éliane. "Les politiques identitaires dans les universités américaines." *L'Homme et la société*, no. 149 (2003): 57–74.

Eribon, Didier. *Faut-il brûler Dumézil? Mythologie, science et politique*. Paris: Flammarion, 1992.

Fanon, Frantz. *Black Skin, White Masks*, trans. Charles Lam Markmann. London: Pluto Press, (1952) 1986.

Fanon, Frantz. *Écrits sur l'aliénation et la liberté*, ed. Jean Khalfa and Robert Young. Paris: La Découverte, 2015.

Fanon, Frantz. *The Political Writings from Alienation and Freedom*, ed. Jean Khalfa, Robert J. C. Young, and Steven Corcoran, trans. Robert J. C. Young. London: Bloomsbury Academic, 2021.

Fanon, Frantz. *The Wretched of the Earth*, trans. Richard Philcox, with forewords by Homi K. Bhabha and Jean-Paul Sartre. New York: Grove Press, 2004.

Farge, Arlette. *Vies oubliées: Au coeur du XVIIIe siècle*. Paris: La Découverte, 2019.

Farris, Sara R. *In the Name of Women's Rights: The Rise of Femonationalism*. Durham, NC: Duke University Press, 2017.

Fassin, Éric. "Identités politiques," blog, *Médiapart*, September 29, 2019.

Fassin, Éric. "L'appropriation culturelle, c'est lorsqu'un emprunt entre les cultures s'inscrit dans un contexte de domination." *Le Monde*, August 24, 2018.

Fassin, Éric. "Le racisme anti-Blancs n'existe pas." Podcast, "Les idées claires," France Culture, October 10, 2018.

Faure, Sonya. "Faut-il utiliser le mot 'race'?" *Libération*, September 25, 2020.

Faure, Sonya. "Un credo pour les antiracistes. *Libération*, June 29, 2018.

Fausto-Sterling, Anne. *Sexing the Body: Gender Politics and the Construction of Sexuality*. New York: Basic Books, 2000.

Ferry, Jules. "Discours devant la Chambre des deputés." July 28, 1885. https://www2.assemblee-nationale.fr/decouvrir-l-assemblee/histoire/grands-discours-parlementaires/jules-ferry-28-juillet-1885.

Finkielkraut, Alain. *L'identité malheureuse*. Paris: Stock, 2013.

Flaubert, Gustave. *The Letters of Gustave Flaubert*, ed. and trans. Francis Steegmuller. Cambridge, MA: The Belknap Press of Harvard University Press, 1979.

Foucault, Michel. "À quoi rêvent les Iraniens." *Dits et écrits 3: 1976–1979*, pp. 759–62. Paris: Gallimard, (1979) 1994.

REFERENCES

Foucault, Michel. "Une poudrière appelée islam." *Dits et écrits 3: 1976–1979*, pp. 688–98. Paris: Gallimard, (1978) 1994.

Foucault, Michel. "Je suis un artificier," in Roger-Pol Droit, *Michel Foucault: Entretiens*, pp. 89–135. Paris: Odile Jacob, 2004.

Fournier, Gilles. "La guerre de demain est déjà déclenchée." *Europe-Action*, no. 16 (April 1964): 20–1.

Frances, Allen. "The new crisis of confidence in psychiatric diagnosis." *Annals of Internal Medicine*, 159, no. 3 (August 6, 2013).

Freud, Sigmund. "A child is being beaten: A contribution to the study of the origin of sexual perversions." *International Journal of Psycho-Analysis*, 1 (1920): 371–95.

Freud, Sigmund. "On the universal tendency to debasement in the sphere of love," in Sigmund Freud, James Strachey, Anna Freud, and Angela Richards, *The Standard Edition of the Complete Psychological Works of Sigmund Freud*, vol. 11, pp. 177–90. London: Hogarth Press, (1912) 1966.

Freyre, Gilberto. *The Masters and the Slaves (Casa-grande & Senzala): A Study in the Development of Brazilian Civilization*, trans. Samuel Putnam, 2nd English language edn., rev. New York: Knopf, (1946) 1987.

Fukuyama, Francis. *The End of History and the Last Man*. New York: Free Press, 1992.

Geisser, Vincent. *La nouvelle islamophobie*. Paris: La Découverte, 2003.

Genet, Jean. *The Blacks: A Clown Show*, trans. Bernard Frechtman. New York: Grove Press, (1958) 1960.

Giesbert, Franz-Olivier. "Récit: Cendrillon au pays des mille et un jours." *Le Point*, December 5, 2003.

Gildea, Robert. *Empires of the Mind: The Colonial Past and the Politics of the Present*. Cambridge: Cambridge University Press, 2019.

Gilroy, Paul. *Postcolonial Melancholy*. New York: Columbia University Press, 2005.

Ginzburg, Carlo. *The Cheese and the Worms: The Cosmos of a Sixteenth-century Miller*, trans. John and Anne Tedeschi. Baltimore: Johns Hopkins University Press, (1976) 1980.

Giraudoux, Jean. *Pleins pouvoirs*. Paris: Gallimard, 1939.

Glissant, Edouard. *Introduction à une poétique du divers*. Paris: Gallimard, (1995) 1996.

Gramsci, Antonio. *Prison Notebooks*, trans. Joseph A. Buttigieg and Antonio Callari, 2 vols. New York: Columbia University Press, 2011.

Grandmaison, Olivier Le Cour. *La République impériale: Politique et racisme d'État*. Paris: Fayard, 2009.

Guchereau, Alexiane. "L'American Library Association a dévoilé lors de la semaine nationale des bibliothécaires la liste des 11 livres les plus censurés aux États-Unis en 2018." *Livres Hebdo*, April 12, 2019. https://www.livreshebdo.fr/article/etats-unis-les-11-livres-les-plus-censures-en-2018.

Guillot, Vincent. "Intersexes: Ne pas avoir le droit de dire ce que l'on ne nous a pas dit que nous étions." *Nouvelles questions féministes*, 27, no. 1 (2008): 37–48.

Hacking, Ian. *Rewriting the Soul: Multiple Personality and the Sciences of Memory*. Princeton, NJ: Princeton University Press, 1995.

Haddour, Azzedine, "Fanon dans la théorie postcoloniale." *Les Temps modernes*, nos. 635–636 (December 2005–January 2006): 136–59.

REFERENCES

Halperin, David M. "The normalization of queer theory." *Journal of Homosexuality*, 45, nos. 2/3/4 (2003): 339–43.

Harpigny, Guy. "Edward Saïd, *L'Orientalisme, l'Orient crée par l'Occident*." *Revue théologique de Louvain*, 12, no. 3 (1981): 357–61.

Hefez, Serge. "Familles en transition." *Libération*, October 6, 2020.

Herculine Barbin: Being the Recently Discovered Memoirs of a Nineteenth-Century French hermaphrodite. Preface by Michel Foucault. Translated from the French. New York: Pantheon Books, 1980.

Hoffmann, Léon-François. "Victor Hugo, les Noirs et l'esclavage." *Francofonia*, 16, no. 31 (1996): 47–90.

Hoquet, Thierry. *Sexus nullus, ou l'égalité*. Donnemarie-Dontilly: Éd. iXe, 2015.

Houel, Jean-Charles. "Ce qu'il faut penser de Dieudonné par Jacky Dahomay, Antillean philosopher," blog, January 28, 2014. https://louviers-2008.blogspot.com/2014/01/ce-quil-faut-penser-de-dieudonne-par.html.

Houellebecq, Michel. *Submission*, trans. Lorin Stein. New York: Farrar, Straus & Giroux, 2015.

Hugo, Victor. "Hugo reading the future: The visions of a visionary." *The New York Times*, June 2, 1879, p. 3.

Hugo, Victor. *Choses vues: souvenirs, journaux, cahiers 1830–1848*. Paris: Gallimard, 1997.

Hugo, Victor. *Jargal*, trans. C. E. Wilbour. New York: Carleton, (1826) 1866.

Hunt, Lynn. *Family Romance of the French Revolution*. Berkeley: University of California Press, 1995.

Huntington, Samuel. *The Clash of Civilizations and the Remaking of World Order*. New York: Simon & Schuster, 1996.

Illand, Joseph. "L'honneur d'un ingénieur général: Réponse aux accusations de Vincent Geisser." *Le Monde*, July 9, 2009.

James, C. L. R. *The Black Jacobins: Toussaint L'Ouverture and the San Domingo Revolution*. New York: Vintage Books, 1963.

Joubert, Claire. "Théorie en traduction: Homi Bhabha et l'intervention postcoloniale." *Littérature*, no. 154 (2009): 149–74.

Juillard, Jacques. "La démocratie en danger." *Le Figaro*, October 5, 2020.

Kaganski, Serge. "Faut-il brûler *Blow-Up*, le chef d'oeuvre d'Antonioni?" *Les Inrockuptibles*, December 15, 2017.

Kaufmann, Francine. "L'œuvre juive et l'œuvre noire d'André Schwarz-Bart." *Pardès*, no. 44 (2008): 135–48.

Keck, Frédéric. "Le sacrifice des insectes: Caillois entre Lévi-Strauss et Bataille." *Littérature*, no. 170 (2013): 21–32.

Keucheyan, Razmig. "Le moment américain: Sur la mondialisation des pensées critiques." *Revue française d'études américaines*, no. 126 (2010): 21–32.

Khalfa, Jean. "Ethique et violence chez Frantz Fanon." *Les Temps modernes*, no. 698 (2018): 51–69.

Khemilat, Fatima. "Épistémicides: L'impérialisme m'a TueR [sic]." YouTube, June 18, 2015.

Khiari, Sadri. *La contre-révolution coloniale en France: De de Gaulle à Sarkozy*. Paris: La Fabrique, 2009.

Khiari, Sadri. *Pour une politique de la racaille: Immigré.e.s, indigènes et jeunes de banlieues*. Paris: Textuel, 2006.

Kinsey, Alfred C. *Sexual Behavior in the Human Male*. Philadelphia: W. B. Saunders, 1948.

REFERENCES

Kintzler, Catherine. *Penser la laïcité*. Paris: Minerve, 2014.

Kirk, Stuart, and Herb Kutchins. *The Selling of DSM: The Rhetoric of Science in Psychiatry*. New York: A. de Gruyter, 1992.

Kohut, Heinz. *The Analysis of the Self: A Systematic Approach to the Psychoanalytic Treatment of Narcissistic Personality Disorders*. New York: International Universities Press, 1971.

Krafft-Ebing, Richard von. *Psychopathia sexualis, with Especial Reference to Contrary Sexual Instinct: A Medico-legal Study*, trans. Charles Gilbert Chaddock. Philadelphia: F. A. Davis, [1886] 1893.

Kutchins, Herb, and Stuart Kirk. *Making Us Crazy. DSM: The Psychiatric Bible and the Creation of Mental Disorders*. New York: Free Press, 1997.

Lacan, Jacques. "The mirror stage as formative of the *I* function as revealed in psychoanalytic experience," trans. Bruce Fink with Héloïse Fink and Russell Grigg, pp. 75–81. New York: W. W. Norton, (1940) 2006.

Lacorne, Denis. *La crise de l'identité américaine: Du melting pot au multiculturalisme*. Paris: Fayard, 1997.

Lacoste, Francis. "L'Orient de Flaubert." *Romantisme*, 119 (2003): 73–84.

Lacoste, Yves. "Le postcolonial et ses acceptions contradictoires dans trois récents recueils d'articles." *Hérodote*, no. 128 (2008): 143–55.

Laforgue, Pierre. "*Bug-Jargal*, ou de la difficulté d'écrire en 'style blanc.'" *Romantisme*, 69 (1990): 29–42.

Lama, Murat. "*Destin français* de Zemmour: Le livre le plus antisémite de la Vᵉ République," blog, Médiapart, October 18, 2018. https://blogs.mediapart.fr/murat-lama/blog/111018/destin-francais-de-zemmour-le-livre-le-plus-antisemite-de-la-veme-republique/.

Laqueur, Thomas. *Making Sex: Body and Gender from the Greeks to Freud*. Cambridge, MA: Harvard University Press, 1990.

Lasch, Christopher. *The Culture of Narcissism: American Life in an Age of Diminishing Expectations*. New York: W. W. Norton, 1979.

Lasch, Christopher. *The Minimal Self: Psychic Survival in Troubled Times*. New York: W. W. Norton, 1984.

Laugier, Sandra. *Politics of the Ordinary: Care, Ethics, and Forms of Life*. Leuven: Peeters, 2020.

Laurens, Henry. "Dans l'Orient arabe toujours plus compliqué." *Le Monde*, March 12, 2004.

Laurens, Henry. *Orientales*. Vol. 1, *Autour de l'expédition d'Égypte*. Paris: CNRS Éditions, 2004.

Laurent, Sylvie. *Pauvre petit blanc: Le mythe de la dépossession raciale*. Paris: Maison des sciences de l'homme, 2020.

Lavallée, Joseph. *The Negro Equalled by Few Europeans* (Dublin: P. Byrne et al. (1789) 1791.

Lazarus, Neil, ed, *The Cambridge Companion to Postcolonial Literary Studies*. Cambridge: Cambridge University Press, 2004.

Le Bras, Hervé, Michel Wieviorka, Rebecca Lemos Igreja et al. *Diviser pour unir? France, Russie, Brésil, États-Unis, face aux comptages ethniques*. Paris: Éditions de la Maison des sciences de l'homme, 2018.

Le Nevé, Soazig. "Les sciences sociales dans le viseur du politique." *Le Monde*, December 3, 2020.

Leménager, Grégoire, and Laurence Marie. "Traversées de frontières: Postcolonialité et études de 'genre' en Amérique," *Labyrinthe*, no. 24

208

REFERENCES

(2006): 11–37. https://journals-openedition-org.proxy.library.cornell.edu/labyrinthe/1245.

Lemonnier, Marie. Interview with Joan Scott. *L'Obs*, September 7, 2018.

Levenson, Michael. "University to Investigate Professor Who Tweeted about 'Black Privilege.'" *New York Times*, June 5, 2020.

Lévêque, Antoine. "L'égalité des races en science et en philosophie (1750–1885)." Ph.D. dissertation, Sorbonne-Paris-Cité University. https://www.academia.edu/40729847/The_se_LEVEQUE_04.

Levisalles, Natalie. "Jacky Dahomay: 'Il y a une mémoire qui libère et une mémoire qui emprisonne.'" *Libération*, May 22, 2015.

Lévi-Strauss, Claude. *Race and History*, translated from the French. Paris: UNESCO, 1952.

Lévi-Strauss, Claude. *The Elementary Structures of Kinship*, ed. Rodney Needham, trans. James Harle Bell, John Richard von Sturmer, and Rodney Needham. Boston: Beacon Press, (1949) 1969.

Lévi-Strauss, Claude. *Tristes tropiques*, trans. John Russell. New York: Atheneum, (1955) 1963.

Lilla, Mark. *L'esprit de réaction*, trans. Hubert Darbon. Paris: Desclée de Brouwer, 2019.

Lilla, Mark. *The Once and Future Liberal*. New York: HarperCollins, 2017.

Lilla, Mark. *The Shipwrecked Mind: On Political Reaction*. New York: New York Review of Books, 2016.

Loi n° 2005-158 du 23 février 2005 portant reconnaissance de la Nation et contribution nationale en faveur des Français rapatriés. https://www.legifrance.gouv.fr/loda/id/JORFTEXT000000444898/.

Loret, Éric. "L'homme couvert d'infâme." *Libération*, May 28, 1998.

Mabanckou, Alain, and Dominic Thomas. "Pourquoi a-t-on si peur en France des études postcoloniales?" *L'Express*, January 20, 2020.

Mabanckou, Alain. "Je n'ai pas besoin d'afficher une rancœur pour affirmer mon identité." Interview with Valérie Marin La Meslée and Christophe Ono-dit-Biot. *Le Point*, August 13, 2020. https://www.pressreader.com/france/le-point/20200813/282948157586633.

Machado, Pauline. "L'histoire émouvante de Lilie, 'née dans un corps de petit garçon.'" *Terrafemina*, September 11, 2020. https://www.terrafemina.com/article/enfant-transgenre-l-histoire-de-la-petite-lilie-emeut-la-france-video_a355051/1.

Maistre, Joseph de. *Considerations on France*, translated from the French, ed. Isaiah Berlin and Richard A. Lebrun. Cambridge: Cambridge University Press, (1796, 1821) 1994.

Mancerone, Gilles. *Marianne et les colonies: Une introduction à l'histoire coloniale de la France*. Paris: La Découverte, 2003.

Mannoni, Octave. "The Decolonization of Myself." *Race*, 7, no. 4 (1966): 227–35.

Mannoni, Octave. *Prospero and Caliban: The Psychology of Colonization*. New York: Praeger, (1950) 1964.

Maruchitch, Raphaëlle. "Changer de sexe, un long parcours chirugical." *Le Monde*, May 28, 2019.

Marx, Karl, and Friedrich Engels. *Manifesto of the Communist Party*. Moscow: Progress Publishers, 1977.

Massad, Joseph. *Desiring Arabs*. Chicago, IL: University of Chicago Press, 2007.

REFERENCES

Massad, Joseph. *Islam in Liberalism*. Chicago, IL: University of Chicago Press, 2015.

Mauco, Georges. *Les étrangers en France: Leur rôle dans l'activité économique*. Paris: Armand Colin, 1932.

Merle, Isabelle. "Les *subaltern studies*: Retour sur les principes fondateurs d'un projet historiographique de l'Inde coloniale." *Genèses*, no. 56 (2004): 131–47.

Merrill, Mia. "Metropolitan Museum of Art: Remove Balthus' suggestive painting of a pubescent girl, Thérèse Dreaming." Posted November 30, 2017, on Care2 website. https://www.thepetitionsite.com/157/407/182/ metropolitan-museum-of-art-remove-balthus-suggestive-painting-of-a-pubescent-girl-th%C3%A9r%C3%A8se-dreaming/?taf_id=46585122&cid= fb_na#bbfb=809455636.

Meynier, Gilbert, and Pierre Vidal-Naquet. Review of Olivier Le Cour Grandmaison, *Coloniser, exterminer: Sur la guerre et l'État colonial. Études coloniales*, May 10, 2006. http://etudescoloniales.canalblog.com/archives/ 2006/05/10/2311101.html.

Michéa, Jean-Claude. "Orwell, la gauche et la double pensée," in Jean-Claude Michéa, *Orwell anarchiste tory*, 5th edn. Castelnau-le-Lez: Climats, 2020. https://lesamisdebartleby.wordpress.com/2020/11/11/jean-claude-michea-orwell-la-gauche-et-la-double-pensee/.

Miles, William F. S. "Caribbean hybridity and the Jews of Martinique," in Kristin Ruggiero, ed., *The Jewish Diaspora in Latin America and the Caribbean: Fragments of Memory*, pp. 139–62. Brighton, UK/Portland, OR: Sussex Academic Press, 2005.

Milner, Jean-Claude. "Entretien." *Le Philosophoire*, 43 (2015): 9–55.

Minc, Alain. "Le terrorisme de l'esprit." *Le Monde*, November 7, 2001.

Money, John. "Hermaphroditism, gender and precocity in hyperadrenocorticism: Psychologic findings." *Bull. Johns Hopkins Hosp.*, no. 6 (1955): 253–64.

Montaigne, Michel de. *Essays*, trans. George B. Ives. Cambridge, MA: Harvard University Press, 1925.

Montaigne, Tania de. *L'assignation: Les Noirs n'existent pas*. Paris: Grasset, 2018.

Montesquieu, Charles de Secondat, baron de. *Mes pensées*, ed. Catherine Volpilhac-Auger. Paris: Gallimard, 2014.

Moran, Mark. "Spitzer issues apology for study supporting reparative therapy." *Psychiatric News*, June 15, 2012. https://psychnews.psychiatryonline.org/doi/ full/10.1176/pn.47.12.psychnews_47_12_1-b.

Mornet, Joseph. "Commentaire à la preface de Jean-Paul Sartre pour *Les Damnés de la terre* de Frantz Fanon." *Vie sociale et traitements*, no. 89 (2006): 148–53.

Murat, Laure. "'Blackface,' une histoire de regard." *Libération*, April 10, 2019. https://www.liberation.fr/debats/2019/04/10/blackface-une-histoire-de-regard_1720559/.

Murat, Laure. "*Blow-Up* revu et inacceptable." *Libération*, December 12, 2017. https://www.lesinrocks.com/actu/new-york-une-petition-seleve-contre-un-tableau-de-balthus-erotisant-une-tres-jeune-fille-125792-08-12-2017/.

Murat, Laure. "La *cancel culture*, c'est d'abord un immense ras-le-bol d'une justice à deux vitesses." *Le Monde*, August 2–3, 2020.

REFERENCES

Nahon, Claire. "Destins et figurations du sexuel dans la culture: Pour une théorie de la transsexualité." Ph.D. thesis, University of Paris 7, 2004.

Nandy, Ashis. *L'ennemi intime: Perte de soi et retour à soi sous le colonialisme*, trans. Annie Montaut. Paris: Fayard, 2007.

Nandy, Ashis. *The Intimate Enemy: Loss and Recovery of Self under Colonialism*. Delhi: Oxford, 1983.

Negy, Charles. *White Shaming: Bullying Based on Prejudice, Virtue-Signaling, and Ignorance*. Dubuque, IA: Kendall Hunt, 2020.

Noiriel, Gérard. *Le venin dans la plume: Édouard Drumont, Éric Zemmour et la part sombre de la République*. Paris: La Découverte, 2019.

Noiriel, Gérard. "Patrick Boucheron: Un historien sans gilet jaune," blog, February 11, 2019. https://noiriel.wordpress.com/2019/02/11/patrick-boucheron-un-historien-sans-gilet-jaune/.

Nora, Pierre. "Malheureuse, oui, mais pourquoi?" *Le Débat*, no. 179 (March–April 2014): 4–6.

Observatoire de la laïcité. Annual report for 2019–2020. December 1, 2020. https://www.gouvernement.fr/communique-de-presse-0.

Olender, Maurice. *Les langues du paradis. Aryens et Sémites: Un couple providentiel*. Paris: Gallimard/Seuil, coll. "Hautes études," 1989.

Olender, Maurice. *Race sans histoire*. Paris: Seuil, coll. "Points Essais," 2009.

Olivier, Maud. "Rapport d'information fait au nom de la délégation aux droits des femmes et à l'égalité des chances entre les hommes et les femmes, sur les études de genre, par Mme Maud Olivier, Députée." October 11, 2016. https://www.assemblee-nationale.fr/14/rap-info/i4105.asp.

Onfray, Michel. "La gauche acéphale." *Le Figaro Magazine* (June 19, 2020): 54.

Orwell, George. *1984: A Novel*. New York: New American Library, (1949) 1983.

Paxton, Robert O. *Vichy France: Old Guard and New Order 1940–1944*. New York: Knopf, 1972.

Peeters, Benoît. *Derrida*, trans. Andrew Brown. Cambridge: Polity, (2010) 2013.

Perrot, Michelle. *Mélancolie ouvrière*. Paris: Grasset, 2012.

Picco, Pauline. "Penser et dire la race à l'extrême droite (France–Italie, 1960–1967)." *Vingtième siècle*, no. 30 (2016): 77–88.

Pinguet, Maurice. *Voluntary Death in Japan*, trans. Rosemary Morris. Cambridge: Polity Press, (1984) 1993.

Plato. *The Symposium*, trans. M. C. Howatson. Cambridge: Cambridge University Press, 2008.

Porot, Antoine. "Notes de psychiatrie musulmane." *Annales médico-psychologiques*, 74, no. 9 (May 1918): 377–84.

Potier, Frédéric, and Claude Ribbe. "Rétablissons la statue du général Dumas." *Le Journal du Dimanche*, July 4, 2020.

Pouchepadass, Jacques. "Les *subaltern studies* ou la critique postcoloniale de la modernité." *L'Homme*, no. 156 (2000): 161–86.

Proteau, Laurence. "Entre poétique et politique: Aimé Césaire et la 'négritude.'" *Sociétés contemporaines*, no. 44 (Presses de Science Po, December 2001): 15–39.

Puar, Jasbir K. *Terrorist Assemblages: Homonationalism in Queer Times (Next Wave)*. Durham, NC: Duke University Press, 2007.

Raspail, Jean. "Big Other," in *The Camp of the Saints*, trans. L. F. Mares, xxiii–xliii. Petoskey, MI: Social Contract Press, (2011) 2018.

REFERENCES

Raspail, Jean. *Moi, Antoine de Tounens, roi de Patagonie*. Paris: Albin Michel, 1981.

Raspail, Jean. *The Camp of the Saints*, trans. Norman Shapiro. New York: Scribners, (1973) 1975.

Rauti, Pino. "L'Europa e il terzo mondo." *Ordine nuevo*, 10, nos. 5–6 (June–July 1964): 1–11.

Rebreyend, Anne-Claire. "Quand la médecine fait le genre." *Clio: Femmes, genre, histoire*, no. 37 (2013): 251–4. https://journals.openedition.org/clio/11110.

Renault, Matthieu. "Heidegger en Inde: De Jarava Lal Mehta aux *subaltern studies*." *Revue Asylon(s)*, no. 10 (July 2012–July 2014). http://www.reseau-terra.eu/article1293.html.

Rennes, Juliette, ed. *Encyclopédie critique du genre*. Paris: La Découverte, 2016.

Revault d'Allonnes, Myriam. *L'homme compassionnel*. Paris: Seuil, 2008.

Rey, Jean-François. "L'épreuve du genre: Que nous apprend le mythe de l'androgyne?" *Cités*, no. 44 (2010): 13–26.

Ricoeur, Paul. *Oneself as Another*, trans. Kathleen Blarney. Chicago, IL: University of Chicago Press, (1990) 1992.

Riebsamen, Hans. "Heftiger Streit um Adorno-Preisträgerin." *Frankfurter Allgemeine Zeitung*, August 28, 2012.

Rimbaud, Arthur. *Lettres du voyant: 13 et 15 mai 1871*. Geneva: Droz, 1975.

Rivet, Daniel. "Le fait colonial et nous: Histoire d'un éloignement." *Vingtième siècle*, no. 33 (1992): 127–38.

Rivière, Pierre. *I, Pierre Rivière, Having Slaughtered My Mother, My Sister, and My Brother: A Case of Parricide in the 19th Century*, ed. Michel Foucault, trans. Frank Jellinek. New York: Pantheon, (1973) 1975.

Roger, Philippe. *L'ennemi américain: Généalogie de l'anti-américanisme français*. Paris: Seuil, 2002.

Ronell, Avital. Preface, *SCUM Manifesto*. Reedition. London: Verso, 2006.

Rosanvallon, Pierre. *The Populist Century: History, Theory, Critique*, trans. Catherine Porter. Cambridge: Polity, 2021.

Roth, Philip, *The Human Stain*. Boston: Houghton-Mifflin, 2000.

Roudinesco, Élisabeth, ed. *Mais pourquoi tant de haine?* Paris: Seuil, 2010.

Roudinesco, Élisabeth. "Geisser: Une pétition à l'aveuglette." *Libération*, June 25, 2009.

Roudinesco, Élisabeth. "Georges Mauco (1899–1988): Un psychanalyste au service de Vichy. De l'antisémitisme à la psychopédagogie." *L'Infini*, no. 51 (Fall 1995): 69–84.

Roudinesco, Élisabeth. "Jacques Derrida: Spectres de Marx, spectres de Freud," in *Un Jour Derrida*, colloquium proceedings, ed. Daniel Bougnous and Peter Sloterdijk, pp. 51–60. Paris: Bibliothèque publique d'information, 2006.

Roudinesco, Élisabeth. "La décolonisation de soi: Un souvenir d'analyse," in Anny Combrichon, ed., *Psychanalyse et décolonisation: Hommage à Octave Mannoni*, pp. 97–106. Paris: L'Harmattan, 1999.

Roudinesco, Élisabeth. "Le foulard à l'école, étouffoir de l'altérité." *Libération*, May 27, 2003.

Roudinesco, Élisabeth. "Se poser en victime d'un complot de l'extrême droite, le tour de force de Yann Moix." *Le Monde*, September 1, 2019.

Roudinesco, Élisabeth. *La famille en désordre*. Paris: Fayard, 2002.

Roudinesco, Élisabeth. *Pourquoi la psychanalyse?* Paris: Fayard, 1999.

Roudinesco, Élisabeth. *Retour sur la question juive*. Paris: Albin Michel, 2009.

REFERENCES

Roudinesco, Élisabeth. "Lacan and Derrida in the history of psychoanalysis," trans. Richard Hyland, *JEP European Journal of Psychoanalysis*, no. 2 (Fall 1995), http://www.psychomedia.it/jep/number2/roudinesco.htm.

Rougier, Bernard. *Les terroristes conquis de l'islamisme*. Paris: Presses universitaires de France, 2020.

Royer, Solenn de. "L'épopée des Kurdes de l'*East Sea*: Drame en cinq actes." *Confluences Méditerranée*, no. 42 (2002): 13–21.

Rushdie, Salman. *The Satanic Verses*. London: Viking, 1988.

Rutherford, Jonathan. "The third space: Interview with Homi Bhabha," in *Identity: Community, Culture, Difference*, pp. 207–21. London: Lawrence and Wishart, 1990.

Said, Edward. *Joseph Conrad and the Fiction of Autobiography*. Cambridge, MA: Harvard University Press, 1966.

Said, Edward. *Orientalism*. New York: Pantheon Books, 1978.

Said, Edward. *Out of Place: A Memoir*. New York: Knopf, 1999.

Samuels, Maurice. "Dès 1789, le républicanisme français s'est montré ouvert au particularisme religieux." *Le Monde*, January 1, 2021.

Sartre, Jean-Paul. "Black Orpheus," trans. John MacCombie. *The Massachusetts Review*, 6, no. 1 ([1948] Autumn 1964–Winter 1965): 13–52. https://www.massreview.org/sites/default/files/Sartre.pdf

Sartre, Jean-Paul. "Preface," in Frantz Fanon, *The Wretched of the Earth*, trans. Richard Philcox, pp. xliii–lxii. New York: Grove Press, 2004.

Sartre, Jean-Paul. "The Republic of Silence," translated from the French. In *The Republic of Silence*, ed. A. J. Liebling, pp. 498–500. New York: Harcourt, Brace, (1944) 1947.

Saussure, Ferdinand de. *Course in General Linguistics*, trans. Wade Baskin. New York: Columbia University Press, (1916) 2011.

Scheffer, Edith. *Asperger's Children: The Origins of Autism in Nazi Vienna*. New York: Norton, 2018.

Schwartz-Bart, André. *A Woman Named Solitude*, trans. Ralph Manheim. New York: Atheneum, (1972) 1973.

Schwartz-Bart, André. *The Last of the Just*, trans. Stephen Becker. London: Secker & Warburg, (1959) 1981.

Scott, Joan W. *The Politics of the Veil*. Princeton, NJ: Princeton University Press, 2007.

Seba, Kemi. *Les Inrockuptibles*, September 16, 2017.

Sedgwick, Eve Kosofsky, "Queer and now," in Eve Kosofsky Sedgwick, *Tendencies*, pp. 1–19. London: Taylor & Francis Group, 1994.

Selin, Shannon. "When Napoleon met Goethe." https://shannonselin.com/2016/10/napoleon-met-goethe/.

Senghor, Léopold Sédar, ed. *Anthologie de la nouvelle poésie nègre et malgache de langue française*. Paris: Presses universitaires de France, (1948) 1969.

Senghor, Léopold Sédar. *Liberté*, vol. 1: *Négritude et humanisme*. Paris: Seuil, 1964.

Serres, Michel. "Faute." *Libération*, November 18, 2009.

Simon, Catherine. *Algérie, les années pieds-rouges*. Paris: La Découverte, 2011.

Simon, Patrick. "Pour lutter contre le racisme, il ne faut pas invisibiliser la question de la 'race.'" *Le Monde*, June 12, 2019.

Smouts, Marie-Claude, ed. *La situation postcoloniale: Les "postcolonial studies" dans le débat français*. Paris: Presses de Sciences Po, 2007.

Solanas, Valerie. *SCUM Manifesto*. London: Verso, (1967) 2001.

REFERENCES

Solanas, Valerie. *Scum Manifesto: "Association pour tailler les hommes en pieces."* Paris: Mille et Une Nuits, 2005.

Solomon, Andrew. *Far from the Tree: Parents, Children and the Search for Identity.* New York: Scribner, 2012.

Sorman, Guy. "Finissons-en avec cet odieux discours réactionnaire!" *Le Monde,* October 1, 2016.

Spivak, Gayatri Chakravorty. "Can the subaltern speak?" In *Marxism and the Interpretation of Culture,* ed. Cary Nelson and Lawrence Grosberg, pp. 66–111. Urbana: University of Illinois Press, 1988.

Spivak, Gayatri Chakravorty. *A Critique of Post-Colonial Reason: Toward a History of the Vanishing Present.* Cambridge, MA: Harvard University Press, 1999.

Spivak, Gayatri Chakravorty. *Can the Subaltern Speak? Reflections on the History of an Idea,* ed. Rosalind C. Morris. New York: Columbia University Press, 2010.

Springora, Vanessa. *Le consentement.* Paris: Grasset, 2020.

Starobinski, Jean. *The Invention of Liberty, 1700–1789,* trans. Bernard C. Swift. Geneva: Skira, 1964.

Sternhell, Zeev. *The Anti-Enlightenment Tradition,* trans. David Maisel. New Haven: Yale University Press, (2006) 2010.

Stoller, Robert. *Sex and Gender: On the Development of Masculinity and Femininity.* New York: Science House, 1968.

Stora, Benjamin. "Je ne suis pas pour effacer les traces, je suis pour renforcer l'histoire." *La Marseillaise,* June 14, 2020.

Stora, Benjamin. *La guerre des mémoires: La France face à son passé colonial.* La Tour d'Aigues: Éditions de l'Aube, 2007.

Storti, Martine. *Pour un féminisme universel.* Paris: Seuil, 2020.

Tadié, Alexis. "Edward Said et Joseph Conrad: La critique de l'illusion coloniale." *Tumultes,* no. 35 (2010): 67–80.

Taguieff, Pierre-André, and Laurent Bouvet. "Les bonimenteurs du *postcolonial business* en quête de respectabilité académique." *L'Express,* December 26, 2019.

Tin, Louis-Georges. *Les impostures de l'universalisme: Conversations avec Régis Meyran.* Paris: Textuel, 2020.

Tocqueville, Alexis de. *Democracy in America,* trans. Arthur Goldhammer, vol. 2. New York: Library of America, (1840) 2004.

Toranian, Valérie. Interview with Charles Enderlin. "Il est du droit de tout Juif de se déclarer non sioniste." *Revue des Deux Mondes* (October 2020): 36. Published online September 25, 2020. https://www.revuedesdeuxmondes.fr/charles-enderlin-il-est-du-droit-de-tout-juif-de-se-declarer-non-sioniste/.

Uhlig, Marion. "Quand *postcolonial* et *global* riment avec 'médiéval': Sur quelques approches théoriques anglo-saxonnes." *Perspectives médiévales,* no. 35 (2014). https://doi.org/10.4000/peme.4400.

Valéry, Paul. *Essais quasi politiques.* In Paul Valéry, *Œuvres.* vol. 1. Paris: Gallimard, coll. Bibliothèque de la Pléiade, (1919) 1957.

Vatin, François. "Octave Mannoni (1899–1989) et sa psychologie de la colonisation: Contextualisation et décontextualisation." *Revue du Mauss,* 37, no. 1 (2011): 137–78.

Vergès, Françoise. *The Wombs of Women: Race, Capital, Feminism,* trans. Kaiama L. Glover. Durham, NC: Duke University Press, (2017) 2020.

REFERENCES

Vergès, Françoise. *Un féminisme décolonial.* Paris: La Fabrique, 2019.

Veyne, Paul. *Foucault: Sa pensée, sa personne.* Paris: Albin Michel, 2008.

Vincent, Catherine. "Querelle républicaine autour des statistiques ethniques." *Le Monde*, September 12, 2020.

Voltaire (François-Marie Arouet). *The Philosophy of History*, translated from the French. Glasgow: Robert Urie, (1756) 1766.

Voltaire (François-Marie Arouet), "Of the discoveries of the Portuguese," in *The [Prose] Works of M. de Voltaire: Additions to the Essay on General History*, trans. T. Smollett, T. Francklin, et al. London: J. Newbery et al., 1763, vol. 22, p. 227.

Weil, Patrick. "Racisme et discrimination dans la politique française de l'immigration, 1938–1945/1975–1995." *Vingtième siècle*, 47 (July–September 1995): 77–102.

Weinberger-Thomas, Catherine, "Cendres d'immortalité: La crémation des veuves en Inde." *Archives de sciences sociales des religions*, 34, no. 67.1 (January–March 1989): 9–51.

Weinberger-Thomas, Catherine. *Ashes of Immortality: Widow-Burning in India*, trans. Jeffrey Mehlman and David Gordon White. Chicago, IL: University of Chicago Press, (1996) 1999.

Wieviorka, Michel. "Penser le malaise." *Le Débat*, no. 75 (May–August 1993): 122–27.

Williams, Thomas Chatterton. "A letter on justice and open debate." *Harper's Magazine*, July 7, 2020. https://harpers.org/a-letter-on-justice-and-open-debate/.

Williams, Thomas Chatterton. *Self-Portrait in Black and White: Unlearning Race.* New York: W. W. Norton, 2019.

Yacine, Kateb. "Toujours la ruée vers l'or," in *Le Poète comme un boxeur: Entretiens 1958–1989*, pp. 121–33. Paris: Seuil, 1994.

Yacine, Kateb. *Nedjma: A Novel*, trans. Richard Howard. New York: G. Braziller, (1956) 1961.

Yonnet, Paul. "Sur la crise du lien national." *Le Débat*, no. 75 (May–August 1993): 128–39.

Yonnet, Paul. *Voyage au centre du malaise français: L'antiracisme et le roman national.* Paris: Gallimard, 1993.

Young, Robert J. C. *White Mythologies: Writing History and the West.* London: Routledge, 1990.

Zemmour, Éric. *Le suicide français.* Paris: Albin Michel, 2014.

Zemmour, Éric. *Destin français.* Paris: Albin Michel, 2018.

Zemmour, Éric. *Mélancolie française.* Paris: Fayard/Denoël, 2010.

Žižek, Slavoj. *The Sublime Object of Ideology.* London: Verso, 1989.

INDEX

abortion 35, 109
Abou, Father Sélim 5
Aeschylus
  The Supplicants 129–30
Afghanistan 86, 134
Africa
  colonization 45
  decolonization 47, 52
  and Negritude 49
Algeria 71, 111
  and Derrida 72–3
  FLN (National Liberation Front)
    57, 58, 60, 115
  and Islam 58–9
  Jewish community 72–3
  writers and decolonization 54–64
Algerian War 57–8, 60
  Manifesto of the 121 45, 58
Alleg, Henri 58, 113, 120
Amira, Sheik Issam 138
amputomania 15
anatomical sex
  and Freudian theory of sexuality
    11, 12–13
  and gender 13–14, 18, 23, 26–7
  and the queer theory of education
    33–4
Andrade, Oswald de
  "Cannibalist Manifesto" 99, 127
androgyny myth 11

anti-Semitism 6, 39–40, 62
  and Arabs 82
  and Césaire 61–2
  and colonialism 44, 45, 51
  and "great replacement" theory
    145–6, 152, 154, 155–6
  and intersectionality 110, 111
  and nationalist identitarianism
    146, 148
  and postcolonialism 72
  in the United States 142
  and Zemmour 157
  see also Jews
anticolonialism 42, 44–7
Antilleaneity 65–7, 68, 70, 71
the Antilles 71, 72
Antonioni, Michelangelo
  Blow-Up 20–1
apartheid 53, 71–2, 74, 75
Arab spring 137
Arabic humanism 4
Arabs
  and "great replacement" theory
    146, 155–6
  and the Indigenes 116–17
  and Orientalism 82
  women as neofeminists 114
  Zemmour and Arabness 157
Aragon, Louis 115
Arendt, Hannah 39, 101

216

INDEX

Aristotle 11
Armenian genocide 111
Aron, Raymond 119
artworks
  feminist rereadings of 18, 19–20
  and racism 127
Atwood, Margaret 134
Audin, Maurice 58, 120
authoritarianism 140
autism 29, 34
Ayouch, Thamy 101–2

Badinter, Élisabeth 115, 121
Bailly, Jean-Sylvain 68
Balthus
  Thérèse Dreaming 19–20
Bantigny, Ludivine 119
Barbin, Herculine 90, 92
Bardot, Brigitte 126
Barenboim, Daniel 81
Barma, Catherine 158
Barrès, Maurice 145–6
Barthes, Roland 154
Baudelaire, Charles 82
BDS movement 31
Beauvoir, Simone de 158
  and the Indigenes 113, 114, 115,
    118
  Le deuxième sexe (The Second Sex)
    10–11, 12
Becker, Jacques 139
Bell, David 29
Benoist, Alain de 152
Benslama, Fethi 138
Bergé, Pierre 159
Berkeley, California 8–9
Berlin Wall, fall of the 8, 133, 136
Bernabé, Jean 67
Bhabha, Homi
  The Location of Culture 98
  theory of hybridity 98–102
Biassou, Georges 46
Bible
  Book of Revelation 150
bin Laden, Osama 124
bisexuality 11, 17, 31

Black Lives Matter 130, 134, 143
Blanchard, Pascal 104–5
Blanchot, Maurice 45, 58, 73
Blanrue, Paul-Éric 40
Blow-Up (film) 20–1
Bonnefoy, Yves 153
Boulez, Pierre 30
Boupacha, Djamila 114–15
Bourdieu, Pierre 45, 153, 158
Bouteldja, Houria 113, 116, 117–18,
    119, 120, 159–60
Bouyahia, Malek 105
Bowlby, John 29
Braudel, Fernand 2, 108, 158
Brazil 99
Breivik, Anders Behring 139
Breton, André 42, 127
  Manifesto of Surrealism 99
Brexit 141
Brisson, Thomas 77
Brissot, Jacques-Pierre 68
Brunet, Philippe 129
Buddhism 147
Butler, Judith 10, 26, 93, 100
  Gender Trouble 30–1

Caillois, Roger 42, 43, 50
Camus, Albert 73, 91
Camus, Renaud 154–7
Canada
  Metropolitan Center of Surgery,
    Montreal 32
cancel culture 126–7, 130
"Cannibalist Manifesto" 99, 127
Caribbean
  and Negritude 49
  San Domingo slave revolt 46
Carter, Jimmy 88
censorship 4
Certeau, Michel de 5
Césaire, Aimé x, 54, 60, 61, 64–5,
    68, 69, 70, 102, 160
  and Derrida 73
  Discourse on Colonialism 50–1,
    53
  and the Indigenes 115, 119

217

INDEX

Césaire, Aimé (*cont.*)
  and Negritude 48, 49, 50–1, 52–3,
    58, 59, 64–5, 65–6, 71, 72,
    118
  *Notebook of a Return to the
    Native Land* 61–4
  on the slave trade 112
  and Zemmour 159
Chakrabarty, Dipesh
  *Provincializing Europe:
    Postcolonial Thought and
    Historical Difference* 95–7
chameleon syndrome ix, 136
Chamoiseau, Patrick 67
Charles VI, King of France 145
Charlie Hebdo murders 124–6, 151
Chateaubriand, François-René de 82
children
  sex and gender 14, 28–9, 33
  Solomon's study of families and
    identities 34–5
  in transgender families 32–3
China 142, 147
Chirac, Jacques 88
Churchill, Winston 134
cisgender identity 18
Clemenceau, Georges 42, 45, 47, 66,
    113
Clinton, Bill 152
Coffin, Alice 91
  Le génie lesbien 36
colonial fracture 104–5
colonialism 39, 42, 53
  and anticolonialism 42, 44–7,
    48–53, 75, 97, 111
  Algerian writers 54–64
  and cancel culture 127
  hybridity 99, 100
  and the Indigenes x, 105,
    113–15, 119–20
  Césaire on 50–1
  decolonization 47, 71, 140, 147
  and Derrida 72–5
  French neocolonialism 51–3
  and the French Revolution 67–70
  and hybridity 102

and intersectionality 108, 113
and Negritude 48–53, 58, 59,
    64–6, 67, 68, 71
and the Occupation of France 49
and Orientalism 82
the psychology of colonization
    54–7
  see also postcolonialism
Columbus, Christopher 133
communism 74
  in China 142
  collapse of Communist regimes 52,
    75, 140
  and Judeo-Bolshevism 107
  and statue toppling 133
Communist Manifesto (Marx and
    Engels) 75
communitarianism 3, 108, 147, 159
Confiant, Raphaël 65, 67–70
Congress of Black Writers and Artists
    48
Conrad, Joseph 84
  Heart of Darkness 80, 98
conspiracy theories 145, 150
Copjec, Jean 100
cosmopolitanism 5, 153
Coulibaly, Amedy 126
CRAN (Representative Council of
    Black Associations) 121–4, 130
Creolity 65, 67, 70, 71, 72, 73
  and Derrida 72, 73
CRIF (Representative Council of Jews
    in France) 121, 122–3
Critical Race Studies 85, 86
Crusius, Patrick 139
cultural appropriation 126–7,
    127–30
cultural hegemony 158
cultural relativism 43
culture and race 40–1, 42, 64

Dahomay, Jacky 69–70
Daoud, Kamel 91
Deaf people 34, 35
Declaration of the Rights of Man and
    of the Citizen 44, 47, 67–8

218

INDEX

decolonial studies x, 56, 78, 79, 84, 89, 101, 102, 104
deconstruction 76, 78
Defense Union Group 109
Deguy, Michel 153
Deleuze, Gilles 89, 102, 106, 158, 160
Delphy, Christine 119
democracy
  and Bhabha's hybridity theory 99
Derby-Lewis, Clive 74
Deroin, Laurence 115
Derrida, Jacques x, 13, 30, 45, 72–5, 76, 78, 79, 86, 94, 102, 153, 160
  background 72
  and Bhabha's hybridity theory 100
  and intersectionality 106, 112–13
  and monolingualism 73, 98
  Of Grammatology 92
  and Said 81
  Specters of Marx 74, 75, 96
  and Zemmour 158
Descartes, René 78
  Discourse and Method 11
Despentes, Virginie 37, 91, 125–6
Diallo, Rokhaya 120
Dieudonné M'Bala M'Bala 69, 121, 125
Diop, Alione 48
disability studies 34
discrimination
  and socially constructed identities 34
  transgender and intersexual persons 31
Douste-Blazy, Philippe 111
Down syndrome 34, 35
drag culture 16–17
Drumont, Édouard 157
  La France juive 145
DSM (*Diagnostic and Statistical Manual of Mental Disorders*) 21–3, 85, 106
Dubois, W.E.B. 121
Duby, Georges 91, 153

Dumas, General Alexandre 64, 68
Dumézil, Georges 153
Duras, Marguerite 154
dwarfism 34, 35

Eagleton, Terry 97
Eco, Umberto 153
economic globalization 5
education
  prohibition of religious markers in French schools 5, 30
  queer theory of 33–4
Einstein, Albert
  essay on race and racism 121–2
Elizabeth II, Queen 88
Eloge de la créolité (Bernabé, Chamoiseau and Confiant) 67
Enderlin, Charles 110
Enlightenment 3, 4, 140–1
  and Bhabha's hybridity theory 99
  and colonialism 47
  and identitarianism 108, 137
  and slavery 53
Epstein, Jeffrey 19
Erdoğan, Recep Tayyip 141
Ernaux, Annie 119
ethnicity, concept of 147
European culture
  and Bhabha's hybridity theory 99
Evans, Marcus 29

families
  raising gender-neutral children 33–4
  Solomon's study of families and identities 34–5
  transgender 32–3
Fanon, Frantz x, 47, 56–60, 61, 62, 65, 69, 73, 78, 86, 102, 112, 160
  background 54
  and Bhabha's hybridity theory 100–1
  Black Skin, White Masks 54–5, 56–7, 98
  death 60

INDEX

Fanon, Frantz (*cont.*)
and the Indigenes 119, 120
and intersectionality 106, 132
The Wretched of the Earth 45,
58–9, 59–60, 62, 100–1
Farge, Arlette 91, 153
Farris, Sara R. 115
Fassin, Éric 126–7, 131, 132
Faurisson, Robert 109
Fausto-Sterling, Anne 26–7
feminism
and fundamental freedoms 18–21
identitarian 35–7
and the Indigenes 115–16
neofeminists 114, 130
pornography and female sexuality
85
postcolonial feminists 105
and transsexualism 15
and women in India 94
femonationalism 107, 115–16
Ferry, Jules 44, 45, 47, 113
First World War 75
Flaubert, Gustave 82–4
Floyd, George Perry 130
Foucault, Michel 9, 13, 30, 63, 78,
84, 86, 87, 100, 102, 158, 160
and intersectionality 106, 117
"Parallel Lives" collection 90
and race 132
Fouque, Antoinette 115
Fourest, Caroline 121
French citizenship 2, 3, 113
French Constitution 43, 144
French Guiana 51, 71
French identity
and nationalist identitarians
139–40, 144–5, 153
Zemmour on 157–9
French language
and Negritude 48
French Revolution 64, 67–70, 135,
145
chouans in western France 46
Freud, Sigmund 84, 92, 94, 98
and anti-Zionism 40

Civilization and Its Discontents
141
and Derrida 74
and the Enlightenment 141
Freudian psychiatry 22
and hybridity theory 102
and the Indigenes 118
Interpretation of Dreams 11
theory of sexuality 11–13
Freyre, Gilberto
The Masters and the Slaves 98–9
Fukuyama, Francis 74, 86

Gabin, Jean 139
Galen 11
Gaulle, Charles de 51–2, 156
Gaulle, Geneviève de 115
Gauthier-Fawas, Arnaud 37–8
Gay International 117
Gayssot law 111
gender x, 10–38, 161
disseminating human gender 33–7
the "gendered gaze" 20
and identity politics 76
and imperialism 105
and sexuality 10–18
see also feminism; queer theory/
movement; sex and gender;
transsexualism; women
gender studies 13–16, 76, 92, 101,
104
and intersectionality 105–6, 108–9,
110–14
Genet, Jean 24
genocide 148
Germany 141
Giesbert, Franz-Olivier 87
Gildea, Robert 126
Ginzburg, Carlo 90
Giraud, Christophe 36
Giraudoux, Jean 146
Glissant, Édouard 65–7
globalization 41, 88
Godard, Jean-Luc 30, 126
Goebbels, Joseph 40
grammatology 92

220

INDEX

Gramsci, Antonio 88–9, 90, 158
"great replacement" theory 140, 141, 145–60
GRECE (Group of Research and Study for European Civilization) 152
Greece 141
Grégoire, Abbé 62
Guadeloupe 51, 63
Guattari, Félix 78, 158
Guggenheim, Father Antoine 123
Guha, Ranajit 89, 95
Guillot, Vincent 27

Habermas, Jürgen 30
Halimi, Gisèle 58, 114–15
Hamlet (Shakespeare) 75, 96
Hanem, Kuchuk 82–3, 88
Hani, Chris 74, 75
happiness 140–1
Harlem Renaissance 132
Heart of Darkness (Conrad) 80
Hefez, Serge 32
Heidegger, Martin 97
Heritier, Françoise 153
hermaphroditism 13–14, 17, 26–7, 31
heteronormativity 18, 25, 27
hierarchies of identities 6
historians
  and identitarianism 111–12
'history from below' 89–91
Hitler, Adolf 40, 50–1
Hitlero-Trotskyitism 107–8
Hölderlin, Friedrich 141
Hollande, François 108, 110
Holocaust 40
homonationalism 103, 107, 115
homoracialism 117
homosexuality 6
  as an identity 17
  conversion therapy 23
  depsychiatrization of 17, 21
  gay identity 16, 17
  and "great replacement" theory 152, 154, 155

and identitarians 35–6, 108–9, 139
and the Indigenes 116–17
and nationalism 102–3
pinkwashing 103
Zemmour on 159
Houellebecq, Michel 37
  Submission 151
Hugo, Victor 45–7, 64, 65, 82, 137
  Bug-Jargal 46
Human Rights League 121
humanism 55
Hungary 141
Huntington, Samuel 74, 96
hybridity, Bhabha's theory of 98–102

identitarianism 126–35, 136–45, 161–2
  far-left Identitarians 151–2
  far-right Identitarians 138–60, 161
  and gender 33–7, 105–6, 108–9, 110–14
  and "great replacement" theory 140, 141, 145–60
  and historians 111–12
  Indigenes of the Republic x, 105, 113–20, 121, 127, 158
  and intersectionality 76–7, 106–24
  nationalist 141–50
  neologisms 84–5, 98, 106–8, 116, 117
  and postcolonialism 76–9, 84–8
  and radical Islam 86–8, 151
  subaltern identity x, 84, 88–103
  see also intersectionality
identity culture 8–9
identity loss 7–8
identity politics 76, 88
  and gender studies 13
  and the systematization of phobias 106
  and transsexuals 16
  see also identitarianism
identity studies 85–6
immigrants
  fear of 146–7
  naming of children 157–8

221

INDEX

immigration
and postcolonialism 72
remigration 156–7
imperialism 53, 97
and gender 105
India 47, 52, 71, 77, 89
Modi government 141–2
sutteeism 93–5, 96
Indigenes of the Republic x, 105,
113–20, 121, 127, 158
Indochina (former) 47, 52, 111
insurrectional movements 79
International League Against Racism
and Anti-Semitism 121
intersectionality 76–7, 104–35
and the colonial fracture 104–5
CRAN (Representative Council of
Black Associations) 121–4
iconoclastic rage 132–5
the Indivisibles 120–1
and "Je suis Charlie" 124–6
and new "phobias" 106–7
see also identitarianism
intersexuals 17, 26, 27–8, 29, 31
Iranian revolution (1979) 86–8
Iraq 103
Islam
and Algeria 58–9
and "great replacement" theory
148, 156
headscarf wearing 4–5, 19, 30, 114
and the Indigenes 116, 117
Islamo-leftism 107, 110, 139, 160
Muslims in India 141–2
radical (Islamism) 74, 86–8, 104,
108, 117, 134, 135, 137–8,
142–3
and republican secularism 107,
109–10, 125
Islamophobia 88, 107, 116, 121,
125, 137
Israel 82
and anti-Zionism 40, 110
colonial policy 53
Israeli-Palestinian conflict 4, 30–1,
61, 62, 79

and Jews 70
Six-Day War 62, 80–1
Italy 141

Jacob, François 153
Japan 147
Jeanson, Francis 56
Jewish Defense League 69
Jews
in Algeria 72–4
and Arabs 82, 148
CRIF (Representative Council of
Jews in France) 121, 122–3
and "great replacement" theory
155–6
and the Indigenes 117–18, 119
and the Israeli-Palestine conflict
30–1
Jewish identity 1–2, 3, 69–70
in Martinique 61, 67
Nazi extermination of 69, 91, 153,
159
and postcolonialism 72
and race 50, 51
and Zemmour 159, 160
Zionism and anti-Zionism 39–40,
110, 117–18
see also anti-Semitism
Judeo-Bolshevism 107

Kanata, performance of 128–9, 130
Kant, Immanuel 141
Kanwar, Roop 94
Kassir, Samir 4
Kauffmann, Vincent 8–9
Kennedy, John F. 124
Khiari, Sadri 113, 116, 117
Khomeini, Ayatollah 87
King, Martin Luther 119, 130
Kinsey, Alfred 10
Kohut, Heinz 10
Kojève, Alexandre 74
Korean War 52
Kouachi, Chérif and Said 126
Krafft-Ebing, Richard von 32
Krisis (journal) 152–3

222

INDEX

Ku Klux Klan 142, 143
Kubrick, Stanley 124

Lacan, Jacques 30, 54, 55, 56, 79,
  92, 98, 100, 102, 157
  and intersectionality 106
Lantieri, Father Laurent 123
Lanzmann, Claude 158
Laqueur, Thomas 11
Lasch, Christopher 7
Latin America 78
Laufer, Laurie 101
Laurent, Sylvie 143
Lawrence, T.E. 82
Le Bras, Hervé 122
Le Pen, Jean-Marie 6, 69, 118, 125
Lebanese identity 3, 38
Lee, General Robert E. 133–4
Leiris, Michel 127
Lepage, Robert 128–9
lesbians 16, 17
  feminists 35–6
Lévêque, Antoine 47
Lévi-Strauss, Claude xi, 43, 45, 47,
  66, 67, 73, 135
  and cancel culture 127
  and race 43, 45, 47, 50, 51, 64
  Race and History 39, 40–2
  structuralism 92
  Tristes tropiques 42
  Zemmour on 158–9
Levinas, Emmanuel 31
Levy, Bernard-Henri 158
Lewinski, Monica 152
LGBTQIA+ communities 17–18, 25,
  27, 33–4, 78
  and the Indigenes 116
  and pinkwashing 103
liberation movements ix
Lilla, Mark 9, 134, 136, 140
linguistic nationalism 73
Louis XVI, King of France 148
Louverture, Toussaint 68
Lozès, Patrick 121, 123, 124

Mabanckou, Alain 132–3

Macron, Emmanuel 157
Madagascar 71
Madonna 127
the Maghreb 47
Maistre, Joseph de 144
Manceron, Gilles 121
Mandela, Nelson 72, 73–4, 75, 119,
  122
Mandouze, André 113
Mannoni, Maud 55
Mannoni, Octave 65
  "The decolonization of myself" 56
  Prospero and Caliban: The
    Psychology of Colonization
    55–7
Martin-Baud, Lucie 91
Martinique 51, 53, 134
  Jewish community 61, 67
Marx, Karl 74, 75, 96–7
Mascolo, Dionys 58
Maspero, François 119, 120
Massad, Joseph 116–17
Massignon, Louis 82
Mauco, Georges 146
men
  and feminist identitarians 35–7
Merah, Mohammed 117
Merrill, Mia 20
MeToo movement 19
Meynier, Gilbert 51
Michelet, Jules 2
Middle Ages 85
Minc, Alain 87
Mirabeau, comte de 68
Mitterrand, François 152
mixed-race identities 6, 49, 54,
  64–70
Mnouchkine, Ariane 128–9, 130
Modi, Narendra 141–2
Modiano, Patrick 159
Mohammed, Prophet 87
Money, John 13–14, 26
Montaigne, Tania de 132
Montandon, Georges 146
Montesquieu, Charles de Secondat,
  baron de 5–6, 144

223

INDEX

Morocco 111
multiculturalism 76, 77, 100, 148
"multiple personality" disorder 22
Murat, Laure 20, 129–30

Nabe, Marc-Édouard 109
Naipaul, V.S. 98
Napoleon Bonaparte, Emperor 12, 82, 159
narcissism 7–8, 10
national identity xi, 108
nationalism 41, 42
  and homosexuality 102–3
nationalist identitarianism 141–50
Nazism
  and colonialism 52
  extermination of the Jews 69, 91, 153, 159
  French anti-Nazi Resistance 54, 61, 62
  and Hitlero-Trotskyitism 107–8
  neo-Nazis 148
  and race 39, 44, 50–1, 132
Ndiaye, Pap 122
negationism, crime of 111
Negritude 48–53, 58, 59, 64–5, 66, 67, 68, 72, 118, 122, 147
Negy, Charles 143–4
neo-colonialism 45
neofeminists 114, 130
neologisms 84–5, 98, 106–8, 116, 117
Netherlands 141
Noiriel, Gérard ix, 111–12, 159
non-binary sex identity 18, 25, 26–7, 37–8
Nora, Pierre 111
North American multiculturalism 77

Obama, Barack 37, 143
Occidentalism 78, 82, 84
Olender, Maurice 153
Onfray, Michel 160
Orientalism 78, 81–4
Orpheus myth 50
Orwell, George 151–2
  1984 150

Pakistan 77
Palestinians 4, 30–1, 53, 61, 62
  and the Indigenes of the Republic x, 105, 113–20
  and Said 79, 80–1
Papon, Maurice 60
Parks, Rosa 76
Paxton, Robert 91–2, 159
Perec, Georges 34, 85
Perrot, Michelle 13, 91, 153
Pétain, Marshal 54, 91, 159
Pewapsconias, Janelle 128
phallocentrism 11
phobias
  new "phobias" and intersectionality 106–7
Picasso, Pablo 127
Piccoli, Michel 126
pinkwashing 103
Plato 92
  androgyny myth 11
Plutarch 90
Poland 141
Popper, Julius 3, 112
populist movements 141
Porn Studies 85
Porot, Antoine 57
positive discrimination 78
postcolonial studies x, 56, 72, 78, 81, 84, 89, 104
  Bhabha's hybridity 98–101
  and intersectionality 105–6, 108
postcolonialism 71–103
  and Césaire 64
  and identitarianism 76–9
  origins of the term 77
  and Said 78, 79–83, 84
  the subaltern identity 84, 88–103
poststructuralism 76, 92
Pouillon, Jean 153
Présence africaine (journal) 48
psychiatry/psychoanalysis 10, 21
  the *DSM* and identity disorders 21–4, 85, 106
  Freudian 12–13
  and hybridity theory 102

224

INDEX

and identitarianism 151
and "multiple personality" disorder 22
post-Freudian 7, 85
and queer theory 25
race and colonialism 54–7, 65
and Zemmour 157
Puar, Jasbir 103
Putin, Vladimir 141

QAnon 142
queer theory/movement 10, 24–33, 76, 131
theory of education 33–4

race x, 39–70, 76
and Bhabha's theory of hybridity 99
CRAN (Representative Council of Black Associations) 121–4, 130
Critical Race Studies 85, 86
and culture 40–1, 42, 64
"ethnic group" concept 147
Fanon on racial identity of colonized peoples 54–5
and the French constitution 131, 132
and the Indigenes 114, 119
and the Indivisibles 120–1
Lévi-Strauss on 40–3
mixed-race identities 6, 49, 54, 64–70
"racial" identity in the United States 142–4
"racialized" neologism 84–5
racialist theories 44, 47, 50, 51, 85
Whiteness Studies 85–6
see also colonialism; Negritude
racism 39–40, 42, 42–3, 44, 45, 46, 76
and antiracism 77–8, 131–2
neoantiracism 153–4
and artworks 127
and Bhabha's hybridity theory 100

and the Indigenes of the Republic 114, 118, 119
and the Indivisibles 120–1
and nationalist identitarianism 142–3, 146–7
and Negritude 49, 50
racialist colonial psychiatry 57
scientific 42
systemic 131
white racism/supremacy 139, 143–4, 148
see also anti-Semitism
Ramadan, Tarik 137
rape 20
Raspail, Jean 154
Le Camp des Saints (The Camp of the Saints) 148–51
Rebérioux, Madeleine 58
Rebreyend, Anne-Claire 26
Reich, William 22
Reimer, David 14, 26
religious identity 1–2, 3, 4, 30, 109
see also Islam; secularism
Renan, Ernest 44
Renoir, Jean 139
Réunion 51
Revel, Jacques 153
Rhodes, Cecil 133
Ricoeur, Paul 113
Rivet, Daniel 71
Rivière, Pierre 90
Robespierre, M. 160
Rochefoucauld-Liancourt, duke de 68
Romanticism
and Orientalism 83
Roth, Philip
The Human Stain 152
Rousseau, Jean-Jacques 160
Confessions 11
Rushdie, Salman
The Satanic Verses 87–8
Russia 141

Sacy, Silvestre de 82
Saddam Hussein 103

INDEX

Said, Edward x, 78, 79–83, 84, 86, 92, 100, 102
  and the Indigenes 117, 119
  Orientalism 81–3
Saint Laurent, Yves 159
Saint-Just, Louis Antoine 141, 160
Salan, Raoul 54
Sarkozy, Nicolas 108
Sartre, Jean-Paul 75, 104, 160
  and anticolonialism 42, 45, 47, 66, 73
  and Bhabha's hybridity theory 100
  chosification 69
  and the identitarians 118–19, 138
  and intersectionality 111, 127
  on Negritude 48, 49–50
  preface to Fanon's *The Wretched of the Earth* 45, 59–60, 62, 100–1
  and Zemmour 158, 159
schizophrenia 15, 34
Schneidermann, Daniel 37–8
Schoelcher, Victor 45, 53, 64, 134
Schwartz, Laurent 58
Schwartz-Bart, André 62–4
  The Last of the Just 62
  A Woman Named Solitude 63–4
Schwartz-Bart, Simone 62–3
Schwarzer, Alice 115
SCUM Manifesto 36
Second World War
  the Occupation (France) 49, 146
  Vichy France 72–3, 91–2, 121, 146, 159
secularism 1, 3, 4–6, 162
  and Bhabha's hybridity theory 99
  and the Indigenes 114
  and intersectionality 104, 108
  Islam and republican secularism 107, 109–10, 125, 138
self-affirmation ix
self-identification x
Semoun, Élie 69
Senghor, Leopold Sédar 48, 61
sex and gender 10–18, 23–4, 38
  disseminating human gender 33–7

hermaphroditism 13–14, 17, 26–7, 31
non-binary identity 18, 25, 26–7, 37–8
queer theory/movement 24–33
  see also feminism; LGBTQIA+ communities; transsexualism
Shakespeare, William
  Hamlet 75, 96
  The Tempest 55
Shariati, Ali 59
Sharif, Omar 79
Simon, Pierre-Henri 113
slave trade 111, 112
slavery
  abolition of 44, 45, 53, 63, 68, 77
  in fiction, *A Woman Named Solitude* 63–4
  and intersectionality 111, 112, 121, 123
  and Negritude 49, 53
  San Domingo slave revolt 46
  and the Taubira law 111
social networks
  cancel culture 126
  Transgender Heaven 29
Society of the Friends of Blacks 68
Solanas, Valerie 36–7
Solomon, Andrew
  Far from the Tree: Parents, Children and the Search for Identity 34–5
Sontag, Susan 73
Soral, Alain 109
SOS Racism 121, 153
South Africa 72, 74, 75
Spanish Civil War 133
Spartacus (film) 124
Spitzer, Robert Leopold 22–3
Spivak, Gayatri Chakravorty 92, 93, 94–5
Stalin, Joseph 133
Starobinski, Jean 141
statues, destruction of 130, 132, 133–4, 162
Stengers, Isabelle 119

226

INDEX

Sternhall, Zeev 144
Stoller, Robert 10, 14–15, 16
Stora, Benjamin 105, 113, 134–5
structuralism 76, 92, 97, 152
  and race 41, 42
subaltern identity x, 84, 88–97
  and "history from below" 89–91
  and women 91, 93–5, 96, 97
suicide
  sutteeism in India 93–5
surgical interventions
  sex and gender 13, 14–16, 26, 27,
    28–9, 32, 35, 161
surrogate motherhood 35
Sylla, Fodé 121

Taguieff, Pierre-André 153
Taliban 134
Tarrant, Brenton 139
Taubira, Christine 121
Taubira law 111
Tavistock Clinic 29
Temps modernes (journal) 56
terrorism 87, 107
  the *Charlie Hebdo* murders 124–6
Thatcher, Margaret 88
theatre performances
  and cultural appropriation 127–9
Tillion, Germaine 58, 115
Tin, Louis-George 121, 123–4, 130
Tosquelles, Francesc 57
transculturation 98
transidentity 98
transsexualism 10, 14–16, 30–3
  hormonal-surgical reassignment
    15–16, 28–9, 31–2
  transgender families 32–3
  transgender identity 10, 16–18,
    28–9, 31, 37–8
transvestites 14, 16
Trotsky, Leon 107–8
Trump, Donald 143, 145
Tueni, Gebran 4
Tueni, Ghassan 1–3, 4, 5
Tunisia 111
Turkey 141

United States
  9/11 terrorist attacks 87, 124
  anti-Americanism 144–5, 147–8, 151
  Berkeley, California 8–9
  and Communist regimes 52
  ethnic groups 77
  identitarianism 134, 142–3
  Iraqi prisoners and military torture
    103
  and Orientalism 81
  Queer Nation movement 24
  transgender persons and bathroom
    wars 37

Valéry, Paul 3, 75, 96
Valls, Manuel 110
Vergès, Françoise 114–15
Vergès, Paul 115
Vernant, Jean-Pierre 111, 153
Vichy France 72–3, 91–2, 121, 146,
  159
Vidal-Naquet, Pierre 51, 57–8, 104,
  111, 119–20
Vietnam 52, 71
Vincennes University 9
Virville, Michel de 123
Voltaire 43–4

Waluś, Janusz 74
Warhol, Andy 36–7
Weinstein, Harvey 19, 20
Weizmann, Chaïm 82
"Western" societies and race 41
Westernism versus Islamism 74
"White" identity
  and the Indigenes 119
white racism/supremacy 139, 143–4,
  148
Whiteness Studies 85–6
"whitriarchy" 106, 115, 116
Wieviorka, Michel 122
Williams, Thomas Chatterton 134
Winnicott, Donald Woods 29
women
  and the #MeToo movement 19
  female sexuality 10–11, 12

INDEX

women (*cont.*)
  and "multiple personality" disorder
    22
  and subaltern identity 91, 93–5,
    96, 97
  sutteeism in India 93–5, 96
  see also feminism; gender

Xi Jinping 142

Yacine, Kateb 73
  Nejma 60–1
Yonnet, Paul 153–4

Zemmour, Éric 121, 157–60
  Le suicide français 158–9
Zionism and anti-Zionism 31, 39–40,
    110, 117–18
Žižek, Slavoj 100